Mistakes Worth Making

How to Turn Sports Errors Into Athletic Excellence

Susan Halden-Brown

Human Kinetics

Library of Congress Cataloging-in-Publication Data

Halden-Brown, Susan, 1946-
  Mistakes worth making: How to Turn Sports Errors Into Athletic Excellence /
Susan Halden-Brown.
     p. cm.
Includes index.
  ISBN 0-7360-4171-0 (Soft cover)
  1. Sports—Psychological aspects. 2. Errors. I. Title.
  GV706.4 .H364 2003
  796'.01'9—dc21   2002151789

ISBN: 0-7360-4171-0

Production Editor: Melinda Graham; **Assistant Editor:** John Wentworth; **Copyeditor:** Patsy Fortney; **Proofreader:** Pam Johnson; **Indexer:** Betty Frizzéll; **Graphic Designer:** Nancy Rasmus; **Photo Manager:** Dan Wendt; **Cover Designer:** Keith Blomberg; **Photographer (interior):** pages 9, 38, and 199 ©Joanna Gleason; page 23 ©SportsChrome; pages 51 and 169 ©EMPICS; pages 71, 125, and 210 ©Jennifer Smith; pages 83 and 246 ©Rob Tringali/ SportsChrome; page 96 ©William Crane/David's Photography; page 115 ©George S. Blonksy/ LUNA; pages 143, 227, and 287 ©Human Kinetics; pages 155 and 181 ©Bongarts/ SportsChrome; page 263 ©William Crane; **Printer:** Versa Press

Human Kinetics books are available at special discounts for bulk purchase. Special editions or book excerpts can also be created to specification. For details, contact the Special Sales Manager at Human Kinetics.

Printed in the United States of America

10 9 8 7 6 5 4 3 2 1

Human Kinetics
Web site: www.HumanKinetics.com

United States: Human Kinetics
P.O. Box 5076
Champaign, IL 61825-5076
800-747-4457
e-mail: humank@hkusa.com

Canada: Human Kinetics
475 Devonshire Road Unit 100
Windsor, ON N8Y 2L5
800-465-7301 (in Canada only)
e-mail: orders@hkcanada.com

Europe: Human Kinetics
107 Bradford Road
Stanningley
Leeds LS28 6AT, United Kingdom
+44 (0) 113 255 5665
e-mail: hk@hkeurope.com

Australia: Human Kinetics
57A Price Avenue
Lower Mitcham, South Australia 5062
08 8277 1555
e-mail: liahka@senet.com.au

New Zealand: Human Kinetics
P.O. Box 105-231, Auckland Central
09-523-3462
e-mail: hkp@ihug.co.nz

For Meg

Contents

Part III   Turning Mistakes Into a Competitive Advantage

Part IV   Laying the Foundation of Your Sporting Future

Acknowledgments

I would like to thank Jeff Bond, head of the psychology department at the Australian Institute of Sport, for inspiring me to ask endless questions, and John Crampton, consultant sport psychologist of performance enhancement systems, for encouraging me to find the answers. Only a life spent coaching in the fast lane of sport could ever have prepared me to write this book, so I also thank those whose quest for success I have shared, and who have shared mine—mistakes and all.

PART I

Rethinking the Role of Mistakes

1

The Case for Mistakes Management

In today's sport, where winners are determined by millimeters, thousandths of a second, or a few points at the end of a hard-fought tournament or a grueling season, it seems we are working very close to the maximal performance of the human body. It's becoming increasingly difficult to find legitimate ways to gain a winning advantage over our opponents. Our mission in sport is not merely to become ever more skilled, fitter, stronger, or faster, but to find a winning edge. So if you've been searching for that new training technique, a fresh idea to add to your sports thoughts, or a new weapon in competition, mistakes management is what you are looking for.

■ Mistakes management will give you that winning edge!

This is a new and as yet unexploited resource that has the potential to improve your performance at any level. If you are an athlete or coach who has not yet seriously included mistakes management in your training, now is the time to do so. And hop in quick, before your competitors discover they can use it to beat *you*!

Current Thinking

Most athletic preparation focuses hugely, and necessarily, on technique and requires us to make immense efforts to ignore our mistakes. Burying our heads in the sporting sand in this way and just hoping that mistakes won't happen may sometimes be the best we can do, but it is hardly effective mistakes management. When the chips are down and the stakes are high, we need to do better! We can choose to manage our mistakes as competently as any other aspect of our sport. To do so, is also to choose to win.

While no one doubts that winners make fewer mistakes than losers do, mistakes management is not generally part of the average athlete's training regime. So, we do not learn about the different sorts of mistakes, and we do not develop strategies to control them or recover from them. Yet we spend much precious time and effort making huge numbers of them, both in training and in competition. We also practice many of them—and then wonder why we get to be so good at them!

In many sports, all the top teams now rely on statistical analysts who pick apart videos of the week's game to provide players and coaches with detailed figures of every move. And the opposition isn't spared either, for their game is also analyzed for patterns of play and the players' strengths and weaknesses. These figures are then used to direct training and are also the basis for team selection. Although these statistics certainly show the world how often the good things happen, they also show how often they don't. Every miskick, dropped pass, fumble, and foul is documented for all to see. No longer is there anywhere to hide!

In individual sports, too, many top athletes have long relied on biomechanical data and frame-by-frame video to analyze complex techniques. Their mistakes are also unforgivingly reduced to cold, hard figures.

While some of these errors are productive and eventually lead to learning new skills, there are clearly heaps of others that don't. Remember that these elite athletes are the ones who make the *fewest* mistakes, yet they still generate enough of them to spend huge chunks of their training sessions correcting them—so just imagine how many mistakes your everyday happy sportsperson makes!

It doesn't matter at which level you're involved in sport, or whether you're an athlete or a coach, because mistakes management applies to everyone, at all levels. So instead of expending all this time and effort making these errors, recovering from them, wearing their consequences, or trying not to make them again, consider the possibilities if you were to reduce them, *by just 10%.*

That's *10% more time* to produce skills—instead of mistakes!

That's *10% more energy* for training or competition.

That's *10% more success for every athlete.*

That's *10% tighter, smarter coaching* in every session.

Any way you look at it, *that's a 10% winning edge!*

In the land of milliseconds and 0.1% improvements in the quality of performance, this represents a *huge* increase and a *massive* untapped advantage over your competitors!

GOOD MISTAKES MANAGEMENT

The *benefits* to you are . . .

Fewer mistakes	Less damaging mistakes
Faster recovery from mistakes	Better correction of mistakes
Increased mental toughness	Improved performance

The *consequences* to you are . . .

Stronger confidence	Fewer injuries
Faster learning	Better attitude
Stronger competitive edge	*Winning more often!*
Less disruption to performances	

This is what mistakes management is all about!

A New Look at Perfection

There's no better place to start to dismantle the old myths that surround the making of mistakes than the point at which all the trouble starts—when we take on board the singularly novel idea that we can actually be perfect. Given our track record, either collectively or individually, and whether viewed on a good day or a bad one, this is an inherently fanciful notion. We shall nonetheless explore it since so many of us believe that we must come close to this ideal if we are to win in today's company. So we shall take a very hard look at the *practicalities* of giving that perfect performance. We shall cast an inquisitive eye over this cherished belief and challenge the very possibility of making flawless efforts. To your surprise—and perhaps to your relief—you will find that perfection can never be a reality in sport. We shall explore the reasons for this, then redefine perfection and give ourselves a new perspective on this ultimately elusive goal.

Fact Versus Fiction

Much as we would like them to, we sometimes forget that our minds and bodies do not operate like machines. Even the simplest action is an extraordinarily complicated combination of mental and physical skills that, try as we may, we can't always guarantee to reproduce to order. If you doubt this, try signing your name at normal speed 10 times in succession. You'll see small but quite clear differences among your 10 "performances." In fact, did you know that the absence of these small but telltale differences is exactly how Big Brother would know if *you* didn't sign them! You'll find these tiny variations from the "perfect" norm in even the most apparently faultless performance of anything. And when the action is too fast for the eye to pick up, the midmoment snapshot or slow-motion film shows it all. Perfection is a beautiful idea, but it was invented before the camera. And we'd better believe it—the camera *never* lies.

Absolute Perfection

From our earliest experiences we soon discover that perfection is a principal prize of life and that achieving it brings us both praise and attention. As our understanding of perfection becomes more sophisticated, we learn that it is also, by definition, anything that is flawless and complete. In sport this is difficult, for by now, despite the limitations of our bodies, we were growing to believe that one day this prize could actually be ours. We devote large parts of our lives trying very hard to achieve it. At times this tantalizing carrot appears to be almost within our reach, and established thinking has it that all that stands between us is the required amount of practice, so we obediently train harder, or longer, or both. To challenge this traditional idea is therefore a daring and daunting task. But that's exactly what must be done if we are to move on from good to great performances.

Long before we had film, this seductive idea of achieving absolute perfection had taken a very firm hold. Throughout history it has been alive and well: The ancient Greeks knew about it; the Romans thought they practiced it. Half the world has been captivated by it over most of chronicled time. But we didn't have cameras until today. That excuses our forebears, but not us. Somehow we continue to run with it, and we are deeply, affectionately, and misguidedly attached to this lustrous ideal. In doing so we quite unwittingly set ourselves impossible, unachievable goals. This is despite all the electronic gear we can now use to analyze our sporting efforts with replays that can run until the tape begins to blur and with slow motion by which to examine every detail. When all else fails, there's the pause button because "That's me!" up there on the screen, and who can resist freeze-framing it just one more time!

Returning to Earth

Sooner or later the novelty of your screen career wears off. A friend may let out a tiny sigh as you prepare to watch the next replay. This is a reminder that you do, after all, have feet of clay. Ignore the friend—it is instructive to compare repetitions of a skill. This is easier in individual sports such as skating or swimming than it is in team games such as baseball or hockey, in which a lot can alter the play and influence your responses. It may surprise you to find that even apparently identical efforts that are indistinguishable to the naked eye appear quite different under the scrutiny of the camera lens. A hand travels higher, the flight of a foot is lower, the body twists with more or less speed. If you're still in doubt, look at the face, for no two efforts will ever carry quite the same facial expression. Why? Because the situation in which each effort is made is unique. We also differ in how we feel about a given effort based on whether it's our first effort, third effort, final effort, or our only chance to get it right. So too, performing in front of a small home crowd is a very different experience from performing before a TV audience of millions. Every situation creates its own unique emotional climate that can never be repeated—if only because it's now happening one more time than it has ever happened before. Think about that. . .

This all means that our thoughts at the moment that we call up a performance are being organized in a brand new situation. Nothing else we have ever invented is quite such a kaleidoscope of such moments as sport. So shouldn't we expect that each effort will be slightly different from any other since each has been started from a different place in life?

But let's not get too theoretical here. Remember the women gymnasts at the 2000 Olympic Games who battled to compete on equipment that was set at the wrong height? Those who strove to deliver perfect repetitions of their rehearsed movements came disastrously unstuck. Devastating as it undoubtedly was for them, they were beaten by the more adaptive competitors who were able to produce a realistic response to the *real* challenges of the moment. The winners produced their routines not by denying the extraordinary circumstances, *but by accommodating them.*

- It was a rare and salutary lesson.
- It was a lesson about living in the Now.
- It was a lesson about goal posts and how to keep focused on a moving target.
- It was a graphic demonstration of how irrelevant the idea of absolute perfection can be to the practical *realities* in front of us.
- For the losers, it was a tragic display of how their ideas of absolute perfection kept them from achieving it.
- For the winners, it was a magnificent example of creative, imaginative excellence using routines that were as close to perfect as the circumstances would allow. That's what made it so special. We'll talk more about excellence a little later.

If you are still hung up on achieving the impossible, remember that at the flip of a switch you can relive reality as often as it takes to prove to yourself that there is no absolutely perfect way to do *anything*. So give it a go. Say it slowly: Absolute perfection does not exist.

Apparent Perfection

Having demolished our dreams, what do we have left? We have apparent perfection. Although at first glance this may seem like little more than word play, we have here a very different beast indeed.

We know that we learn in small easy-to-manage pieces. We also know that we then build on those pieces, string them together, and eventually produce a complicated, coordinated, pleasing effort that we call skill. It's a bit like the gold chains so many of us wear, complete with the minute natural impurities in the gold. The fewer of these impurities, the higher the quality of the gold, and the more pleasing and decorative it becomes. It doesn't matter—indeed it's a fact of life, as any jeweler will tell you—that there's no such thing as *totally* pure gold. Nature

■ Even seemingly simple plays require a complex combination of physical and mental skills.

simply doesn't work to that tight a specification. Even what's in the bank vaults shoring up our national debt is only 99.99% gold. Pure gold does not exist. Oh dear. That's another illusion down the tube. While you digest that information, here's a riddle:

What is the 0.01% if it's not gold ?
Nature's mistake.

And there we have it! Even the most precious, most highly prized currency in the universe is not absolutely perfect. Even gold contains mistakes. That doesn't stop it from being synonymous with everything that's best in a dozen different cultures; neither does it interfere in the least with our appreciation of its beauty. All we need to learn from this is that absolute perfection is neither real *nor necessary*. According to the history of civilization, the rest of humanity, and the World Bank, apparent perfection will do just fine.

Putting Imperfection in the Frame

Going back to our chain, let's take a closer look. When compared to machine-made links, handmade links will each be just minutely different from one another. Are we going to mind these tiny flaws in the workmanship? Certainly the fewer there are, the more arresting the finished article will be to our eye. But if the overall impression is one of rhythm, symmetry, and grace, it doesn't matter at all that the links are minutely different.

As we grow more comfortable with the idea of imperfection, we get closer to seeing our chain, and our performance, in a more realistic light. The important thing about the chain links is not that they be utterly identical, but that they *appear* to match. They must also meet our expectations of them if we are to find the end result satisfying. In connecting these small gold rings, we create something timeless that has found expression in every sophisticated culture yet invented. The 0.01% of flaws is too small to detract from the illusion of absolute perfection, so we can go on believing in it. Now we *know*—we know the flaws are there, *but if they're too small to notice, they don't matter anyway.* To our enormous relief we've discovered that nature isn't perfect after all. *And we don't have to be perfect either!*

Isn't it time then to bring mistakes in from the cold? Can we get our head around the idea that nature's tiny mistakes actually contribute to the gold? Can you think of them as the glitter in the gold? If you can, then like the twinkle in your eye, or the highlights in your hair, you can think of tiny mistakes or brilliant recoveries as the sparkles in your performance. Having the creative courage to make efforts knowing they will be constantly different, and at the same time OK, will vitalize your performance like never before. It will add a high shine to everything you do.

- We've now seen with the help of the camera's eye that even our best performances are flawed by tiny mistakes.
- We've also realized that, like the links in the chain, this doesn't have to detract at all from their ultimate success.

Every sport skill, from the simplest and most basic to the complex and most spectacular, is constructed like the chain. For ease of reference later, each link now needs a name. We will call them *miniperformances.* As long as none of these miniperformances falls noticeably below the general skill level, only some of them need to be superskilled or superbeautiful for the rest of the world to be suitably impressed.

Let's give the chain another twirl. The links don't have to be exactly the same to look good—they just have to *appear* to be the same, despite the tiny differences among them, which are undetectable to the naked eye.

It's the same with us. Our miniperformances, with their inherent flaws (otherwise known as mistakes!), don't need to all be exactly the same—they just need to *appear* to be. When they all meet our expectations of an apparently perfect performance, then that is just exactly what we will achieve—*apparent* perfection!

Redefining Perfection

Sadly perhaps, we'd better agree now that perfection is an illusion. For ease of language, we will take perfection to mean apparent perfection rather than absolute perfection. In fact, we will dismiss absolute perfection altogether as a myth that does not exist in the real world. Perfection is a range of miniperformances that includes some flaws (alias small mistakes) but that we *perceive* to be perfect.

So our conclusion now reads: Perfection is in the eye of the perceiver! But since our intellect now knows that perfection is inevitably flawed, our reason now says: Perfection is the *management* of these flaws.

This puts us in the box seat, for we can now *choose* whether to continue to be a slave to absolute perfection or to embrace our newfound reality of apparent perfection, complete with mistakes. We can also choose to minimize our mistakes and choose how to control our responses to them. This is what mistakes management is all about.

When you feel comfortable with all of this and can cheerfully acknowledge the natural flaws in your "perfect" performances, you will be able to choose to get rid of the old pressure that your striving for absolute perfection created. *This is one of the biggest benefits of good mistakes management.* As you know, pressure creates mistakes, so your new thinking has already reduced these. When you doubt this conclusion, feel free to revisit a video of your last competition.

The Price of Perfection

Here are a few cautionary words. Since believing in perfection is about on a par with believing in Santa Claus, it's a guaranteed way to set yourself up. Sooner or later you're going to feel disillusioned, disappointed, short-changed, or all of the above. Not a happy spot to be. So let's move on . . . anyway, where does excellence come into the picture?

A New Look at Excellence

As every performer knows, in the heat of the action excellence is a trade-off between the perfect and the possible. It is a working compromise between what we know to be wonderful and the degree of wonderful that we can make happen at that moment. So excellence is approximate perfection.

The one enormous difference between excellence and perfection is that excellence is *real* (table 1.1). It is something everyone can achieve, if only in a small way. It can be reached at any standard, in anything we do, whether preparing a pitch or playing on it. The experience of creating excellence enlivens our self-esteem, enriches our memories, colors our dreams, and lives to haunt our critics. Try it. Do something—anything you want—and go on doing it until it's excellent. Feel the flood of success that comes with the knowledge that you have achieved so well. Bask in that feeling.

■ Let a little excellence light your day.

Excellence is to be lived, loved, and endlessly repeated. You don't have to be a megastar all the time, but if you choose to become that good at something as a way of life, then excellence can be your daily

Table 1.1 Perfection Versus Excellence

Concept	Status	Definition	Action
Absolute perfection	Obsolete	An impossibility	Discard— permanently
Apparent perfection	Alive and well	An illusion— which you can create for others to see	Be proud of this —despite the mistakes—if it achieves your purpose
Excellence	Within your reach	Achievable, believable, and real for you	Make a little excellence part of your day

reality. That leaves perfection very much where it belongs—out in the cold as the unreality that no one can ever quite reach no matter how much they practice or how hard they try.

A Word of Reassurance

In case you are beginning to wonder, there are some very practical reasons for sorting out these ideas. As part of the mistakes-management strategies in part II you will need to seriously redesign your goals. Real-life, working definitions of perfection, excellence, and mistakes will be vital to that. So take time to think about these things. They could change your life.

Coaches' Corner

Well, if ever there was an opportunity to lead from the front, this is it. Naturally, embracing mistakes management involves letting go of old ideas. This is always an uncomfortable business because then you have to cross the no-man's-land where the old ideas won't do but the new ones haven't yet been tried, tested, or found to be worth the effort. Be brave. Let these words rattle your cage—then open the door and fly free! You'll wonder what all the fuss was about before you even get your brand new bird's eye view in focus!

Action Pact

In your coaching, do the following:

- Redefine the word *perfection* to represent a more realistic range of minutely, but naturally flawed, effort. Can you kindly but firmly bring the expectations of a perfection-orientated athlete back to earth? Have you actually ever done this? Do it again, today.

- Verbalize your ideas to your athletes. Taking "progress" on board is on thing, but it's no good arriving one day with a whole new spin on the world and no explanation to go with it. Your athletes must always know where you're coming from, so discuss these new ideas with them.

- You no longer need to contemplate this mythical perfection. Neither can you ever again in good faith encourage its pursuit.

- Instead, encourage excellence, secure in the knowledge that everyone can achieve it—yourself included.

Coach Note

Now that you're finding out all about mistakes management, your last excuse for neglecting to teach and coach it has just evaporated! To install it in your training programs, begin as you would with any other aspect of the athlete's preparation, with just a few basic principles. Even one new idea a week is more than your competitors will be doing! Gradually build on those principles and practice the skills of mistakes management until they become comfortably integrated into the training and can then be carried forward into competition. Nothing new about any of that except that your athletes now have skills the opposition doesn't own!

When is coaching like gardening?
When you're weeding out the mistakes!

Summary

We agree that absolute perfection is a myth and is therefore not achievable by normal mortals. We will settle for apparent perfection, which is an illusion. We can create illusions. We know this is the case because the camera says so.

■ Excellence is approximate perfection. It is achievable, believable, and *real*.

We have discovered that . . .

- Performance is made up of lots of miniperformances.
- Some miniperformances will be wonderful.
- Others will be less than wonderful. These will be flawed, though mostly we won't notice that.
- If we do notice our flaws, we will call them mistakes.
- We agree that mistakes will happen whether we like it or not.

Mistakes are what we'd rather do differently next time. Believe that they happen in *every* performance as surely as the sun rises every day.

The bottom line is, you can *choose* to move away from an outdated, romantic notion of what really happens. Or buy a camera.

2

A New Look at Mistakes

It's time to redefine the general image of mistakes. To do this, we need to remove their "bad boy" tag and repackage them as user-friendly items over which we have much more control. It's also time to revisit and revalue some common responses to mistakes in order to feel comfortable about having made even the worst of bloopers.

Redefining Mistakes

Understanding the structure of a performance and how it is made up of lots of miniperformances with plenty of natural differences between them turns mistakes from unpleasant, abnormal intrusions into everyday parts of our sporting effort. They now become merely variations of performance. Whether they are so tiny that we need a camera to see them, or so big they disrupt what we're trying to do, mistakes are all just normal and usual parts of everyday life.

Plan A

Now that we have taken the unexpectedness out of making mistakes, that really takes the sting out of the scorpion's tail! Mistakes will happen. We no longer need to waste precious energy pretending that we should, or might, or ever could perform without them. Instead, let's use that energy to minimize them, manage them, and respond more positively to making them. Now there's a turnaround!

By now it's quite exciting to have mistakes squarely in the picture. Just accepting them as a fact of life will have already revitalized your performance.

Mistakes are OK. *You're* OK. If you no longer have to think about that one, you have made major progress!

But let's not get ahead of our game here. Remember the miniperformances? Two things are important about them:

- They are always plural. That's because there are always lots of them in any performance.
- Each one is a stand-alone opportunity; we may do it better or worse and (guaranteed) different from before.

But when is a variation in your performance sufficiently different from what you expected to call it a mistake? Clearly if you knock your coffee over, that is a mistake. But if you make it a tad stronger than usual, is that also a mistake? Perhaps as long as the coffee is drinkable you wouldn't think so. This is where you find that you actually have quite a lot of tolerance for difference. You're taking another step forward in acknowledging that. It's the *amount* of difference that matters.

Let's follow the same thinking out onto the track. Say you break from the blocks—OK, that's a mistake. But if you run more slowly than you did yesterday, is that also a mistake or just a natural variation in your performance that results in a different time today? Perhaps it wasn't realistic anyway to think you could go on running faster and faster times indefinitely, but when does a slower time become a bad time? What about the circumstances of today—how or why were they different from other days? Perhaps they easily account for your slower times—maybe they were actually very good given you only had three hours of sleep, you had a sore heel, the track was slow, or whatever. Find reasons, not excuses. Keep asking questions until you get to the bottom of the differences in your performance. There are no wrong answers.

So here's another riddle:

When is a mistake not a mistake?

Anytime you like!

We choose whether to label something a mistake. One person's best effort is another's worst nightmare. A variation that is comfortably tolerated by one athlete may be seen as a disaster by her best friend. This might also depend on where and when the action takes place, for we often have more tolerance of differences in performance when we're training than when we're in competition. Or maybe we're more critical of ourselves in front of significant others than in less threatening situations. We all have a comfort zone inside of which we will tolerate differences of performance and outside of which we'll feel we've made a mistake.

Meanwhile, it seems we're quite good at moving our own goalposts, and yesterday's triumph can easily become today's disaster. So it seems that mistakes can be pretty slippery customers. In fact, it's not the mistakes that change, just our appreciation of them. As our frame of reference moves, so our classification of mistakes changes too. What were acceptable performances become unacceptable. Minor mistakes assume major proportions as we move into progressively smarter company. Some mistakes may "disappear" by becoming so small that we no longer notice them because they've slipped out of our field of vision. In fact, sometimes they may not have disappeared at all and may come back to haunt us much later when we have forgotten all about them. Others may grow so large that we can't see past them. This is where our coach comes in, hopefully with 20/20 vision on what's happening.

If you have previously thought of mistakes in very finite terms, you may feel very unsettled to discover they are so apparently changeable. But don't abandon ship just yet—there are better things to come.

Plan B

If we think of mistakes as the things we could, would, should, or might do differently *but not necessarily better*, then we soon see that there are lots of opportunities to do this. In a good performance, mistakes are just the less-than-wonderful-but-still-marvelous parts, like strawberries in a glass of champagne. In a poor performance, mistakes are more obvious and a good deal less palatable, like lumpy custard.

Years ago there was a cookbook all about dealing with cooking mistakes. It didn't tell you how to make custard—it told you how to get the lumps out of what you had already carefully manufactured. It also explained how to make burnt potatoes edible and why your soufflé looked like scrambled eggs. It was one of the most useful cookbooks ever written. It was every humble foodmaker's ultimate plan B.

Life doesn't always run on well-oiled, supersmooth, unlumpy rails. More often for some than for others, it comes comprehensively off those rails. At such times we don't just need a glittering plan A—we need a very sternly functional plan B. We also need to know why we had to use plan B at all. If we accept that inevitably we're going to use our plan B because of the mistakes we make executing our plan A, then we immediately cope better with swinging into it because it was squarely in the cards when we started. Plan B need not necessarily be any less wonderful than plan A. What's important is that it be different. It may differ radically, or it may only differ in the details, but as surely as custard gets lumpy all on its own, you're going to need it. Every plan B must offer practical, workable options that still lead you in the direction of your original goals. We shall develop these.

A Call for Quality Control

As we reinvent each performance, we must learn to pay much closer attention to the variations within it so that we don't practice those variations indiscriminately. Otherwise we may become extremely competent at making ongoing, seriously inhibiting mistakes and grow vastly experienced in every aspect of their mismanagement. That way we could inadvertently get very good at making very bad mistakes indeed.

It is not in our best interest to unthinkingly practice mistakes. We need to learn the different types of mistakes we make and deny ourselves opportunities to practice those that are destructive to our performance. That way we will only make mistakes worth making! These will be the ones from which we learn and grow. Using constructive mistakes well, and avoiding destructive ones through better knowledge of how and when they appear, is probably the single most immediate improvement you can make to your performance. Constructive mistakes will . . .

Build confidence   Facilitate learning
Cause fun   Speed progress

Destructive mistakes, on the other hand, will . . .

Destroy confidence	Inhibit learning
Cause misery	Slow progress

Revaluing Mistakes

Sometimes it's not just the mistakes themselves to which we should pay attention—it's the way we look at them. Do you still see mistakes as the villains of the piece, lying in wait to sabotage your every move? That's probably the most common attitude toward them. How much better if we can recast them as teachers or even heroes who help us learn a million skills in life and bridge that yawning gap between mediocrity and excellence. Cheer for the heroes every time!

To put a friendlier face on our mistakes, let's think how they might be of use to us. For instance, try to see your mistakes as . . .

- Challenges that spur you to greater effort
- Events that help you focus more strongly on your goals
- Opportunities that motivate you to do better
- Markers of your progress
- Dress rehearsals, long-odds efforts, or optional extras

Your choices are limited only by your imagination. It doesn't matter how you make it happen, but somehow you have to turn around that gloomy, negative image of mistakes until you see them as bright, shining, and positive. Work on it! You can give them names or call them by number, keep a list of them under you bed or leave them to your next of kin, *but get fond of them somehow.*

Only when you've brought your mistakes in from the cold are you going to want to do anything positive about managing them. When you do, that's not just going to improve your performance—that's going to rewrite it.

A Scale of Mistakes

The first thing to take notice of is how big your mistakes are and whether they are detracting from your performances (table 2.1). This will be very useful later in deciding what to do about them.

Table 2.1 Levels of Mistakes

Mistake	Characteristics	Consequences	Training remedy
Micro-mistakes	Elite-level errors. Only visible to biomechanics with stop-watches, cameras, or high-tech gear. Mainly relevant to individual sports.	Can decide the medals in elite company. Not relevant to ordinary mortals.	High-tech analysis and biomechanical/ specialist correction of technique. Sports psyche details can make a difference too.
Mini-mistakes	Still very elite-level errors. We make these all the time. Most are natural, unnoticed variations in performance.	Will cost a win in hot company. Most don't matter and will only cause trouble if ignored.	Correct details of technique. Use video. Increase quality of practice. Improve quality of mistakes-manage-ment. Apply the sports psyche.
Maxi-mistakes	Our everyday errors. In team and individual sports. Noticed by judges, teammates, officials, and ourselves.	Will cost a win at most levels. Provide clues for further training. Give measures of progress. Cause us to make further mistakes if not corrected.	Correct fundamen-tals of technique. Raise standards of mistakes-manage-ment. Ignore them at our peril! Learn the elements of sports psyche.
Mega-mistakes	Dramatic disasters.	Cause injury or loss of confid-ence. Seriously interrupt progress. No fun. Can mostly be avoided.	Improve and apply risk-management. Employ mistakes management. Observe sports best practices. Observe rules of sports. Re-set goals to be within skill levels.

Micromistakes

Micromistakes are the tiny ones only the camera can see. They fascinate the biomechanical buffs. If you're into that too, then get wired up, get your coach on the easy end of a video camera, and establish the range of miniperformances within which you must work if you are to end up on the awards podium. If you operate within the micromistake range most of the time, you'll probably come home with a bagful of medals. The days that you don't, it will be someone else's turn to win. If you're not at this end of the sport spectrum, or they're not relevant to your sport, ignore these mistakes.

Minimistakes

Minimistakes are the next size up from micromistakes. They are still very high-quality bungles and will only be in the cards for pretty sophisticated performers. How much of a performance is devoted to them will depend on your skill level and the success of your mistakes-management strategies.

By engineering standards, the physical tolerances of even the most accurate sporting performance are quite broad. The eye that judges them need not be particularly acute to detect differences of skill. Individuals generally operate within quite roomy comfort zones with any number of fail-safe systems in place to preserve their tenure. This all adds up to having quite a lot of latitude in which to make minimistakes on all fronts without necessarily compromising the performance at all.

Having said that, at elite levels too many minimistakes will probably keep you off the awards podium, although they may still go unnoticed by all but the expert eye. At subelite levels, whether or not you pay attention to them and try to correct them will depend on the quality of your training and whether you're going for the big stuff later.

The winning performance, therefore, is not the one without mistakes but the one with the least number of mistakes *that matter at that level.*

A nice by-product of almost any skill is that it's pleasing both to watch and to perform. Whether it is in the magic lines of a javelin thrower, the grace of a gymnast, or the rhythmic power of a football player, the skilled movement of the human body is something we enjoy immensely. None of these performances need be at all compromised by the smaller mistakes in them (even if you or your coach notice them) unless somebody else notices them too. If they don't, you have successfully created the illusion of perfection.

Maximistakes

Maximistakes are the errors that really matter. These are the ones that intrude unpleasantly on our efforts, the bloopers and blunders and everyday errors of life. We can't help but notice these and wish we hadn't made them. In the grand scheme of things we've already been making a fistful of less spectacular mistakes, although they have not necessarily had a dramatic effect on our performance. But suddenly we're in trouble. Or so it seems. Perhaps the writing has been on the proverbial wall for quite a while, but we were just too busy performing to see it. Usually there's nothing really sudden about these maximistakes other than our waking up to them.

Maximistakes are not unannounced disasters. They are clear indications that we've missed the warning signs of trouble. If we can repackage them, then we can begin to make use of them. We can redefine them as less a mistake and more as a signpost from which to backtrack on our progress and pick up on those minimistakes we previously missed. We can use them to realign our performance and choose training programs that are better tailored to helping us reach our competition goals. In this way, although maximistakes are uncomfortable, they need not feel like catastrophes.

Megamistakes

Megamistakes are the calamities of consequence. This is where your hopes and dreams come seriously unstuck. If they're caused by equipment failure, you can usually find the necessary adjectives and move on. If they're sitting fairly at your own feet, then that becomes a lot more challenging. Megamistakes do not compromise a performance—they usually conclude it. As with all other errors, of course, you must get to the bottom of why they happened if you want to avoid repeating them. It's especially important to do this with these monsters, as they have an unreasonable potential to destroy confidence on all sides, and confidence, as we all know, is the glue that sticks everything together. The main cause of megamistakes is insufficient preparation for the task, and they are always a warning that serious maximistakes have been overlooked.

A word here about the curious tendency of mistakes to snowball. They tend not to stay one size but to grow gradually over time. If you don't pick up on them early, they often quietly and remorselessly gather momentum until they burst into your life and you are forced to acknowledge their presence. Minimistakes often grow into maxies over time, and it's not a pretty picture. The thing is to get to them *early*. The more that things go wrong, the more you need to look to the fundamentals of your skills and the less you should focus on the high-quality details. It's in the fundamentals that you'll find the cause of your mistakes. Early corrections that were misinterpreted, first principles that were misunderstood, foundation skills that were not sufficiently cemented before the next story was built on them—these are what cause real trouble later on, when you had long forgotten any original difficulties you may have

■ First recognize that mistakes are part of your performance—now deal with them!

had learning new skills or getting your head around new ideas. For years you may have assumed that your skills were rock solid. Perhaps they were, but so may your mistakes have been, carefully embedded in your early work. So take care and notice with an uncompromising eye for detail the size and quality of your mistakes. Then ask yourself . . .

- Would I like my performance to improve by 10%?
- Are my mistakes getting in the way of winning?
- Are my mistakes undermining my confidence?
- Have my mistakes already caused me—or do they have the potential to cause me—injury?

If the answer to any of these is yes, then you have a strong case for better mistakes management, beginning with plan A. Establish an overview of your current mistakes-management plan by doing the following:

- Identify the size of your mistakes.
- Decide which ones you can tolerate (this depends on the standard you want to reach).
- Decide which ones you need to manage.
- Establish how often you're making these mistakes.
- Keep this overview of your performance to compare with later ones.

Plan B may be one of the following:

- Reread chapters 1 and 2 until you can commit to action.
- Do nothing.
- Give this book away and continue making mistakes that spoil your show.

We'll assume you've taken the positive, proactive path here. You've now discovered that the most important thing to know about mistakes is that they are absolutely inevitable, and that they come in different sizes. You're close to accepting that you can't get through life without making them. So rather than trying to exclude them from your training, you're now resigned to include them and to quickly get good at making the best of them. Let's see what you can do.

Survival Mistakes

Let's begin with some of your earliest, most experimental mistakes. Undoubtedly some were life threatening, and clearly these are the most important ones from which to recover well. As a kid, you probably tried to drink scalding-hot soup, possibly tried piloting your skateboard up a tree or into a wall, and maybe later tried the same thing with a car but fared no better. Having survived the consequences, your survival mistakes have served as crucial lessons in how to successfully interact with your environment. The more adept you become at minimizing these mistakes, the better your chances of reaching a fine old age.

Exactly the same principles apply to sporting performances. The first and most important thing to learn in sport is how to survive it. To do that we make some necessary, and possibly hair-raising, discoveries. We fall off bicycles, skates, high bars, and horses. We slip, skid, and slide into goalposts, guardrails, and similarly unforgiving furniture. We get in the way of bats, rackets, sticks, and other gear and innocently confront seriously destructive missiles hit, hurled, or flung at us with murderous intent. We inevitably fail to duck some of this potentially deadly shrapnel and may thereafter bear the lifelong imprints of it on our bodies or embedded in our psyches. We may try drowning. We might break a bone or two. We get run into, run over, stamped on, and squashed. All this we survive but only by getting a handle on the activities. Otherwise, soon enough, we'll be in the sort of drama that doesn't leave much to be negotiated.

For those of us who take a little longer to learn how to organize a pain-free lifestyle, here is a new sticker—just as a reminder—for your refrigerator door:

■ It's smarter to survive.

Example

Attempting a new ski run is a good way to cartwheel into the snow (minimistake, but no harm done). Failing to train for the challenges of the run is definitely setting yourself up for a fall (maximistake, and possibly painful). Ignoring good advice that the run is altogether too difficult for you is a recipe for disaster (megamistake, which may conclude your skiing career).

Training Strategies

To make only minimistakes, try this good advice:

- Always observe the best practices of your sport. Education is the key to this. Know the risks. Learn the form.
- *Never* take liberties with ill-fitting or unsafe gear.
- *Do not* break the rules; they are there for good reasons.
- *Listen* to experienced, qualified people who want to help you.
- Always train and compete using your sport's best practices to minimize the possibilities of making maxi- or megamistakes. As your skills improve, some risks may lessen, but don't bank on it.

Biggest Risks

- Ignorance (which really is bliss)
- Complacency (which really can hurt)

Coaches' Corner

To take your coaching responsibilities seriously, follow these guidelines:

- Make sure your practice sessions are appropriate for the skill level of your athletes *and for your skill level as a coach.* This means not asking for jumps that are too high, dives that are too difficult, routines that are too complex, and so on. Pride, peer pressure, and other people's expectations need to take a back seat.
- Make sure that your training regimes are appropriate for your athletes' fitness levels. Many mistakes happen when muscles, or minds, become fatigued, so be sure to build up mind and body fitness gradually and conscientiously over time.
- Make sure that the training covers all the demands of upcoming competitions. It's important for your athletes to train for *every element* of the competition. That includes, of course, their mistakes management.

Feel-Good and Follow-Up Mistakes

Another mistake we learned very early in life was the *feel-good mistake.* This mistake leaves us feeling better than we did before we made it. As children we particularly enjoyed that these mistakes attracted lots of people to our rescue. This pleasure does not diminish as we are scooped up by friends, coaches, and teammates later in life. In competition, these mistakes may even rally the whole crowd to our support, and in so doing are useful in wrong-footing our opponent. When this happens, we have made a feel-good mistake, and regardless of what the scoreboard says, we are the winner.

For a while in international soccer, feel-good mistakes were overused as players writhed in apparent agony to enlist the crowd's sympathy and disrupt the opposition's play. However, because such antics interrupted the flow of the game, the rules were changed to prohibit it. As a result, when players discovered that they weren't being noticed, they sprang hastily to their feet and hurried back to their positions. That didn't feel good at all.

Feel-good mistakes are the ultimate spontaneous mistake. They are also the easiest and fastest mistakes from which to recover. But beware! They have an idiosyncrasy all their own. Because they impact well on your performance, it is easy to underestimate the extent to which they can distract you from your task. This very often results in a *follow-up mistake* that may be very costly and negate the positive effects of the feel-good mistake. Follow-up mistakes, as their name suggests, happen on the heels of the main mistake. Usually they are a result of the distraction and disorder caused by the original mistake, and before you know what's hit you, you are in even worse trouble! They are real confidence-shakers because after two different types of mistakes in a row, it's practically impossible not to expect a third. If you make another mistake now, your first thought is that your whole performance is falling apart.

Example

You mis-hit a drive up the fairway, but it somehow makes it onto the green (feel-good mistake). The crowd roars its approval, but unless you move on and successfully refocus, the long putt is likely to be a follow-up error. Let that one get to you and you miss the short putt too.

Training Strategies

- The disruption to the rhythm of your performance caused by feel-good mistakes is what you have to train for. Refocusing is the key here. You need to practice challenging your concentration with all sorts of distractions and then refocusing on your task.

- See just how many popped balloons or car horns it takes to put you off your stride or disrupt your game. Take time to refocus and measure your success by the presence or absence of follow-up errors. Then get quicker at doing this.
- Never let your sense of humor desert you. If the fun goes out of the training sessions, then the fun will also go out of the competitions. Once that happens, you're on the road to burnout.
- Run a fun check from time to time. When did you last laugh in training? When did you last laugh at something you did?
- Talk to your coach. He needs to keep the fun in the sport too.

See table 2.2 for a summary of survival, feel-good, and follow-up mistakes.

Table 2.2 Sorting Out Your Mistakes

Type of mistake	Characteristics	Consequences	Action
Survival mistakes	Not usually much fun. Always in the cards but mostly avoidable.	Can be huge! Real confidence-wreckers and injury prospects if mismanaged.	Practice risk management and respect your sport.
Feel-good mistakes	The ultimate spontaneous mistake. Feel better after mistake than before. Easiest mistake from which to recover.	Attracts lots of attention. Brings others to our "rescue." Positive impact on performance. Can be distracting and lead to more errors.	Join in the good humor. Enjoy! Take care to refocus.
Follow-up mistakes	Follows a previous mistake. Usually caused by distraction.	Negates effects of a feel-good mistake. Shakes confidence.	Get body and mind back on the job. Use positive imagery. Focus, focus, focus!

Biggest Risks

- Underestimating the ability of the feel-good mistake to distract you.
- Making follow-up mistakes that move in with a vengeance.
- Having the fun go out of your sport. That's a shortcut to dropping out.

Coaches' Corner

The choices your athletes make are driven by their value systems. If these are different from yours, they may be the reason mistakes remain uncorrected or corrections go unheeded. The more closely you and your athletes can align your values regarding mistakes, the sooner your feedback will be regarded as a constructive, appropriate response to their efforts, and the more tolerant they will be of mistakes on your part (which you *will* make!). As you know, it's sometimes very important that corrections be accepted spontaneously and with trust. There's often just not time for challenges and doubts to get in the way.

If you do not come to some agreement with your athletes regarding your attitudes toward mistakes, disparities between your two value systems may result in constant friction. Your athletes then do not accept your corrections unconditionally, and as a result their improvement is slow and their motivation falters. This is a difficult negative spiral from which to extricate yourselves. Better to see it coming and choose another path.

Action Pact

Here are some ideas to think about. Openly discuss attitudes to mistakes with your athletes and their significant others in a comfortable, nonthreatening environment when you all have time to enjoy the conversation.

For Yourself

Discuss your attitudes with other coaches or with a mentor. This might be your own coach, a knowledgeable friend, or a sports-wise person whose judgment and impartiality you trust. If you don't have a mentor, find one in the next week. They are every coach's sanity and salvation. They are the absolute best way not to get stale, insular, or stuck in a rut. Furthermore, because coaches get very used to being right, it doesn't hurt to be told you're wrong from time to time, especially by a significant other to whom you might just listen.

For Others

You absolutely *must* preserve the fun in sport for everyone who participates—and at all levels. Check that your coaching style contributes to, and does not detract from, the fun for everyone, including yourself. If you have *any* doubts on this score:

- Praise more often and more generously.
- Lower your stress level before starting each training session (through meditation, yoga, exercise, whatever).
- Listen for laughs—they should be part of each session.
- Invite a co-coach to a session to help you generate some new ideas.
- Visit other coaches' sessions and check for fun content.
- Talk to your mentor.
- Find a mentor if you still don't have one.

The Feel-Good Trap

It's easy to get caught in the feel-good trap of being too easy on your athletes. In your efforts not to be too hard on them after they make all sorts of mistakes, you may unwittingly be too warm and fuzzy in your feedback. This will certainly make them feel good, but it may also mislead them into thinking they are better-skilled than they actually are, which might have these consequences:

- They may develop lopsided and unrealistic images of their abilities. That's not fair. Next thing you know, they'll be repeating the mistakes in search of more fuzzies. That's not fair either.
- Errors may become just another comfort zone. That's unfortunate. There are more productive places to be.
- They will soon see mistakes as "events with a view." That's sports-speak for a desirable outcome. That's misleading. Attention can be gained in more positive ways. Anyway, mistakes are something to be managed, not manipulated.

- The line between fuzzies and flattery becomes blurred. You are a mirror of effort, not a soul-soother or a mind-bender.

So the buzzword is *integrity*. No overpraise. No undercorrection. No ego massage. No unearned brownie points—just good, honest coaching.

Summary

Yes, there's something to this mistakes-management stuff, but no more than there is to learning any other aspect of sport, such as mental skills training, weights, fitness, ball handling, stick skills, rules, flexibility, and so on. We now agree that mistakes are part of the normal universe, nothing more than variations in performance. In so doing we have begun to put a fence around our mistakes, sorting them into the following sizes:

- **Micromistakes:** The camera tells us they are there, but no one else does, although they may cost us a medal or two in smart company. They are not relevant for subelite performers.
- **Minimistakes:** These will tip us off the awards podium and are warnings of worse to come. These also don't matter unless you're among the top competitors.
- **Maximistakes:** These put us on notice that things are coming seriously unstuck. These are the typical mistakes of most sporting mortals.
- **Megamistakes:** These indicate that disasters are on the move and headed in our direction. These are the errors everyone wants to avoid because they are definitely not worth making!

Types of mistakes include . . .

- **Survival mistakes:** These are vital tools for learning to engage in life—and sport. We need to respect our sport's best practices to avoid making ongoing, unnecessary survival mistakes in the future.
- **Feel-good mistakes:** These make us feel great, as long as we don't take them too seriously. They are usually unplanned, harmless, and fun.
- **Follow-up mistakes:** These land on us like a bag of sand, but we can avoid them through ferocious refocusing.

- **Feel-good trap:** This is when the coach or athlete falls into a sticky soup of flattery and fiction. It's a recipe for indigestion.

Why is a mistake your best friend?
Because it tells you things that no one else would dare to!

That's why we will try to accept all mistakes, somehow.

3

The Emotional Cost of Mistakes

If we were to apportion a hypothetical sport pie, mistakes would take up only a very small slice of the overall effort. What gives them clout way beyond the time and effort we expend making them is their link with emotion. Being distracted by our emotions often causes mistakes, and mistakes invariably trigger emotions. So emotions, not mistakes, are the real villains. While sport psychologists have known this for years and have long tried to train us to perform dispassionate sport, that's only half the story. The other half is that understanding the links between emotion and mistakes vastly improves our management of mistakes, through encouraging us to take responsibility for the emotional climate we create. We can then stop blaming the mistakes, or ourselves, for our performance deficits and make real progress toward improving our performance.

When we learn to control the emotional climate of our performance, we will

- make fewer mistakes,
- recover faster and better from the mistakes we do make,
- maintain our confidence, and
- enjoy more serious fun.

There is a small flaw in the sports psychologists' approach of learning to control our emotions. Throughout our attempts to produce a dispassionate performance, we are somehow expected to ignore the fact that sport is *the* most collectively emotional experience in life. Clapping our hands into a putty in the theater, or even shivering our way through the exquisite agony of the best horror film in town doesn't hold a candle to being one in a hundred thousand on the roller-coaster ride of high drama that unfolds during your average clash at the Rose Bowl. To the casual observer, this gathering of the faithful to rock the stratosphere on a peaceful afternoon must look like pretty marginal behavior!

Has anyone asked *why* we behave in this extraordinary way? Perhaps it doesn't matter. When we're so wrapped up in the emotion of the moment, such erudite questions are simply irrelevant. But small wonder that when we're on the production end of all this passion, we feel the heat of it. Getting it right in front of so many intensely ambitious eyes is a fantastic high. But getting it wrong can dig you into a hole so deep you may never get out again. Consider the Olympic ski jumper—just a teenager—who stood at the head of the ramp with his nation's gold in his grasp if he got it right, and a lifetime's remorse if he didn't. He didn't. Poor kid. Was there ever a more frightened face in the history of sport? All the world watched his fear and failure, and then the cameras moved in for close-ups of his despair.

For the competitor, the impracticalities of ignoring all of this emotion are very real. That's probably why we're not able to do it very well, or very often. So we will abandon current thought and devise our own alternatives. They will be practical, plausible, and *possible*.

Serious Fun

Happily, sport is not all doom and gloom. Many good times ensure that we hang in there and repeat our sporting experiences. We can eventually turn around even the worst experiences until we see them as opportunities to learn or grow; had we gotten everything right the first time around we would not have had this chance. Such thinking can become something of an art form. Try seeing life as one big trampoline—on the way up you can do spectacular things, but to go up again you first have to come down. That down doesn't feel so bad when you know it's just part of the serious fun of your life. Anyway, it stops you from getting bored with the view up there! The mental skills you will learn in taking this perspective will generalize into other areas of your life and enable you to take a sunnier view of the future, confident that you can turn even the most heavy-duty gloom-laden events to your ultimate advantage.

Innumerable sports exist to suit all manner of temperaments, and they offer us a positive galaxy of opportunities for emotional satisfaction. This makes riding the sporting roller-coaster such serious fun. Fun, however, means different things to different people. For one it is achieving those amazingly complicated kinesthetic feats on the way down from a diving board, and for another it all happens on the way up to the dizzy heights of the pole-vault bar. Some get their buzz in the water, while others never leave the land. By the looks of it, fun is about as individual as it gets and a good deal more serious for some than for others. Nevertheless, it's pretty fundamental because only if we have fun do we come back for more.

The moment the fun goes out of our sport, our efforts start to feel like nothing more than hard work. We no longer enjoy producing what has become just time consuming, overvalued effort. So how do we keep the serious fun in our sport? One of the best ways is to remember what *exactly* it was that gave us so much pleasure from the activity in the first place. Was it the clean, sharp hiss of a skate as it cut into the ice, or the revving of a high-tech engine on the track? Was it winning on our own account, or being one of a team? We need to know this to keep the fun happening.

So, now we're getting into it. List five reasons why you enjoy your sport. Now list five things that you feel detract from that enjoyment. Draw up five strategies to remedy the things that detract from your enjoyment. Having fun was the principal reason for starting sport in the first place, and if you want to enjoy your sport on through the years, you must keep the element of fun in it.

Serious fun is not just the recreational element in sport. It is the marvelous feelings of satisfaction and enjoyment that only your involvement in your particular sport can bring. Maybe it's the flow of the water over your skin, the zing of the ball off the racket strings, or the companionship of good team spirit. These are simple pleasures. Despite this, we often lose our way in the course of our sporting career and forget that fun can be had at all levels of participation and for a host of different reasons. If we lose that fun, we lose one of our most important motivating factors. Usually it's more a matter of focus than any actual withdrawal of what we enjoy. The fun is still there, but we have just stopped paying attention to it. This is a shortcut to early burnout. Remember—having serious fun is seriously important to your career prospects.

■ It's a simple equation: *Serious fun = Your reward*

Serious fun is not the same as frivolous fun. Having serious fun gives us that basic satisfaction that tells us we're doing the right thing with our lives. Frivolous fun may temporarily entertain us, but its overall impact is shallow and transient. Make *no* mistake here—we all need our share of serious fun in our lives.

Emotional Matters

The first, last, and *only* cost of a mistake is the emotional cost, because if we didn't care—if it didn't *matter* whether things were good or bad or right or wrong—then mistakes wouldn't matter. They would never be noticed, much less corrected, because they wouldn't even exist. Sometimes the quality of our performance matters very much, to the point of becoming a jubilant player, furious contestant, tear-streaked winner, or devastated loser. Mattering may be neither fashionable nor newsworthy, but it is a very emotional issue. Without attention as to how we're going to deal with mistakes, our sporting success is on the line. Get this one straight: Mattering makes the difference between a champion and an "also ran." And the next thing to handle is that mistakes are a major part of all this because they can have major consequences in your sporting career.

So it is a fact of our sporting times that *mistakes matter hugely*. Before moving on, accept this basic tenet: Mistakes are very emotional indeed.

If you're about to skip the next 10 pages, do so at your peril. You'd be better off learning what to expect and how to deal with it. Maybe some of us are tougher to chew on than others, but when it comes down to it, we all have to learn the same emotional lessons to survive and get along with each other. In sport those lessons can be hard, and we have all kinds of huge expectations for ourselves as we try to learn them.

To begin with, we have to get past some of the old-fashioned cultural stuff and accept that being or getting "emotional" is not a sign of weakness. Indeed in the 21st century, being able to experience *and share* the whole range of human emotions is now recognized as a strength. What's important is how we manage these emotions and that we express emotions that are appropriate to the situation.

Anger

Most people get angry. It's a part of life, and it's certainly a part of sporting life. Anger is only a problem if it gets in the way of producing your best performance. Let's be quite clear about this: It's not you that's the problem—it's only the angry *behavior* that sometimes needs a new script.

There are lots of good books on anger, but right now we're interested in anger as a reaction to making a mistake. Nobody has written much about that so it seems we're on our own here.

Anger can be useful. It can bolster apparent strength, and it can add a good deal of zest to gross motor skills such as running, punching, jumping, lifting, or pulling. But anger can be counterproductive to any performance needing good balance, good judgment, steadiness, or fine motor skills. It can also do drastic things to your memory, causing you to forget the rules, your strategies, tactics, or manners.

The worst aspect of anger is that you are no longer focused on your performance. Why? Because it takes time, effort, attention, confidence, and practice to be satisfactorily angry. Since you need all of those things for your performance, it is not useful to be busily applying them to something else. When you make a mistake, you need them more than ever, so it is then *highly* inappropriate to be using them elsewhere.

As usual, the choice is yours. If your fuse burns short, will you let rip now and blast your opponent (together with your performance) off the planet, or will you stamp out the sparks and set fire to the whole show some other time? Taking the deferred option in the face of judges, coaches, umpires, and other officials, not to mention however many spectators and the serious prospect of defeat, isn't always easy. In the heat of the moment you may also forget the presence of the media or others you later wish you hadn't quite so readily obliged. No one is saying the choice is easy, but it's always there.

Example

Another player barges into you with serious intent to do you damage. He nearly succeeds. It really, *really* hurts, and for a horrendous few moments you see yourself sidelined for the rest of the season with a leg

■ Feeding off your emotion is one thing—losing yourself to anger is another. Do you know which is which?

in plaster. How angry do you get about *that?* There are several advantages to getting angry:

- You could probably run the other player down faster.
- You could definitely hit him harder.
- You'd scoop up a satisfactory amount of revenge.
- You might establish a reputation for being aggressive.
- You might reroute future similar assaults.
- It's probably the easier option.

But there are also disadvantages to getting angry:

- You could make an all-time enemy . . . or a whole team of enemies!
- You could get injured.

- You might come off second best.
- Your pride could take a beating.
- You could attract penalties.
- You might miss out on the rest of the game.
- You might compromise further selection for your team or squad.
- It will distract attention and effort from your performance skills.
- It's very hard work.

Training Strategy

In real-life situations you don't have time to run through all the previous options. You have to make a snap decision. Sometimes that decision will be right, and sometimes it will be wrong. The time to work it out is during your debriefing session, which is the time to learn from your decisions and decide whether to repeat them next time. *It is a megamistake not to address your anger.*

Unresolved anger will get in the way of your progress, inhibit your training, damage your performances, and impair your success. That should be sufficient encouragement for you to do something about it. If it isn't, then you are definitely not championship material. In fact, you could probably better spend your time doing something else altogether. Well now, *that's* putting the cards on the table. While you're still smarting from the assault on your ego, but *only* if it's part of your game plan, get angry and run or jump or lift better than the absolute best of them. If it's going to compromise your day, then save it for the debriefing when you can decide . . .

- What exactly you were angry about
- How angry to get
- Whether being angry improved the situation
- Whether it was to your advantage to get angry
- Whether a different response could have gotten you a better outcome

By this time you probably have regained sufficient composure to ask yourself (nicely) these questions:

- Could I have had a more positive response?
- What might that response have been?

Mentally rehearse that response every day for a week, or until it feels natural. In the short-short term, if the anger is still getting in the way, some helpful strategies might include a few of these old favorites:

- Whack a pillow with your hockey stick or beat the ground with your bat.
- Sound off to a friend.
- Run it off, swim it off, walk it off, or go pump iron.

When all else fails,

- some less physical people write the anger out of their system,
- others play music until the dust settles, and
- a few sleep it off.

Choose whatever makes you feel better as long as it doesn't harm anyone else.

- Start every training session with a positive mental rehearsal of your most angry situation.
- The most explosive and destructive spin-off from a mistake is undoubtedly anger.
- Anger is by far the most common result of a mistake.
- Not many people deal well with anger in any context. In the highly charged atmosphere of sport it is therefore not surprising that most of us struggle from time to time to contain our anger, or to discharge it in an appropriate way. *It follows that if you deal with anger well, you will have an immediate advantage over a great many of your opponents.*

Frustration

When you feel frustrated it tells you there's a gap between what you want and what you have. It is the expression of the difference between your goals and your performance. When that performance falls short of what you hoped or needed it to be, you feel frustrated. Anger often follows. Sometimes it's hard to tell the difference.

Recognize frustration for what it really is—a temporary shortfall in the grand scheme of things. This helps to keep it in perspective. Sure, you feel it, but you don't necessarily have to act on it when that action would be a cast-iron guarantee for making things worse. You don't have to let your emotions rule your intellect. Not every time. Not this time. You have choices again.

Example

Let's suppose you're a golfer who is languishing in the rough for want of a win. It's worse than Tiger Woods' fall from grace, or a year in jail, or writer's block. Your life is suspended in some sort of limbo that feels halfway between being caught in a rip and wading through a ton of molasses. You're not in control any more, and despite your best efforts, your performance continues to be dysfunctional. Your disgust and anger grow. Before long you feel disillusioned, distressed, angry, and above all, frustrated.

Training Strategy

Feeling frustrated is not a comfortable place to be. If you are to move out of it, you have two options. Either improve your achievements until they reach your expectations or modify your expectations to match your achievements.

Both are easier said than done. Improving your achievements takes considerable presence of mind and presumes that you have the necessary skills and that they are at hand. If you can withstand the challenge to your concentration that the feelings of frustration pose, then you may be able to summon these skills and to rescue the situation from disaster. Modifying your expectations is no less difficult and requires that you keep a cool head in the heat of the moment and refocus your efforts on more immediately achievable goals. These are the only two ways you can resolve feelings of frustration. Failing this, the next step is to get very angry indeed, which is to acknowledge defeat well before it is endorsed by the final score.

Embarrassment

Mistakes that result in embarrassment are the ones we all love to hate the most. It doesn't matter how you try to package it, it never feels good. There's only one way to deal with it—*move on.*

Example

Imagine any mistake that makes you wish you were somewhere else on the planet. Whether you sky an easy shot or split your shorts, the fallout feels much the same.

Training Strategy

Refocus on the job. Regroup. Regather. Practical help may be difficult to come by in public circumstances, but training should be geared toward repair or reinstatement of your glass bubble if cracks have appeared under stress. What is a glass bubble? Talk to your coach about using your mental skills to create an imaginary but impenetrable glass bubble around yourself that will shield you from anything that might distract you from doing your job. You can retreat inside it, blow it up and make it bigger, toughen it, strengthen it, color it, or do whatever else you can think of to make it "real" enough to be useful. The whole idea is to create an inviolable personal space in which to operate—one in which you have complete control and which is insulated from the pressures of the game, the crowd, or any other perceived intrusion. While your glass bubble is a safe haven, it is also a workplace; the association must be to withdraw into it to work, not to escape. It is especially useful if you're in an individual sport. If you're a contact player, you might need to think in terms of playing in a wafer-thin steel suit, or of using some other imaginary device to separate yourself from the outside environment and protect your concentration. Use your glass dome now. Or retreat to a quiet spot for a quick re-read of this paragraph.

Giving Ourselves the Benefit of the Doubt

Sometimes we are so genuinely disgusted with ourselves that we let ourselves down by producing below-standard technical skills at critical times. When this happens, we need to be more forgiving of our efforts and to understand or at least tolerate the complexity of our bodies and the enormity of what they have to do to produce even a simple action. We often underestimate how many variables in the physical and emotional environment impact on our performance. At times we need to give our bodies the benefit of the doubt. They may have been temporarily busy with other business when we called up that particular skill *because we didn't tell them to be otherwise.* We only put ourselves under further pressure when we denigrate the effort of the moment. We don't have to have liked it, but we don't need to be disgusted by it either. Our body is still our friend. Friends do not always perform on call or live up to our expectations. They are no more perfect than we are. Treat your body as the friend it truly is, and try to be tolerant of its occasional lapses—you'll find it will reward you richly when it matters most.

Disappointment

Disappointment is a big one because it hooks into the loss cycle to which most of us are remarkably sensitive. It's also one we can't avoid because by the nature of the beast we are not going to win every time we go out. Disappointment is part of the life of any sportsperson. It's quite useful to learn to deal with it effectively. Disappointment, by definition, implies hope. There has to be hope before there can be disappointment. When that hope is misplaced, oversized, or crushed, we can feel bitterly disappointed. We can tear through the loss cycle, covering the entire spectrum of emotions in a matter of minutes, or it may take us days, weeks, or even years to work our way to the end of it. We may get stuck at any point and be unable to move through to the next stage of resolving our feelings and reaching a point of equilibrium.

The loss cycle begins with disbelief. Who has not denied a mistake within milliseconds of it happening? As the line umpire calls the ball out, you respond with, " I don't *believe* it !" That says it all. Next on the list is denial. The horrified "Oh *no!*" is a dead giveaway. This is followed by that moment when you wish the ground would open up so you can escape the gaze of so many critical eyes. Then, as you move on, you get angry. Now at least you know where you are, and that you're well on the way to getting out of the current hole. You may have a moment or two of misery before you finally accept what's happened. When that passes, you'll have reached the other side of the incident and can then get on with the rest of your life.

Mistakes are substantial triggers for this reaction and your newfound knowledge will make you much more aware of just how often you cover this wide spectrum of emotions, and of the large amounts of energy it takes to do so. Disappointment is often the starting point for this cycle. You need to be mentally tough enough to take disappointments in stride if you are to survive a career in sport. Mental toughness and mistakes management go hand in hand. Being good at one of them will automatically enhance the other. So, better get busy.

Example

You've been training for months. It's been a hard season. You've worked like a dog and held your place in the rankings against stupendous odds. Then you come out on the big day, and your star weapon just won't function. Bereft of your favorite shot or your signature move, what is there left to do this side of the sun?

You must always and forever have a well-practiced, in-every-way-functional plan B. You cannot afford to be without one. Only the quality of your plan B will save your day. Better decide now whether your day is worth saving, then have the best plan B in town. And you better have the presence of mind to put it into action.

Fright

Many sports, from skydiving to scuba diving, can be life threatening. Any of these can generate strong feelings of fear, but like skiing down a mountain (which isn't for the birds either), we do it in droves. Here are a few worthwhile strategies for dealing with the fear that can be a full-time occupation in some sports.

When you make a mistake that sends a spike of fear through your stomach, you'd better *keep thinking*. If you seriously want to make matters worse, now is the time to mentally abandon ship. But it's better to make smart choices to get yourself out of trouble.

- *Choose* to keep focused.
- *Choose* to actively keep doing your sport skills.
- *Choose* to override your fear.

There's nothing quite like a mistake to trigger fright. This is particularly true in the high-risk sports, in which the mistake happens so fast that it often isn't until later that the fright hits you. This is why the old adage tells you that when you fall off a horse, you'd better get right back on again. Doing so is supposed to keep you from mulling over how much harder the ground has gotten since you last hit it.

When we frighten ourselves it usually undermines our confidence, which then needs repair before we can get on with fixing the technicalities of our performance. This means backpedaling onto safer, easier ground. In competition, this is not always possible. Consider the enormous courage required by athletes such as ice skaters who, after a fall, must get up, regroup, and immediately repeat the same jump or perhaps an even more difficult one. Gymnasts and equestrians also face similar situations. Getting a handle on your fear at such times is quite a challenge. That's where the legendary "nerves of steel" come in.

Instant mental rehearsal can be done at any time in any place. Because it is so quick and *safe* and you can always get it right, it is the best confidence booster around. It is only effective, however, if you have top-of-the-range concentration skills that are not overpowered by your fear. Only then will you be able to control the focus of your thoughts and steer yourself out of trouble.

Coaches' Corner

■ Tip of the decade: Always address the emotion first—then crack into the technique.

The most sure-fire way to defuse the intensity of any emotion is to tell the athlete swept up in it that you read her loud and clear. If you can acknowledge her feelings and say, "I know it's exasperating/frustrating/upsetting/embarrassing. . ." it will be music to her ears. That tells her that she has been heard. That's often enough to have her give you some airtime.

The next thing to do is to remind the athlete of her options. Do this by giving her cues for refocusing on the job, *fast,* before she decides to continue being angry, embarrassed, or whatever her emotion is.

It's difficult to go on being swept overboard by any emotion if you are being called on to do something—anything—else. It's just as effective to have a job distract you from an emotion as it is to have an emotion distract you from a job. Reread that if you need to.

Significant Others

It is well understood in sport that being watched by people with whom we have a strong emotional connection or who are important to us in any particular way can substantially influence the way we perform. The fact that these watching eyes belong to someone who matters to us can create an explosive emotional cocktail that can blow our performance right out of the water. When our skills are well honed, we generally feel positive about the presence of significant others at our sporting events, whether they are family members or scouts or a home crowd. This characteristically "lifts" our performance. If, however, our skills are still rough, the presence of an audience can be detrimental to our performance. Given that in training we are frequently practicing our *less*-learned skills, the presence of significant others may place us under very real pressure. The frequent result is "unexpected" mistakes, which of course are entirely to be expected. This explains why it is not a good idea to have Dad looking on as little Johnny releases his first hammer. It could just land in his lap.

Coaches' Corner

Here are some considerations to help you accelerate your athletes' progress:

- On behalf of your athletes, manage significant others as you would any other element of the training environment.
- Never underestimate the influence of significant others.
- Use significant others to enhance the performance and *at the same stages at which you would use video.*
- Brief significant others on appropriate performance indicators and expectations.
- Never allow negative comments from significant others to go unchallenged. They can undo in one sentence what it has taken you a year to put together!
- Remember that significant others are just that—*significant!*
- Explain all this to significant others. They may have no idea how much of an influence they are.

The following suggestions are based on sound learning theory. Few are currently implemented, despite that ignoring them slows skill acquisition to a crawl and can damage confidence and self-esteem. They are especially important when coaching children.

- Take care that the training sessions viewed by significant others are those with the best-practiced skills, and not those that concentrate on the athlete's new skills.
- To maximize training progress, do not encourage the presence of significant others (or the use of video) until new skills are well integrated into the athlete's skill base and are at least to the intermediate learning stage.

- Whenever possible, stay within the well-confirmed skills in front of significant others to maximize the experiences of success for the athlete and minimize the possibilities of mistakes (which the athlete *must* be able to correct). The mistakes that do occur will be more significant to the athlete and will carry this emotional tag even when the significant other is no longer there.

- You may want to discourage significant others from attending *any* training sessions. From a purely pedagogical point of view, it is not supportive to have Mom on the sidelines or the girlfriend in the gallery. It can slow the athlete's rate of progress and ultimately undermine his confidence. On a regular basis it is a disaster. Do not believe the athlete who tells you his significant others make no difference to his performance. Believe only that he is not yet aware enough to register that difference. There is plenty of research to substantiate that significant others *do* make a difference, and so do audiences, crowds, and peanut galleries. As a stand-alone stressor, a significant other is hard to beat, but combine it with the inherent stresses of training or competition, add early skills, and see the results for yourself.

- Significant others are one of the most sensitive triggers for mistakes in training. If a significant other of one of your athletes shows up unexpectedly at training, in your athlete's interests, immediately revise your session plan to include well-confirmed skills only. By doing this you will effectively plan out many mistakes. *Do not be tempted to have the athlete show off the latest new skill.*

The bottom line is that, from a learning point of view, it's no more appropriate for Dad to be on the sidelines while little Johnny learns to play baseball than it is for him to sit in the back row of Johnny's math class while he learns long division. If you're stuck with Dad, then at least know the consequences for little Johnny *and know that you'll only get the best out of little Johnny if you "train" his Dad too!* Educate Dad about the influence of significant others, and don't take any stuff about "toughening up little Johnny" as an excuse from Dad not to change his ways. Little Johnny will get mightily tough in the course of his sporting career with no help at all from Dad!

Remember that you too, as coach, are a significant other for athletes. You can help by taking a lowered profile when athletes are practicing new skills. That's not to say you should look like a piece of furniture, but it is a good time to be less critical, less incisive, and perhaps a little more tolerant. This is often at odds with our instincts to be Mr. or Ms. Fix-it, but we can be most helpful at these times by just backing off a little and giving athletes some space. Of course they will get it "wrong," and it doesn't matter a bit. What you're looking for is experimentation. We all have to learn what a new skill feels like. That means pushing our minds into new spaces and our bodies into new muscular and neurological responses that are unknown and unknowable until we actually do them. Naturally, we make misjudgments and miscalculations in the process, but learning to meet the challenges of being outside our comfort zone delivers an excitement like no other.

Summary

Fact: No matter what emotions may have been roused by your successes or failures in sport, they will impact tremendously on your performance.

- Mistakes, by their very nature, trigger emotional responses, which therefore have a similar potential.
- You can learn to control your emotional responses.
- You can also learn new responses, new behaviors, and new coping strategies.
- Emotional responses can impact positively or negatively on performance.
- It's up to every athlete and every coach to *choose* whether that impact will be positive or negative. Every time.

Significant others are just that—*significant.* Their presence has the potential to enhance or destroy a performance, so make sure they are as well-trained as the rest of the production team.

4

Redefining Success

It's all very well to turn perfection on its ear and bend the bars around mistakes, but where does that leave our ideas of success? Clearly there's more to think about before heading off into the action.

Let's first acknowledge that success comes in a number of different packages. It means very different things to different people, so you need to decide for yourself exactly what kind of success makes you happy. You also need to explore with your coach and significant others what they mean by success and what will make them happy about your performance. If, for you, success is doing your best but for them it's a trophy on the mantle, then unless you talk about it, at the end of the day you will feel used and resentful of them and they will feel frustrated and angry with you. It's in everyone's interests to establish these parameters early. Also, other people's goalposts are very often just out of our range. Some have a habit of moving. This eventually wipes the smile from anybody's face.

So What Is Winning?

Here are some ideas. Winning is . . .

- Beating someone else
- Taking home the trophy
- Coming in first
- Being the best

This list defines winning from other people's point of view (because they all represent comparisons with someone else's efforts). It is the traditional, dare we say old-fashioned, way of thinking about winning that wrests control of the outcome from the athlete and places it in the hands of unknown others. Once you give up control, you also give up taking responsibility for making it happen. The only "advantage" to this scenario is that it can always be "their" fault if you didn't win, which is quite handy if you're into blaming others for your own shortfalls, but doesn't sit well with the true sportsperson. Worst of all it is guaranteed to rob you of your fun.

If you run with these outcome-focused goals that emphasize the end result and not how you get there, you'll find that they will knock the stuffing out of your training objectives and wreak havoc with your competition results.

Let's take another look at winning, this time from *your* point of view. Winning can mean . . .

- Being your best
- Achieving your goals
- Fulfilling your dreams
- Meeting your standards
- Making your deadlines
- Completing your competition in your time and in your way

This is the antiadversarial view of winning, and it works. When you define winning in this way, you set performance-focused goals that are based on how you do things, not on what you get for doing them. This sort of winning measures your courage and your determination in trying to achieve the goals you set. Obviously you will do your best. Who wouldn't? If you don't achieve your goals, then clearly the goals need adjusting because every goal you ever set should be within your reach.

Also, you need to have a fallback position since it's possible your goals just weren't within your reach on that day. So that's the way it is.

Personal Bests

Personal bests are another idea that needs an update. Why wouldn't you give your best to an activity you train your socks off for, might get wiped out at, don't get paid for, and risk public humiliation for—all in one afternoon! Get real. Personal bests are *out*. Give yourself credit every time for doing your best at that time. Presumably, you either could not change the space you were in, or didn't wish to. So take your courage in both hands, turn and face the world, and *be your own person*.

The extent to which anyone can do this is perhaps the ultimate measure of their success and maturity in any field of endeavor. It is

■ Don't put so much emphasis on personal bests—always give yourself credit for doing the best you can at each moment.

particularly difficult to do in sport because the stakes are often so high, but continuing to try is a pretty fair way of winning.

Aside from these ideas on private winning, a frequent consequence of public winning is publicity. Whether you have a modest local write-up or international banner headlines, the role model you become can be an immensely powerful icon, especially for younger athletes. To do anything well enough to attract large-scale public attention is to wield huge power—which in turn confers huge responsibility. What you define as success and how you handle all the trappings that go with it are then very much on display. Others will copy your attitudes, your vocabulary, your mannerisms, and your sport style. As either athlete or coach, be sure to take good care of those formative lives that for a short but immeasurably precious time you hold in the palm of your hand.

P.S.

Postscripts are sometimes more important than the rest of the message. Dream your own dream, not someone else's. Set your own standards against which to perform, then show the world that you can do just that. Do a Kathy Freeman—even if your 400 meter takes half an hour!

What About Losing?

It's surprising just how many times we lose in the course of a successful sporting career. That's not because we're not good; it's just that sometimes the opposition is better. No sporting great has ever been such a freak as to wipe out the opposition 100% of the time. Even an all-time icon like Muhammad Ali was beaten before (and after) he became "The Greatest." Being beaten is a fact of sporting life. How we cope with it, and how it figures in our career, is a different matter altogether.

Let's do a few sums. The date is A.D. 2000; the venue, Sydney, Australia. A total of 10,300 athletes from 199 countries gather for the Olympics. Athletes are vying for 3,100 medals in 28 sports. Only 1,000 of them are gold. Does that mean that 9,300 of those athletes are losers?

To continue, there are 3,100 medals altogether, counting the silver and the bronze. It seems there are still not enough to go around. In the end, 7,200 athletes go home empty-handed. (Actually it's more than that, of course, because some athletes go home with a bagful.) Did 7,200 people make a horrendous mistake the day they paid for their plane fares? Did they think they were winners? Were they all proved wrong?

Culturally, we've taken the hard line on winning. It means everything in most sports. It's generally neither fashionable nor profitable to take a "softer" line, despite the fact that it may help us live healthier, happier lives. It's win or bust, and our society has little patience with anything less.

So, returning to our sum, do we cheer the 7,200 empty-handed athletes? Yes, of course we do. In raising our voices, we're saying that winning is not everything after all. It seems that somewhere there may be room, if not in our heads then perhaps in our hearts, for acknowledging all those hours of training and the huge commitment of so many lives to the sporting ideals and illusions of our time. Surely it is a small step to take, to extend our generosity from these to the elite nonwinners, to our own sporting peers, or to the junior battler down there on the local oval next Saturday afternoon . . . or to ourselves after giving our less-than-winning all.

Other People's Success

It's difficult to be generous about other people's success sometimes, especially when we thought their win was our due. We're apt to make unkind assumptions (most of which have no basis in fact), perhaps attributing their success to more opportunities or better luck. This does not do us credit. How we deal with other people's success is a reflection of how we deal with our own. If we take responsibility for our own efforts, then we will be able to give due credit to others who have done the same. Understanding performance in these terms, and deciding when we are winners and what success means, will improve our tolerance of ourselves when we sometimes produce performances we don't want or didn't expect. We will win on merit, by luck, and by others' mistakes, and they by ours. Try as we may, neither of us will ever have complete control of the process. Better get used to that.

What Is Failure?

This is tricky. Let's choose a definition we can live with and leave the more destructive ones to the pessimists out there. How about any or all of the following:

Insufficiency *for the moment*	Lack of achievement *as yet*
Work in progress	Potential success
Success in the making	Tomorrow's win

If you don't like any of these, think up one of your own. You need to sort this out. By all means do it your way, but just don't wander around the planet with blurred vision and then wonder why you walked into a wall. By then it will be too late. Anyway, we don't do well against walls.

You need to be able to let yourself fail sometimes. It's not the end of the world, and it's not the end of your world either. It's just the beginning of a new one. Everybody fails from time to time, so you're not that special. Just decide to fail well! Decide to handle it better, more constructively, and more usefully than others do. Decide to applaud yourself for how well you manage your failure. Decide to succeed at failing! We've all heard of bad losers. No one really wants to be bad at anything. Anyway, it's possible to get very good at sometimes being not very good at all. (Reread that one if your eyes walked over the top of it.) Now that's a real success story.

Some people need to fail more than others do. You are what you think you are, and you behave how you think you should because of your thoughts, which ultimately drive your body in the directions you decide to go. It's all about choosing what you want to be.

There's more to this story, too. For those athletes whose self-worth does not add up to the price of a milkshake, any kind of success is anathema since their need to validate their low self-worth may be far greater than any need to succeed in worldly terms. Sometimes being right, and therefore in control of this thing called life, is more important and a good deal less scary than trying to do things on other people's terms and coming up wrong. It follows that for some athletes making mistakes will be a critical part of ensuring their "failure." Their mistakes will be as well timed and highly orchestrated as any of their other skills. But hang on a second! If you are achieving your objectives so well, how can you be doing anything other than succeeding? To be sure, there is a different, but not unusual, frame of reference in use here, but if that's not causing you problems, then who's to say you aren't succeeding brilliantly? So failure in the eyes of others may actually be success in your book, and vice versa.

Oh dear. We've done it again. There goes another illusion. Until now, we thought we knew what success and failure were all about. It did seem pretty straightforward when we started. Now we find success can be failure and failure can be success—how confusing is that! That leaves winning and losing very much in the melting pot. If there's a lesson in all of this, it may be to take care before adopting hard-line

positions and arriving at judgmental conclusions in case we find ourselves somewhere we did not expect to be.

Let's move back onto safer ground by sticking with what matters to
us—as individuals. Let's decide now that the rest of the world does not
live in our head and has no right to move in either. We will make up
our own minds about how we choose to live with these issues, what
for us is winning or losing, and what we each see as success or failure.
Do we have a deal? Good.

It is important to straighten these matters out. Only then will we be
able to measure our successes, and failures, against our goals.

Owning Your Mistakes

If we are to reach our goals, we must learn how to correct the mistakes
we make along the way. This means we must first admit to them, confess
to them, or otherwise own them. This does not come easily to all of us.
But consider that the very best fishing stories are always about the one
that got away. Somehow it lends authority in almost any company to be
known to have just missed that fish, and nobody minds at all that it was
a toss-up between bad luck and bad management that you came home
with a sardine instead of a salmon! On a nonwinning day, your experiences—which are clearly extensive—can still buy you subhero status.
Your obvious ability to dust yourself off and—in the face of almost impossible odds— hang on, hold on, and strike, swing, or claw your way
back into the frame is soon legendary. It's good talk in anyone's language,
and most conversations can be steered around to it sooner or later.

This clearly shows that owning your mistakes can have its advantages.
It also shows that it's not always necessary to win in order to cash in on
the free-floating accolade due to those who take home the trophy. Most of
us have made good use of this at one time or another to reconstruct ourselves after a less than successful outing. You can do so without a guilty
conscience because everyone needs a helping hand now and then.

It's also interesting to note that people who talk just about winning
are not usually as popular as those who tell how they overcame their
mistakes along the way. Certainly our sporting heroes are the ones who
bring home the glory, but our outright adulation is often reserved for
those who—win, lose, or draw—managed to survive a few adventures
in the course of combat. If we weren't sure whether we could relate to
these superbeings before, we've just discovered that we can. And we've
just worked out how, for while most of us cannot identify with their

feelings of megasuccess, we can certainly identify with their feelings of having made mistakes. Mistakes bridge the gap between us and our heroes because everyone can pick up on the disappointment of losing an important match, or the exhilaration of recovering well from a mistake. We've all been there and know what it feels like, and we are endlessly curious to know how others cope in such circumstances. So if you won, tell the world how you did it in spite of your mistakes, and if you missed out on the winning, at least enjoy losing in style. Before you can blink, you'll be the most popular kid on the block.

With all the good intentions in the world, however, you will never correct a mistake *until and unless you declare that it is yours*. This is first base. You must reach the stage at which you really do embrace your mistakes as a genuine part of your very own best effort.

What's the worst mistake on the planet?
Believing you didn't make it!

Coaches' Corner

Tackling ideas of success and failure is so fundamental to coaching that it really should be required thinking in every coaching course. If you've missed out in the past, now's the time to fix it.

There are no apologies for the fact that all this can be a prickly issue. Many younger athletes may have outdated views they have not yet questioned. Some will be in a state of flux, others in an undecided muddle. As their role model and significant other, you need to get your act together for their sake. You'll find your mentor valuable here. Still haven't got one? Better hurry before the water gets any deeper and you discover you forgot to bring your water wings.

In the interests of harmonious and ongoing relationships with your athletes, listen to them. Encourage them to listen to you. If you can't get things to match up between you, then one of you has to move on. There are no halfway houses.

Action Pact

Spend 15 minutes answering these questions:

- What has been your greatest public success to date? How did it feel then, and now?

- How does your greatest public success compare with your greatest private success?
- Do you believe in successful failure? Explain it in three sentences.
- How is winning different from success?
- Compare and contrast public and private winning. Work out which is most important to you. List five reasons for your choice.
- Can you turn mistakes into positive, constructive events for your athletes? How can you do this?
- Can you explain losing in positive terms? Try.
- How is losing different from failing?
- Can you coach significant others in these matters? Practice this today.

If all this brain work is getting difficult, try harder. If you've run out of time, give yourself an extension. If you've run out of excuses, you're making marvelous progress!

Little Homily

Back at the paddock or down at the gym, you may have to interact with a variety of people with whom you have no chance to discuss these ideas and whose views are clearly very different from your own. Angry parents, frustrated fans, unappreciated volunteers, irate officials—their feelings will all run high at the end of the day. This is because the outcome matters to them. It is *only* because the outcome matters. Maybe they haven't sat down and thought about the answers to these questions, which are all about outcomes. Maybe they've just inherited a whole bunch of secondhand views and didn't even realize how tacky some of them were. Lots of people have done that. In the interests of good coaching, you can now choose not to be one of them.

Summary

This chapter discussed many weighty issues and arrived at no conclusions. You were encouraged to develop your own working definitions of

- winning,
- not winning,

- losing,
- succeeding, and
- failing successfully.

If you are an athlete, such personal definitions will help you establish a framework around your performance by which you can measure your efforts. If you are a coach, it's time to sort out the views, beliefs, and opinions that will drive your coaching and propel you and your athletes in the direction you all want to go.

PART II

Putting Excellence Into Action

5

Planning Your Success

It's time to get on with the show. Here's where you start to put together your new sporting life in terms you've never used before. Once upon a time, your dreams may have been enough to fire your enthusiasm and send you scampering out onto the court or puffing around the track. But now it's time to face the fact that you'll spend an awful lot of time and energy rushing around in circles—unless you have a *plan*. This chapter will show you how to develop a plan. Having now decided what success means to you, you will find it easy to list your goals, and it will be a breeze to sort out what you must do to achieve them. This plan will be the new blueprint of your life; it will help you structure and organize yourself to achieve your goals.

Why is it so vital to have a plan? Because only when you have a plan can you see if what you're doing is *unplanned*. Plans are a map of your future. If you follow the map, you'll stand as good a chance as we know how to muster of getting where you want to go. If you don't follow the map—or you don't have a map to start with—the chances are you'll get very lost. It's rough country out there. Plans often get amended, lost, or even shelved, or someone else's plan sometimes takes over your own. (Tip: If you find this planning business difficult or disheartening, don't skip the chapter. Decide now to make an easier plan, *but promise the world you're going to stick to it*.)

Drawing Up Your Grand Plan

Get comfortable and make the coffee now. You could be here for some time. You'll need to concentrate on what you're doing too, so take the phone off the hook and put the cat out. You'll find, and quickly, that there's nothing quite like a good plan. It sorts out what has to be done and when to do it. It lets you chew on the awkward parts before getting in on the action. And this is no ordinary plan. This is the new template of your life. This is your grand plan.

With all the advice in the world, no one is better qualified to draw up your plan than you. You don't even have to get it right because a plan is a working brief that comes up for review the minute it's finished. Regardless of whether you never change one word of it or you scrap it inside the hour, just put your future life down on paper. Nevermind if you make mistakes—at least they'll be *yours*.

Deciding On Your Sporting Goals

Remember that good goals are *smart* goals. Never heard of them? Read on. Smart goals are . . .

- Specific
- Measurable
- Achievable
- Realistic
- Timely

Specific

Wanting to be an Olympic athlete is a fabulous dream, but it's not a goal. It's altogether too vague and unfocused. So let's make it more specific by narrowing down your event. Say you're a swimmer. That's fine, but still not specific enough. What is your stroke and your distance? Your goal may now be to become a 400-meter butterfly international champion. Now we're talking! Put a time frame to it (Beijing 2008?), and you're in business. All goals must be accurate and specific. Nonspecific statements are only aims in life. With a little focus, they can become goals.

Write out your specific goals as accurately and with as much detail as you can. Try to make them so clear that even if you explained them to someone who had no knowledge of your sport, they would know exactly where you're heading.

Measurable

This is arguably the most important criterion your goals must meet. There's no getting around it—you *must* specify the actual dimensions of your task. Otherwise you will never know whether you are achieving them. So ask yourself some very straight questions. What standard—*particularly*—do you want to reach? How fast—*exactly*—do you want to run? How far—*precisely*—do you want to throw? You must commit yourself to speeds, distances, heights, weights, or whatever numbers are a part of your sport. Without numbers, your goals are still no more than interesting items on your wish list. You will certainly change the measurements of your success as your standard of performance improves, so don't feel you have to meet Olympic standards in the first season. Be sure to measure your efforts in accordance with your current levels of skill and fitness.

Achievable

Your goals need to match your physical, mental, and emotional capabilities. This is a good thing to discuss with your coach since it's not always easy to be objective about your capabilities. There's no use thinking you'll make an international basketball team if you're only 5 feet, 2 inches tall and built like a brick. Top basketball players just don't come in that sort of a package. But weightlifters do . . .

Realistic

Your goals need to fit with your lifestyle. Whatever standard of competition you're heading for, it won't happen without the relevant training facilities and coaching expertise. This may mean you need to make serious moves to change your lifestyle. If you really do see yourself as a runner, skater, bowler, or goalie, then now's the time to call your own bluff. Is this someone you really want to be or just something it might be nice to do? Now is the time to also take a long, hard look at your bank account to see if it's going to be able to take the strain of supporting your habit. Realism always has a dollar sign in there somewhere. There's no use planning a trip to stardom if you don't have the wherewithal to buy the ticket. Of course you could always use someone else's money, but that's tricky if you don't already have the track record to convince them to give it to you. It's something of a Catch 22 situation: You need the money to get that good, but you need to be that good to get the money. If you are chasing sponsorship, here are a couple of tips: Go for broke (which you're probably doing anyway) and put in for maxidollars. Too often, athletes' proposals are too modest, and the sums are just not big enough to attract corporate interest. Be prepared to work hard for your dollar and know that you'll earn every cent before the day is done. Decide not what your sponsor can do for you, but what you can do for your sponsor! This is a business deal, and as in any other deal, there are services to be rendered (yours), for a price to be agreed (generally theirs), to the benefit of both parties. Being realistic regarding your worth to your "business partner" is entirely to your credit.

Timely

Your goals need to be *reasonably* challenging. If they are too difficult for where you are right now, you will lose heart trying to achieve them. If they are too easy, you will lose interest in making them happen.

Now you are ready to draft your goals. You need to set out clearly and succinctly exactly what you want to do. Feel relaxed about that. Most goals can stand some modification.

Long-Term Goals

Following the SMART formula (table 5.1), write down the principal competitions you want to win (such as a national title in your sport) or the main things you want to do (such as represent your state or coun-

Table 5.1 SMART Goals

Specific	What *exactly* do you want to do?	*When* do you want to do it?
Measureable	How, *precisely*, are you going to measure this?	What performances do you have to beat?
Achievable	Do you have the talent, resources, determination, body, and mind to do this?	Does your coach agree on this?
Realistic	Is this goal *practical* in the context of the rest of your life?	Is this *possible*?
Timely	Are your goals *revelant* to your age, skills, and sports potential?	How hungry are you for success?

try) in as much detail as you can. This should include the *really* important things that you ultimately want to achieve. This, or these, are your long-term goals.

Medium-Term Goals

Continuing to use the SMART formula, work backward from your long-term goals and decide what you will need to achieve, qualify for, get experience in, or get good at to make your long-term goals a possibility. These are your medium-term goals. Now work out your short-term goals.

Short-Term Goals

Still using the SMART formula, turn the possibilities into probabilities by setting out what you need to achieve next week or during your next training session to make it all happen. These are your short-term goals.

You can construct your own time frame as long as you put *end dates* on all your goals (e.g., I plan to win the club championship *next season*, or *in 2005*). Remember to *check all your goals* to see that they meet the SMART criteria.

You now have a large-scale road map of exactly where you're going, one that tells you down to the hour precisely how to get there. It is your very own, very good grand plan.

When you've done all this for your sporting life, do the same thing for any other significant areas of your life. This might include your education, professional career, family life, or workplace progress. Then reconcile these different rafts of goals. Are they compatible in terms of time, money, and effort? Are they geographically and logistically possible? Asking yourself some of the following questions may help you focus your goals.

- Do I have enough hours in the day to do all this?
- Can I afford my sport? If not, what could I do about that?
- Do I have the support (family, coach, etc.) to succeed?
- Does my Olympic (championship) year coincide with my final college year or other major personal event? If so, how could I organize this?
- Are there any major drains on my resources (financial, emotional, physical) that may prohibit my reaching my goals? If so, could I share those obligations with someone else?
- Will I be in a job that will pay me enough to afford my sport? If not, how could I change that?
- Will my job take too many hours out of my training to achieve my goal? What could I do about that?
- Have I got a plan B? If not, why not?

Drawing Up Your Training Schedule

Here's where we move into making it happen. If you already have a viable training schedule, commit it to paper. If you don't, then draft a new one, preferably with the help of your coach. If you don't have a coach, get serious and find one.

Bear in mind the different facets of your training (endurance, strength, speed, etc.) and make sure that the schedule for each dovetails comfortably into your grand plan. Also consider the standard to which you want to perform. If you're heading for the club finals at the end of it all, then training twice a week will probably suffice. If you have greater goals in mind, however, that just may not do.

Fine-Tuning Your Training

Your training schedule is not set in concrete, and you may well want to amend it later. A good one is one that works *for you*. This means that by achieving your short-term goals, you progress toward your medium- and long-term goals. The pace must match both you and your lifestyle. If you are a teenage beginner who is still in school, you will have a different training schedule than a sport veteran with a family to support and a job to hold down.

Good periodization is the key here. You need to generate workable, progressive micro- and macrocycles of training set carefully against your competition calendar and squarely in the context of your "other" life. Be sure to integrate the different aspects of your training associated with your particular sport, such as strength, speed, and so on. Establish where you currently sit on the sport–life continuum. Consider the consequences of moving along that continuum to the heavy end of sport involvement. It's a very different life out there. Almost certainly there will be other people in your life to consider, and the impact of your moves on their lifestyle may not be to their liking.

Your Very Own, Very Good Plan B

Write a list of alternative ways to make your goals happen if every one of your current ideas were to run aground. This is a good exercise in thinking outside the box. You need to be as strong and as flexible as sprung steel. There's nothing like having options to make you feel you can change the world after all.

Managing Your Support Team

It is not possible to achieve sporting prominence as an isolated individual. Every successful athlete is supported by a squad of specialists. This section is all about your support team. Set aside an afternoon and list the advantages, disadvantages, problems, issues, difficulties, and marvels of interacting with each of the specialists on your support team. Set a time to meet with each one and share the things on your list.

Commit to this time and agenda. (This means not postponing or canceling at the last minute.)

Tell each person how you value the efforts he or she makes on your behalf and how—if at all—he or she can change to better help you. It may take only a few minutes, but you'll be amazed at how such a meeting will change the quality of your relationships for the better. In the light of this experience, set another time and review the agenda. *Commit to this new time and agenda.*

Mistakes on an Upper

Of course, you'll draft the perfect preparation plan in which everything runs according to plan, your coach doesn't leave town, there's no time out for injury, and your motivation never falters. It's easy to think that disasters only happen to somebody else.

Think again, my friend! This is the real world we live in. Build in some contingency plans, some "what ifs," some plan Bs. What if your sponsor walks off in the other direction? What if you don't *have* a sponsor? Although positive thinking is all the rage, you need to keep an eye on the reality factor. Believing in your own affirmations is one thing, but believing your own publicity is quite another, so remember that the world is not yet at your feet. You may need to accommodate that, at least for the time being.

Mistakes on a Downer

These kinds of mistakes are more painful. They're the ones you didn't plan for at all. The world is no longer at your feet—it's on your shoulders. You're overcommitted, backed yourself into a corner, created an image you can't live up to. How do we do these things! Somehow your life jumped the tracks when you weren't looking. Now the task of the day is to get it back on the rails.

This starts with a careful, if slightly wary, look at your goals. Somewhere along the line they didn't stand up to the test. The trick is finding out where. It's the questions that matter. Ask yourself, *Is* this possible? *Am* I being realistic? When you're not reaching your goals, it's time to reassess what's happening. Smart folks reassess anyway. Supersmart folks will be doing this with their coach. They've found it's easier to look in the mirror if there's another face in there too.

Coach Note

Everyone wants to coach a champion. Be careful, however, that you pick the right horse before you place your bet. Making sure the horse himself really wants to win is not always easy to do.

Goals and all the planning associated with them are in very personal territory. So goals, by definition, are very personal. Be sure that you respect that. At no time should you try to impose your expectations on your athletes, nor should you try to influence them to adopt unfulfilled goals of your own. *Their* goals call up *their* effort for *their* glory. That's the way it should stay.

Of those you coach some will not set goals as high as yours. Some will be underachievers. Although such athletes' goals may be difficult to reconcile with your own appraisal of what you think they could do, their goals represent no less of a challenge to them than some of the more public prizes. If you're tempted to urge them to bigger and brighter things, back off! You don't live in their head, and you don't know how it feels inside their world. In taking on a more modest challenge rather than throwing themselves at something they were never really in the frame to achieve, it could be that they are being more realistic than you are.

Success With Attitude

It's all very well planning your life down to the last gasp, but if you're going to make it to the top, you'll need to add something extra. We've all heard of the "artistic temperament" of prima donnas in the arts world and that's all very well for them, but what those of us in the sport world need is a bit of *attitude!*

Attitude is the stuff champions are made of. This is the high-drama end of performance that brings the crowd to its feet and has them chanting your name. The goal from an impossible angle that ricochets off the bar, the almost-dropped catch that is juggled for a heart-stopping moment, the slip that turns the stretch into a high-power slam to somehow win the impossible point—these magnificent efforts create the gut-wrenching moments of gasps and yells, the triumphs in the face of impossible odds, and the best action entertainment ever invented. Here's how to put yourself in the box seat every time and turn an ordinary success into your greatest triumph. Stitching such moments into the fabric of your performance is the ultimate in producing not only a winning effort but one with that touch of magic that even years down the track brings a light to your eye. This is where we lift the veils of secrecy and expose *exactly* how it is done.

Let's have no illusions about the size and shape of the task before us. This is going to require a degree of brilliance that borders on genius. And the secret? Easy. Here's another one for the refrigerator door:

■ **Never, never, *never* give up!**

Believe right down to the smell of your socks that nothing is lost until the point, the game, or the day is absolutely over. That glory is still up for grabs until you've run the last yard, hit the last ball, or swum the last stroke. So keep on trying.

Move in to the winner's frame today and every day. *Start* in the winner's frame as you greet the day. Say to yourself a dozen times before breakfast: "I'm a winner until proven otherwise!"

Then *stay* in the winner's frame *regardless of the score* until the action is over. Move on—but not out of that frame—as you live the rest of your day. Post positive affirmations in every room in the house, at work, in the garage, and on the garden shed. Become obsessed with experiencing success 18 hours a day. If you think that's far out, think again. The seriously committed winner *sleeps* in the winner's frame too because there's a whole lot of dreaming to be done before breakfast!

To join the ranks of those who make these great sporting moments happen, you'll need to mend even the tiniest chink in your armor that might let in the smallest worm of suspicion or the briefest moment of doubt that success might not happen. Regard nonsuccess as temporary. Believe that success is the norm. Your norm. Repeat after me:

■ **I was born to succeed.**

Post affirmations on the refrigerator, the bathroom mirror, the front of your closet, and the back of the cornflakes box. Stick multiple copies on the inside of the bathroom door for more lengthy contemplations.

Example

You've just hit a winner off a mis-hit of the last ball of the match. What else is there to say? You acted with all the confidence that only a winner can bring to such a swipe, never doubting that miracles *do* happen.

■ You've got to practice living with a successful attitude to make it a permanent part of your life.

Training Strategies

It's all in your head. This is no time for false modesty and drawing-room manners. You need a ton or two of the best *attitude* in town! Go get a real grip on the world and then snatch the bit that wasn't yours to start with. Make off with the spoils like they were always yours anyway, and snarl a bit at anyone who thinks you should share them. That's putting together a winning attitude. Then, as with the rest of your sport skills, practice takes you to the top, so get busy on living with attitude.

Mistakes take effort. Recovering from them takes even more effort. It's all a question of how hungry you are. When you're *really* ravenous, nothing this side of the sun will stop you from getting what you need. You'll need more than skill, more than luck. You'll need monumental effort . . . and *attitude*. The following can help you create that attitude:

- Check that your self-talk is consistently, reliably, unshakably *positive*.
- Check that your conversations with others are equally as positive.
- Check that your dreams match all of the above.
- Make sure your actions match your dreams.
- Boost your belief in yourself by enjoying praise and believing compliments from others.
- Compliment yourself. Often.
- Build your confidence *on the hour, every hour*, in your sport skills, in your social skills, in your life skills, in yourself. Reward yourself for these too.
- Live with success. Every day do something you *know* you can do well. Then congratulate yourself on a job well done.
- Read, learn, and live by your affirmations. Make winning your way of life.
- When you can do all that, naturally you will have a touch of genius.

So who needs to recover from a success? Well, practically speaking, you do. When you've succeeded, enjoy the exhilaration, don't bother to hide your satisfaction, and give a passing nod to the relief that goes with it. We're too used to agonizing over our losses for far longer than we rejoice in our successes. Now is the time to let your success break over your head like a wave and love every drop of it! Let the crowd roar, and bask in this moment because no price can ever buy it.

That's OK if you finish at a magic moment, but it's a tad trickier if you write success into the script and you're only partway through your game. It's easy to be distracted as you celebrate a great shot or a winning effort. By all means, use your attitude, but don't let it get in the way. You have to refocus quickly to forestall follow-up errors, but we know about them. That takes a touch of brilliance, otherwise known as attitude, but you have that now.

What's a mistake worth making?
One with attitude.

Coaches' Corner

Behind every great athlete is a great coach (or so they say). So hopefully it's safe to assume that your attitude is all organized. You'd better believe it because now's your hour. This is where coaching moves closer to mentoring. You become your athletes' role model and friend as you help them measure their mind-sets, sort out their values, and move to a whole new level in relation to their sport involvement. Most of us feel privileged to be part of the steering gear that a young person uses to chart a course through their sporting life.

To remain a socially bearable human being during the coaching process, it helps to do something occasionally that requires a measure of humility to remind yourself that you're one of the lucky ones in life. Try a new sport or do something you've never done before—preferably something with risk attached. Then do it in front of other people. This will remind you that you didn't always have all the answers and you weren't born perfect after all. At the end of the day we are all very small cogs in a much larger wheel.

Action Pact

Here are the major players:

- **Attitude** is copied, learned, and practiced. Your athletes will learn from you every which way you play, teach, or coach your sport on and off the track, field, or court, in or out of the water or the gym, and from your conduct both in public and in private. Better believe that *once a coach, always a role model.* You're never out of your athletes' frame, so make sure they like what they see, and know that they'll live what they learn . . . from you.

- **Self-talk** is highly reflective of the comments of significant others, including the coach. Stay kind in what you say. Listen to your own mind chatter too. You will have little to give your athlete if you have not addressed yourself.

- **Success** is a very special feeling. Reward your athletes often and well, and let them savor their best moments. We can be miserable on our own, but happiness only really works when it's shared.

- **Confidence** is built one day at a time. Give your athletes opportunities to do that *themselves,* in every training session. Give yourself the same opportunities.

- **Coach till you drop!** If we ever needed a mantra to live by, it might go something like this:

  Stay positive even in the face of drastic odds.

  Never give up, even when threatened with catastrophe.

  And *keep smiling* because you know that . . .

■ Good coaches make champions, *but great coaches make history.*

Summary

You are now convinced of the need to plan. You have learned, or have been reminded, that your goals need to be SMART:

- **S**pecific
- **M**easurable
- **A**chievable
- **R**ealistic
- **T**imely

You also need

- long-term goals,
- medium-term goals,
- short-term goals, and
- a good plan B.

You are also convinced that you need *attitude. Attitude* can be learned, copied, mimicked, or invented. *Attitude* is the difference between success and triumph. Success has a shelf life; *triumph is eternal.*

6

Reasons for Making Mistakes

Perhaps it has come as a bit of a shock to realize that there are many different kinds of mistakes, and it maybe seems unreasonable to think that you'll ever be able to sort them out. But in fact you'll soon get just as quick at recognizing them and taking appropriate action as you already are at reading the play or deciding on your next shot. It's easy to forget that that didn't happen overnight either. Try to look at mistakes management as just another facet of your skill base. It's no more complicated than that.

Correcting Your Mistakes

To make corrections *that will fix your mistakes for all time*, you need to know two things:

- Exactly where to look for the cause of your mistake
- What factors are contributing to the frequency of your mistake

In training you will want to work out the reasons for your mistakes. That's what this chapter is about. You will also want to make particular corrections for various sorts of mistakes. These corrections have been explained in the Coaches' Corners throughout the book. If you skipped those parts, do not pass Go, do not collect $200, and go back to page 1!

In competition, or any time you want to recover immediately from a mistake and move on, you will need the general recovery strategies outlined in chapter 9.

Sorting Out the Systems

To fix your mistakes, you will need a quick and simple system of sorting them out. Think of it this way. Making a mistake in your performance is the equivalent of hearing an unusual noise coming from your car. This noise signals that the system needs repair. It will tell the skilled ear exactly where to look for the problem. Just as your friendly mechanic knows whether to work on the wheel hub or the gear box, so a particular type of mistake will tell your friendly coach whether it is a learning error or a confidence problem.

Sooner rather than later you will regret ignoring the ugly noise in your car because unfixed faults usually get expensive, and often quickly. It is the same with your performance mistakes. Uncorrected errors get progressively more difficult to correct and become rapidly more "expensive" in terms of lost time and wasted effort. They also take their emotional and financial toll, not to mention the lost opportunities for glory. Also, the more you practice, the better you get. This same is true of mistakes; like most things, the longer they go uncorrected, the better you get at repeating them. Most important, the more you use the trigger that prompts you to make the mistake, the more sensitive that trigger becomes and the more easily it is activated. This can cause you to become extremely good at consistently—and instantly—producing the appropriate and well-practiced mistake, right on cue.

Different mistakes require different corrections, so it is vital to know what type of mistake has been made. So you should worry if your friendly coach makes too many *coaching mistakes* because now that you have the inside story on making mistakes, you know the consequences. Think of the "costs" to you if your coach corrects your training mistakes as though they're competition errors, or misreads your faulty attentional focus as an innocent fitness problem. Not to mention those uncorrected errors. So are we all on red alert? Good. This is appropriate because this is where some of your brain should be most of the time if you are to pick up on your mistakes before you get too practiced at them.

This brings us to *the* most seriously important basic rule of good mistakes management: Log on to your mistakes *early*. Live by this rule. Make it a mission.

■ Repair them now—or regret them later!

But before you can fix your mistakes, you must find out the reason things unraveled in the first place. Distinguishing the minor mistake from the major blunder is easy enough (see page 19, "Scale of Mistakes"), but you need to know much more than that. You must find out *exactly* what went wrong because nailing the *exact* cause of your mistake is absolutely fundamental to fixing it. You need to decide which of your performance systems was responsible for the action that you didn't like. Only then can you go looking for what went wrong inside that system.

Performance Systems

You have four performance systems—skill, physical, mental, and emotional. If any one of them is faulty, a variation in your performance will result. If you don't like the variation, you'll call it a mistake. If you do like it, you'll call it a flash of genius.

• **Skill system:** Your skill system is your bank of *learned* sport-specific skills. They will be the patterns of behavior that relate particularly to your sport, such as the technical skills of swimming, pole-vaulting, or football. Variations in these patterns will result in technical mistakes. These will need technical corrections, such as "watch the ball," keep your head lower," "follow through," and so forth. These skills may also include the ability to read plays, read your opponent, judge speed and distance, or strategize.

• **Physical system:** Your physical system is your *body*—its fitness, strength, flexibility, and power. Sometimes we make unreasonable or inappropriate demands on our bodies, which they cannot meet. Mistakes here may be the result of lack of fitness, stiffness, fatigue, previous injury, actual injury, or unsuitability of your system for the job in the first place. Timing is crucial to the body's ability to respond, and although you may even have made a reasonable demand, it could have been at an unreasonable moment, when your body was either too disorganized for the task, or well-organized but for something else. It might just have been busy.

- **Mental system:** Your mental system is your *mind*—its skills drive the whole show. This system includes the ability to choose the appropriate attentional focus, the ability to maintain that focus, imagery skills, control of self-talk, control of tension levels, goal-setting skills, and all the battery of mental skills commonly addressed in sport psychology. This system also includes the intellectual ability to understand a task and direct the practice necessary to developing that task into a high-quality motor skill. Mistakes here may originate in the following system.

- **Emotional system:** Your emotional system is how you *feel* about what you're doing, such as nervous, confident, happy, and so on. Often we're told how we *will* feel rather than how to deal with how we *do* feel, and we have largely been expected to perform in an unemotional way. This has led us to trying to put our emotions in park and perform *in spite of them*. Since we are not machines, we do not do this very well and make many mistakes in the process. How very much more helpful to enlist our emotions and use this mightily influential resource. More on how to do this shortly.

Meanwhile, if one of your performance systems fails, you *must* know which one it is before you start rummaging around looking for spare parts and wrenches to fix it. After all, it's not going to be much help if a mistake happens because your body wasn't strong enough for the task, but you think it was caused by inattention. Paying better attention to your lack of strength is not going to improve your muscle tone! Taking your body down to the weight room could be more productive.

Once you have flagged the system that needs repair, you have taken the first and most important move toward successfully identifying the mistake. Naturally you will sometimes flag the wrong system, but the worst that will happen is that you then won't be able to correct the mistake. This might be irritating, but it won't end the world. Keep thinking, and just bring your coach in on the action. Try a process of elimination if you both get stuck. Your discussion may go something like this: Well, it wasn't a technical mistake because you know the stuff backwards. You were cool as the proverbial cucumber, so it wasn't the emotional stuff. You understand what you're doing, so the mental bit's no sweat, but maybe you just didn't have the ergs as you launched that shot. Muscle fatigue? Not fit enough? Physical system? Gotcha!

Sometimes more than one system fails at the same time. This is when things become tricky. For instance, if you lost the ball to a good tackle, were you outplayed (skill system), were you starting to become fatigued (physical system), did you misread the play (mental system), were you intimidated by the opposing player (emotional system)—or was it a combination of some, or all, of the above? This is when it's particularly handy to have help from your friendly *mistakes-wise* coach. Video will also show you useful replays. But remember it doesn't show you what you were thinking or how you were feeling at the time, and that just may have been critical. To help yourself sort these things out, try asking yourself or your coach these three questions.

Three Big Questions

1. What—*exactly*—did I do? (Be sure to answer this question *positively*.)

   - Do not say, "I hit the ball out." This is of no help.
   - Instead, say, "I hit the ball too far behind the base line." This may later reveal a pattern in your mistakes that can then be corrected.

2. When—*precisely*—did I do it?

   - Do not say, "Again!" or make similarly vague comments.
   - Instead, say, "Following an aggressive move from my opponent," or maybe, "When I felt under stress," or, "At match point." We're looking for a pattern of behavior, remember.

3. Which of my performance systems needs fixing?

   - Were your skills not there when you needed them (is your technique not up to the job)?
   - Did your body not stand up (were you tired, heat-stressed)?
   - Did you not have your mind on the job (where was your attentional focus; what was your self-talk)?
   - Did your feelings get in the way (did nerves get the better of you, were you too excited at the prospect of winning)?

Then *definitely* ask your coach the following questions:

1. What will it cost to fix the mistake? How much will you need to practice to set things straight? This will clarify the job to be done. It will also put a fence around how much effort, how many dollars, and how much ego is on the line.

2.   How long will it take to fix the mistake? Some mistakes are more recalcitrant than others are, and those that answer to the name *habit* are always slow to shift. Those that answer to *bad habit* take longer still. Getting some sort of time scale is useful not only for mapping out the content of your training—it will also help your motivation enormously!

3.   Is the mistake trivial or terminal? Some well-learned, well-practiced, homegrown mistakes are not easily relearned, and most are never entirely forgotten. Better that you know what you're up against here. If your mistake is going to get in the way on a regular or ongoing basis, then you may need to seriously adjust your goals. Well-entrenched mistakes should be kept somewhere absolutely inaccessible! Read chapter 8 to discover how to lock them up and where and when to throw away the key.

All this is the stuff of a good debriefing session. There's nothing quite like it for getting to the guts of the matter. *Win, lose, or draw—debrief like never before!* If you won, then naturally, you'll want to know how to win again. If you didn't, you'll want to know why. If you drew, you'll want to get the rematch in the bag.

The more successfully you can address these matters, the more thoroughly your mistakes will be corrected. Having targeted the cause of your mistakes, you'll be in a much stronger position to customize your future practice to your upcoming competitions. And because you've gotten right down to the bottom of the matter, you know that even if you make similar mistakes in the future, they can never take you unawares again. You've got their number. Your confidence gets a *guaranteed* boost. That's a nice payoff for having debriefed well.

Frequency of Mistakes

It's one thing to know what kind of mistake you've made, and even where to start looking to fix it, but it's quite another to know how often you're likely to make it. The three most significant factors that will directly affect the frequency of your mistakes are as follows:

- The quality of your training environment
- The quality of your practice
- The quality of your coaching

Improving the quality of any or all of these will immediately cut down on the frequency with which you make *any* mistake.

Training Environment Quality

It's just not possible to create magic in a mundane environment. Since it may be difficult to change your facilities, you may have to consider relocating if you're heading for serious stardom.

Neither is it possible to do wonderful things in woeful gear. You can no more play hockey in sneakers than you can play basketball in rubber boots. So fix your gear if it's getting in the way of you reaching your goals. Doing this will immediately reduce the size and the number of your mistakes. Alternatively, remembering you always have choices, revise your goals to match what the quality and range of your gear will currently allow you to achieve.

Choose your gear with care and invest in good-quality brand names whenever you can. Choose your facilities carefully too; because they won't come to you, you just might have to go to them. It will be worth the effort and whatever sacrifices you have to make to rearrange your life.

Practice Quality

This one is all yours. There is no substitute for guided, high-quality trying! Presuming that you have the necessary aptitude in the first place, you will need to devote approximately 10,000 hours to your sport if you are to reach elite level. This will mean devoting about 10 years of your life to practicing, whether you feel like it or not. You would need to devote a similar amount of time and effort to becoming a master craftsman, a top-class musician, a professional dancer, a doctor, or a rock star. Megastars at anything work even harder and usually longer. Millionaires make it a lifestyle.

The equations are as follows:

10,000 hours ÷ 10 years = 1,000 hours per year
1,000 hours ÷ 48 weeks = 20 hours per week (allow 4 weeks of vacation per year)
20 hours ÷ 6 days = 3 hours and 20 minutes per day (allow 1 rest day per week)

Most elite athletes train for at least 20 hours per week. Having reached that level, most work twice as hard to stay there! This is practice only, remember, and does not include competition exposure, which depending on your sport may take another couple of months out of your year.

In light of this information, perhaps now is a good time to review your goals and address your priorities. Given that you are going to commit such a huge amount of time to this occupation, it will be useful to explore exactly what you are going to do. This might include asking yourself whether you can have too much of a good thing. It appears from recent running history that the answer could be yes. Runners have discovered that the human body does not just go on improving indefinitely in response to how much you tax its resources. It seems there is an optimum range of demands that inspire an adaptive response. Beyond that the body is merely fatigued and does not fully recover within the specified micro or macro training cycles. In circumstances that amount to continued overload, the body does not perform at its ongoing and improving best.

The mind becomes similarly fatigued in response to long periods under such regimes. In our quest for "faster, higher, stronger" we had better learn that our bodies are not a bottomless bank account on which we can draw indefinitely. Sooner or later the loan is called up. The body may say, That's it! in a dramatic way, such as a ruptured Achilles tendon or a torn hamstring. You and medical science are then left to mend the pieces as best you can. If it's the mind that says Enough! you may just wake up as an exsportsperson one day and never want to pick up a bat or ball again. Or you may simply experience a long, slow burnout until you finally hear what your mind is trying to say.

Inevitably, in the course of such a long run as 10,000 hours, we are bound to make mistakes. We are just abiding by the statistical probability that, since we are not machines, in spending a long time learning and repeating skills, we will not be able to deliver 100% of the task, 100% of the time. Anyway, even metal fatigues eventually. If that's no consolation, recall that perpetual motion has yet to be discovered or invented.

Put this one on the refrigerator door:

■ Quality performance begins and ends with quality practice.

It's not only *how much* you practice. Above all, it's the quality of your practice that counts. Quality is *everything.* If you only practice mediocre stuff, you'll only learn mediocre stuff. Neither your mind nor your body will ever learn how to be in top shape, much less to stay there, from mediocre practice. Small wonder then that when your practice lacks quality, your competition record reflects it. You cannot suddenly expect to pull off a performance for which you have not prepared. Minds can do extraordinary things sometimes, but bodies generally run pretty much according to plan. You need, from the beginning, to establish the level of quality in your training. This will largely be determined by your end goals. The higher these are set, the higher the quality of your training must be to meet them. So we're not just talking practice now; we're talking 10,000 hours *of supervised, coached, high-quality practice.* That's how it is.

You choose the quality of practice at every single practice session. You may feel that many factors affecting this are not within your control—the track may be wet, the pool may be cold, or you may have had a poor night's sleep. Any of those may be true. What is in your control, however, is your reaction to these matters. You might like to choose wisely here, unless you're into wasting some of those 10,000 hours, and therefore extending them.

You choose which mistakes to practice, which to learn from, which to avoid making, and which you will repeat. Perhaps you need to know a few of the options on this before you'll take that on board, so for now just believe that your mistakes management can be trained, practiced,

■ You want quality performance? Begin with quality practice.

and coached just like any other aspect of your performance. To do this only takes a small mind shift, and once you've moved *all* of your performance into the positive end of the spectrum, you'll feel a noticeable sense of relief. This is one of the most significant moves you'll ever make toward creating your new sporting life.

Coaching Quality

Good coaching will help you . . .

- Lower the likelihood that you'll make more than your share of silly or serious mistakes
- Lessen the number of repeat mistakes that can peg your performance at a low level
- Profit from the coach's experience
- Accelerate your skill learning
- Increase, and share, the fun

However, it needs to be said that mistakes and difficulties will occur in everyone's career, even with very good coaching. Recognize that at the end of the day even the best coaching is no more than facilitation that can only bring out what is already in the athlete. To be sure, your coach may be very skilled and use wonderful educational episodes and inspired teaching. Nonetheless, there's no way your coach can turn you into a champion unless you were born one. Consequently, the buck still stops with you.

The bottom line—*your* bottom line—is as follows:

- *You choose* to play.
- *You choose* your coach.
- *You choose* to continue to be coached.
- *You choose* to listen to—or to ignore—your coach's advice.

As you now begin to map out not only the size of your mistakes, but also how often the ones you know about actually happen, there is one other aspect of them that we should mention. It is their capacity to lie dormant, sometimes for very long periods of time. Because of this they don't necessarily happen in a nice, tidy, linear progression. You don't just stop making maximistakes because you've improved your skills.

You may stop making most of them, but unless you've really cleaned out the bottom of the barrel and improved *all* of your skills, maximistakes will still be in the cards. If you have ignored the early warning signs that they are on their way, they can still be unpleasantly unexpected visitors to your performance. You may experience big gaps between your mistakes, and their arrival may seem random. This is not the case. They merely go into recess. Because they are a response to a fairly infrequent trigger, they just don't surface very often. Instead, they lie dormant until that trigger is activated, then—WOW!—enter the maximistake with a vengeance. Be careful of these mistakes because by their very nature they are real confidence killers. Read chapter 8 with special care if this is your sort of problem.

A Reminder

Before you go into overload, remember that this chapter is about finding the causes and reasons for your mistakes so you can fix them. It's not about dealing with them in the heat of the action. (For all the latest on *that*, see chapter 9.) The information in this chapter is for sifting through with your coach over a quiet cup of coffee, not stuff you need at your fingertips when your world has just fallen apart.

Making New Mistakes

If you're going to continue to make mistakes, then at least move on and make different ones! To continue to improve the standard of your performance, you can't keep repeating the mistakes of your earlier efforts. This requires that you have some preventative strategies in place to guard against practicing your mistakes as thoroughly as you practice the rest of your performance. The cornerstone of any such strategy is your ability to work out, analyze, or otherwise tear to pieces the reasons why your mistakes happen. If you can work that out, then it's easy to decide what to do to fix them, when they are likely to happen again, or how you might stop them from happening altogether. This is where you need to develop something of a terrier-not-to-mention bulldog mentality and refuse to let go until you've solved the problem.

Any time now, you're about ready to take on the world, but before you do, it's time to put a fence around all this. That means keeping things in perspective and *not* beating yourself up. One learning error is not a national disaster. Allow yourself to make mistakes, knowing that in due course you will become free of them without any further proactive intervention on your part. Remember too that a touch of *attitude* here is the best thing in the world to preserve your confidence.

Camera Shy

A word here about the use of video in training—these films are not recreational viewing. They are a powerful training aid to help you do a job. As such, unedited filming of an entire training session can be both inappropriate and damaging for coach and athlete. The most useful video will be snips of action, particular angles and shots, close-ups of legs, arms, or other body parts we may want to watch in action, and sequences of particular techniques or actions that we can later freeze-frame. Many of us become self-conscious in front of the camera. We often regress as a result, and our performance can suffer drastically. Somehow we always look a little different from what we expect on film. We are always a little thinner, fatter, faster, slower, or more or less flexible than we imagined. Then there is our back view, which, unaccustomed as we are to seeing it, we often find curiously disconcerting. It's all too easy to be concerned about what others will think of us, even if we know the film is only for private viewing (which probably means we will entertain not less than three sets of significant eyes). During filming, concentration is easily lost, and the fact that the camera is rolling distracts us from our job of the moment. In short, we respond to the camera in very much the same way we do to a significant other. So the presence of a camera may actually be a reason *why we make mistakes.*

The same rules, therefore, apply to filming as to the presence of significant others. *Do not* film beginner skills because the image of beginner mistakes, which we know to be gross, and which we also know will be exacerbated by the "significant other" presence of the camera, will stick like glue to the athlete's memory. They will be endlessly replayed, are practically impossible to erase, and are highly counterproductive to later learning. Like all first impressions they have a very strong impact. For the athlete, film of their early efforts is the first impression that they will have of themselves in their new skill role. Take care that it is a *positive* one because you can rest assured they will continue to live up to it.

Once the skill base is reasonably secure *and early mistakes can be successfully corrected,* filming can begin. Learning will be greatly enhanced, and progress will be accelerated. Even so, it is wise to restrict the filming to only the best and most impressive efforts and the mistakes that can be successfully corrected. Either edit out or fast-forward through the rest, but preferably don't record it in the first place because, once filmed, it's hard not to want to watch it. This stands as a rule of thumb for the use of all video in training.

Coaches' Corner

When you have the answers to all three big questions, you know you can successfully and comprehensibly correct any mistake thrown across your coaching path. Some questions may be more complicated or take more time to answer than others. Some you may have to think about for days . . . or even weeks. Now and then you'll need to confer with other coaches, other athletes, or a mentor, but nothing this side of the sun should stop you from coming up with an answer. And if it's not the right answer, you'll get right back in and find another one.

Unhelpful Questions

Not all questions are useful. There are some that you will never ask but you will hear them around, usually because they are asked loudly with much exasperation, and in a spirit of condemnation. If you put yourself in your athlete's shoes for a moment, you soon see that these are neither kind nor necessary. Such queries as, "Why did you do *that*?" (well, if he knew, naturally, he wouldn't have done it) or "How could you?" (to which the obvious answer is, *Easily!*). These questions are not serious coaching inquiries aimed at rearranging the result. They are attributions of blame and thinly veiled expressions of disappointment, frustration, and anger. See them for what they are—do not buy into them, and head them off if you see anyone else winding up to them. You can ask better questions that will yield better answers.

No Questions

If there's anything that's worse than asking the wrong questions, it's asking no questions at all. That means you haven't just caught the wrong train, you've missed every train on the timetable. The best that can be said of this mistake is that you've saved the fare. It's a long walk home from here, though. Begin by putting one foot in front of the other and heading in the direction of coach education. Your education. Go back to chapter 1 of this book and as many relevant others as you can beg, borrow, or steal . . . and find that mentor.

Getting It Right

Having asked the right questions of the athlete, now ask the right questions of yourself. This will lead you to the right answers. You will soon have many of your own, but here are a few to get you started:

- What is my reaction to a mistake? (Address this first.)
- Has the athlete done this before, and if, so when?
- What was the trigger(s)?
- Can I identify the faulty performance system?
- What kind of mistake are we dealing with?
- Can I moderate the athlete's reaction (emotional response) to it?
- What are we going to do about this mistake?
- Are my corrections effective?
- If not, am I asking the right questions?

Summary

Identify your mistakes because *different mistakes need different corrections.* Log on to your mistakes early because *old mistakes don't die—they just live on to haunt you.*

You have four performance systems:

- **Skill system:** This is your learned sport-specific skills.
- **Physical system:** This is your body, which does the hard yards.
- **Mental system:** This is your mind, which drives the show.
- **Emotional system:** This is how it feels to do it all.

To correct a mistake, ask yourself these three big questions:

- What did I do?
- When did I do it?
- Which system needs fixing?

Then ask your coach:

- What will it cost to fix this mistake?
- How long will it take?
- Is it trivial or terminal?

There are three factors that influence the frequency of your mistakes:

- The quality of your training environment
- The quality of your practice
- The quality of your coaching

You choose all three.

Never underestimate any of the following:

- The value of a good debriefing session in identifying faulty performance systems
- The value of asking the right questions
- The influence of significant others, or the presence of a camera as a cause of mistakes

7

Accelerating Skill Learning

This chapter is one to share. Sport learning is so much a collaborative effort, between athlete and coach or between athlete and teammate, that knowledge of how this learning works is useful to everyone.

Let's start by blasting another illusion into the upper atmosphere.

Myth: Your coach will teach you the skills you need. Wrong!

You will learn the skills you need because nobody can teach you anything unless you want to learn it! Ah, but what about the "good teacher/ bad teacher" bit. That doesn't change a thing. Good learners will learn in spite of bad teachers. Bad learners won't learn from anyone. But what can be said with great certainty is that good learners will learn better, faster, and more easily from a good teacher. So we see there are now skills to be learned on both sides of this story.

Learning Well

Learning how to learn is a skill all its own, regardless of what you want to learn. Each of us has an individual style of learning. Some like to listen and possibly question an explanation. Some like to read about it. Most of us do better using pictures of what we have to practice, either by watching a live demonstration or seeing a video of the skills. Some of us create our own pictures through imagery, which is a particularly effective way to learn because we can rehearse the skill many times without exhausting ourselves as we would with a similar number of physical efforts. A few of us are impatient to get started and just launch in to trying, but that's ultimately a slow and inefficient way to learn because it usually involves personally reinventing every mistake known to man along the way.

Finding Your Own Learning Style

Remember that your teachers are facilitators, not mind readers. Although experience will tell them what is working and what is not, you can greatly speed up the process by telling them which way you learn best. If you don't know, experiment until you find out. Use the following examples.

To learn a new swimming stroke (even if you're the kind of swimmer likely to drown in the bath) do you prefer to

- *listen* to an explanation (auditory learner),
- *watch* a swimmer in action (visual learner),
- *watch* a training demonstration (audio/visual learner), or
- just *do* it (kinesthetic learner)?

You'll find that one of these works really well for you, although depending on what you're learning, you may want mixed input such as a short demonstration (visual) before a slice of the action (kinesthetic). The closer you can match your training to your preferred learning style, the fewer mistakes you will make and the faster your progress will be. That's good learning. By contrast, your nonpreferred methods will do little to improve either your knowledge or your skill.

Don't get stuck with that if the results matter to you. Knowing your preferred learning style means you can ask your coach to use it. That puts *you* at the helm and very much in charge of your learning. That's exactly where you need to be if you are to maximize your rate of progress. But it's already time you took a long, hard look at how well the teaching in your life actually matches your preferred learning style. Are you tolerating what—for you—is inappropriate teaching? If so, this is your first skill-learning mistake.

Example

If your coach is a wordsmith, that might seem to work fine for the rest of the team, but if you're a visual person, you need to see him do it. Muttering in the locker room later will not make this happen. You need to step out there and tell him what you need. The great thing is, you'll probably find that half of your teammates were thinking the same thing.

Active Versus Passive Learning

Regardless of your preferred style of learning, the more active you are and the more energy you contribute to the process, the faster and more effectively you will learn. Once you have made efforts to determine your learning style, you have already moved from being a passive learner to being an active learner, taking responsibility for your knowledge and skill acquisition. Passive learners do not contribute to the learning process. Their participation is limited to absorbing information and practicing what they are told, but they do not help to steer the process. Active learners work much harder. They use bucketloads of imagination and effort.

You are not a receptacle for information, nor are you a mirror in front of which someone else can parade knowledge. You are a hungry brain inside a body with a mission. Because you are a talented, proactive person, you do inventive and contributory things. You endlessly pursue all possible avenues to your success. You don't always get it right, and you sometimes get it magnificently wrong. You may be exhaustingly energetic, hugely brave, impossibly obstinate, and tiresomely noisy. But you are what makes teaching and coaching such a joy.

You may not have realized it until now, but your learning protocols will run something like this:

- You will relate new information to your past experiences. When learning about the muscle soreness of lactic acid buildup, for example, you may recall the last time you felt stiffness in your muscles after a training session.

- You will open your mind to new information by refusing to let old prejudices, fears, or bad memories get in the way of believing new information—at least until you disprove it.

- You may question new information in a healthy, inquisitive, noncombative way to establish the reasons it might be useful or how it may improve your performance.

- You will try to validate your understanding of new information by asking, *Is this how it's supposed to be done?* or by seeking to identify the physical sensations or feelings associated with a new skill.

- You will want to generalize your understanding of a skill by citing occasions in which you can now recognize the skill being used. This will often take you by surprise and prompt comments such as, Is *that* what she was doing?

All of this activity facilitates and consolidates your learning. Every time you learn in this way, you will accelerate your progress. Later recall of information will be more complete, and later repetitions of skills will be more successful. Throughout the learning process, you will make fewer mistakes of all kinds, which will build "cleaner" experiences and more positive mental associations with the new skill.

When you are an active learner, your confidence will be substantially stronger and the feelings of control, competency, and success that accompany greater confidence will significantly enhance your self-esteem and the building of a robust self-image. This is quite an impressive line-up of good reasons for learning to learn well. As a potential world beater, why would you want to do it any other way?

Typical Mistakes of the Learning Stages

Most experts recognize three learning stages and certain mistakes that are characteristic of each stage. The mistakes are different in quality, quantity, and patterns of frequency. The trick is to spot these differences—and therefore to *expect* them—as you progress through the learning stages in your training. Your coach needs to understand the mistakes in learning stages too so that the coaching is appropriate to your stage of learning, for only then will you be able to successfully correct your skill-learning mistakes and maximize your progress.

Beginner Stage

The beginner stage does not necessarily relate to your overall standard of performance. We should clarify here the difference between being a beginner athlete and being a beginner *at a particular skill*. If you are an advanced athlete and you added a new skill to your repertoire yesterday, then for a time being you are a beginner *at that skill*. It will not compromise your standing as an advanced athlete in all your other skills. If, however, most of your skills are at the beginner stage, then you are a beginner in your sport. We tend to like to put people in boxes, but we all have lots of skills at lots of different levels. It's only the *average* skill level that gets written on the box.

So what about beginner's mistakes? Typically, beginners' mistakes are big, gauche, and gleeful. Many are quite wondrous. There is no finesse about a novice howler. It's not the fine details that come unstitched—it's the whole fabric of the skill that comes unraveled. Confidence is important here as this can be quite disconcerting for both coach and athlete if you're not expecting this degree of disorder. Everyone needs to prepare for beginners' mistakes so that they are expected, accommodated, and survived. Your coach will have a fair idea of what's likely to happen so there should be a few safety nets in place (literally). You may have actual physical catchers or a range of mats, padding, or protective gear. To minimize making survival mistakes, simulations are useful in part or in whole. You can often use an easier, safer environment to practice skills that need to be in place before transferring to a more hazardous scene, for example, learning scuba skills in a swimming pool before going out into the ocean. It's also sometimes initially useful to learn slower versions of a new skill when possible, such as learning control of a car on a skid pan before tackling the rally circuit. Remember—you can be a beginner in the mental skills too and perhaps be unable to maintain concentration for more than a few minutes, control your self-talk, or control your nerves.

Intermediate Stage

Not many of us find the beginners' skill level satisfying enough for more than a short period, so we quickly want to progress to the second stage of learning. This is the intermediate stage. Intermediate learners are reasonably sure that, barring the end of the world, they can make their skill happen. Results may not yet be wholly reliable, and there is still much room for skill development, but the intermediate stage of learning is where most of us are most of the time.

Intermediate learners' mistakes are all about quality control. Reasonably confident that the skills *will* happen, you make technical mistakes in *how* it happens. Your mental skills will also have improved, and at this stage you expect fewer lapses in concentration; useful imagery skills; healthy, positive self-talk; good tension control; and so on. But these too can all break down under pressure.

From the coach's point of view the intermediate stage presents an endlessly interesting kaleidoscope that needs to be analyzed, organized, and corrected, all in the right order. The broader and more in-depth the coach's knowledge is, the better equipped she will be to meet the multiple challenges that the intermediate learner presents.

■ You know you *have* the skills. The question now is can you consistently *use* them?

The vast majority of us find that the commitment needed to develop advanced skills is not in our grand plan. So, only a few of us will move out of the intermediate frame in even our principal sport. If this surprises you, look again at your performance and measure it against the best in the business. Squaring up to the gap is what's called getting to know yourself.

Advanced Stage

The third and last stage of learning is the advanced stage. Here you become highly automated in your performance. You easily and frequently "enter the zone," "go into the flow," "move into the bubble," or whatever phrase describes your focus and tension management. Your skills are deft and your performance is polished. You have well-established preskill routines and postskill recoveries. Since the techniques here are secure and well practiced, mistakes at this level are typically ones of timing. But beware! Faulty timing is only a symptom, not a cause. Under the umbrella of timing we will also include rhythm and pace, for in some sports, such as tennis, these are as critical to a player's game as is the timing of an individual shot. When any or all of these elements are derailed, it is a signal that other more fundamental skills have broken down. It is then time to look at repairing or stabilizing such things as concentration, tension levels, responses to fatigue, and so on, if you are to reestablish the basis for your customarily good timing.

Timing is just as much a learned element of your skills as the physical manipulations of your body. Your sense of timing is responsible for your accurate judgment of speed and distance. It takes much practice to fine-tune the mind–body effort to within fractions of a second. In the process of trying to do this, you make many less-than-useful efforts that end up on the scrap heap. Your timing is extremely sensitive to anticipation, excitement, lack of confidence, nervousness, and similar dynamics. Any of these may result in increases in adrenaline levels, muscle tension, or other physiological disturbances that can then effectively interfere with your timing. Warily, you begin to realize that mistakes in this league are a whole lot more sophisticated. The answers here are not "just" technical corrections. The technical skills are a given at this level. It becomes a matter of addressing what's going on in your mind and intervening to change it.

Some elite athletes can address their mistakes themselves using the range of mental skills already learned from an educated and perceptive coach. Most elite athletes are very self-aware and can shoot down problems from long range and with excellent accuracy. That's part of what makes them who and what they are. If, however, they want to add a few more guns to their arsenal, or buy a bit of extra ammunition for those they already have, their friendly sport psychologist is usually only a phone call away.

Patterns of Mistakes

By now you will have begun to recognize that the mistakes you are making actually fall into a number of patterns. Perhaps you often make a particular one at the beginning, or end, of a game, or in particular situations such as just when you think you're about to win. This implies that mistakes come in multiples. They do.

■ Rule Number 1: Mistakes are always plural.

There's always a first mistake, but there's never a single mistake. It might be the first of a series, or the series may have been going on for some time and this is the first mistake you've noticed. Either way, if you haven't already, you will make the same mistake again.

There may also be more than one pattern of mistakes happening at any given time. This can be confusing, especially if one is a pattern of beginner mistakes relating to a new skill and the other is a pattern of intermediate mistakes related to a more established skill. Most sporting activities are a composite of many skills at which we will be variously competent. The gross nature of beginner mistakes will often mask intermediate ones, which consequently don't get corrected until later, by which time, of course, they've been well practiced.

A word of advice here: Try to keep your skill development as even as possible across the whole plane of activity. Developing one area of skill out of proportion to others, or before base skills are sufficiently consolidated, is what causes this sort of problem. Hurrying through the basic training to reach the more advanced work before the earlier work is properly confirmed means small technical mistakes go uncorrected and surface later as apparently "new" mistakes. Be careful here. The farther you are likely to go in your sport, the more important it is to build high-quality technical foundation skills in the early stages of training. Anything less will not support later demands. In looking to identify the causes of a learning mistake, always begin by

- remembering the characteristics of mistakes at the different stages of learning and
- determining the frequency of the mistake (chapter 8 offers a more in-depth treatment of repeated mistakes)

From there it's only a small step to deciding what to do about it. This is difficult stuff but nothing you can't manage.

Coaches' Corner

This section will give the athlete an insight into the coach's point of view, in the interests of two-way tolerance of everyone's mistakes. In response to the complexities of the coaching task here, we will explore many of these issues in detail. They are fundamental to the athlete's skill acquisition, and therefore fundamental to good coaching.

■ Thought for the day: Coaches go where angels fear to tread!

Feedback: The Vital Link

Few things are more important to the athlete's progress, and nothing determines the standard of coaching more unequivocally, than the quality of feedback. Everyone knows that a chain is only as strong as the weakest link, but perhaps it's not quite such common knowledge that coaching is only as good as the worst feedback.

■ Feedback *is* coaching.

On Wednesdays and Saturdays, write it back to front:

■ Coaching *is* feedback!

Feedback is the blood that runs in the veins of the relationship between coach and athlete. Nothing is more fundamental to good coaching than good feedback.

Feedback From Athlete to Coach

The most important feedback ever given is from the athlete to the coach. The coach must have antennae 10 feet long to receive feedback on all wavelengths from the athlete at all times. Only once you, as coach, have tuned in to your athletes *as people* can you generate appropriate feedback in response to their efforts *as athletes*.

Myth: Feedback is only given from the coach to the athlete. Wrong!

How do you do this? You listen, and you pay attention, very careful attention indeed, to hear what is being said. Listen with every set of antennae that you have ever owned. You might try extending your antennae to pick up new messages that are currently passing you by. Listen with your ears, your eyes, your intellect, and your instincts. Listen to bodies—their postures and gestures, their strength and their power, their precision and control, their fatigue and their failures. Listen to skills—their deftness, timing, confidence, and repertoire. Listen to action, reaction, interaction, and inaction. Listen to voices—to pitch and tone, to color and timbre. Listen to eyes and to faces—their moods and expressions. Listen to changes of breathing and skin color. Listen to all the emotions with as much respect and regard as if they were your own. Listen for harmony across the messages you are receiving, patterns of behavior, misfit information, and discord. And last of all, listen to words, pauses, and silence and to what is never said.

Good listening takes time. Spend time with your athletes in a quiet place. Make opportunities to listen to the person behind the athlete. Then move quietly among their goals and dreams. Listen to their plans and strategies. Share their success and feel their failure and fatigue. Now you are hearing your athlete. It's all out there, so if you think nobody ever tells you anything, try asking, How well did I listen today? And maybe tomorrow you could add, What did I hear today?

Your athletes' choice of words will reveal their preferred learning style if you listen carefully.

- Auditory learners will say, Can you *tell* me that again? or Can you *explain* it again?
- Visual learners will say, Can you *show* me that again? or I don't *see* how I can . . .
- Kinesthetic learners will say, Can I *do* it again? or How do I *do* that?

Be sure to respond to them in their preferred mode if you want to accelerate what's happening.

Reading kinesthetic feedback is very much an acquired skill, rather like driving a car. You certainly weren't born with it, any more than you were born with language skills, and there's no good reason why you should just be able to do it. In most sports, it's severely complicated by fast action and no replays, so you have one millisecond to get it right and that's it. Not only are you trying to read other people's bodies, but you're often trying to read their minds too. Did they really *mean* to do that? Well, it happened anyway, but they may or may not want to do it again. The more accurately you can read your athletes, the more you can give them precise feedback— which in the end is the only feedback that will help them. Without precise feedback they will always be a package of unknown origin and unfulfilled potential.

None of this means that you'll always get it right or understand where your athlete is coming from. It just means you'll have a chance. For most of us that's enough.

Feedback From Coach to Athlete

- **Technical accuracy:** This needs to be as good as you can possibly get. You owe it to those you coach to train your eye endlessly, mercilessly, and with a passion for detail to rival none other.

- **The right half-dozen:** We know that because of the nature of living performances it's always possible to pick up on half a dozen things that could be done better—at any level. (Doubting Thomases may want to reread chapter 1.) Experience will tell you to expect to see those items, and a good coach will put them on the better-next-time list. If you can't see them, then you haven't looked hard enough, or well enough, or often enough, or long enough. Keep training that eye! The trick, however, is not to get stuck in the negatives, but to see just as clearly the *positive* things that are done well, better than ever, brilliantly, or bravely. Then everything rolls into perspective. If you can't look past the bad parts, *re*train that eye.

- **The right order:** Although there is huge satisfaction in being able to pick out what needs to be done, that is only half of the story. The big half is to be able to place the corrections in the right order. This order is critical.

  - Getting the *right* half-dozen in the *right* order will make for immediate improvement. This is what you're aiming to do.

- Getting the *right* half-dozen in the *wrong* order will make little or no difference. These will be some of your coaching mistakes. Think about these.
- Getting the *wrong* half-dozen in the *right* order will make matters worse. This is bad coaching. We all know those people who get everything right and miss the point in the first place. They're usually the ones with the most to say!
- Getting the *wrong* half-dozen in the *wrong* order is no help to anybody. (Take a coaching course and don't give up your day job.) Think about that!

Only guided practice can help you sort out the right order of your corrections. Watching other coaches at work can be helpful. A mentor at your elbow can be worth his or her weight in gold. Only hours and hours and *hours* of second-guessing the instructions given by a trained coach, watching the results of two-way feedback, and assessing the end result of the performance can train you to put these items in the right order.

■ Tip: Fundamentals first—details later.

Never address faulty details without *proving* that the fundamental skill is in place. Any assumptions here will cost you very dearly. If you don't correct faulty fundamentals, the faulty details will flourish indefinitely.

Words, Words, Words

If you're inclined to talk too much, then do so under the shower or at least under your breath. Diluting your message with too many words will only make it less effective. Use lots of action, please, when wearing your coach's hat, and discipline yourself to use only as many words as is absolutely necessary to get the message across. Remember—brief is best.

When is enough feedback too much?
When it's time for action.

Advice or Comment

Hopefully, for the experienced coach there is no need to distinguish between advice and comment. For the less seasoned campaigner, however, it's wise to keep to advice. This needs to be clear, timely, and objective. Casual comments tend to be generalized, are often subjective, and sometimes carry an emotional or judgmental edge that is not helpful.

Knowledge of Results

To be effective, feedback must match the stage of learning of the athlete. *Knowledge of results* is the feedback given to beginners. This makes sense if you think that the first thing beginners need to know is, Did I do OK? In other words, they need to know the *results* of their effort because their skill level is such that they don't yet know what result they produced (table 7.1, p. 103). Remember here that beginners are anyone in the early stage of learning a new skill regardless of the fact that they may otherwise be advanced performers in their other skills. By using knowledge-of-results feedback, the coach gives the athlete immediate confirmation of the result, which may or may not be the one the athlete set out to achieve. It gives no indication of the quality of the result at this point since an approximation of the skill is sufficient in the early stages. Knowledge of results merely gives the athlete information on what took place.

Effective knowledge of results is only given after the task is completed. Giving feedback to beginners while they are still engaged in performing the new task is counterproductive. It will actually slow their progress and inhibit their success. This is because you will create an attentional deficit on the new skill while they listen to what you are saying. Consequently, their execution of the skill will suffer. So the bottom line is: Show and supervise beginners, but above all, *let them learn for themselves.*

Example

After the athlete has performed a somersault for the first time, good feedback would be, "Yes! That's it!" This is knowledge of results at the appropriate time. Bad feedback would be to comment as it's happening since the timing of it will distract the athlete from the task. *Any* comments on the quality of the performance would be inappropriate since the athlete is just starting to learn the skill and is in no position to address the quality of the effort—yet.

We've all been beginners at lots of things. We know how important it is to experience the process and the feeling of a new skill and at our own pace. Being talked to, or at, while we are trying to concentrate on these things is not helpful. It's rather like having a backseat driver in full voice while you're trying to make an unscathed exit from a busy intersection. Somehow you just can't wait to get rid of your passenger! No one begins life planning to be a backseat coach, but a few end up there. Don't be one of them. You have a thousand opportunities to do better.

Praise will also play a role in giving knowledge of results to your athletes. Be generous with it. But also be fair and only give praise when it has been earned by a show of effort, courage, patience, or other appropriate behavior. Often praise is sufficient feedback to prompt the further experimentation necessary to take the learning on to the next stage.

Knowledge of Quality

Once the athlete no longer needs confirmation of the result—that is, she is sure what she did *was* a somersault—it's time to move on to giving her knowledge of quality. This will tell her how good, bad, or ugly it was.

Knowledge of quality is feedback given only to intermediate and advanced performers (table 7.1). This is information on the technical quality of their effort. It must be immediate and should be given *during the task or immediately afterwards.* Don't give knowledge-of-quality feedback several minutes later (e.g., You didn't stretch enough) because by that time the athlete has already forgotten the kinesthetic sensations of the task, making it difficult for him to correct his movements in the next effort. Knowledge of results is not necessary at this stage because athletes are experienced enough to know they got a result; what they need to know now is how good it was.

At the intermediate stage of learning, the athlete is not yet solid enough in the new skill to carry an accurate enough memory of the skill sensations for a long period. Consequently, the benefits of any feedback that is not *immediately* linked to these sensations is lost, and the performance will remain unimproved. This is despite the fact that your technical comments may be right. The athlete not only needs to learn what to rearrange in his effort, but he also needs to learn the precise moment to do it. Left with just the technical information, there are an almost infinite number of occasions when he will experimentally try to make use of it. Do not let this happen. In the heated glare of fruitless repetitions, the motivation of all concerned will dry to a crisp.

Feedback to advanced performers is invariably *only* concerned with knowledge of quality. (Remember that we're relating specific feedback to a particular skill, not to the average standard of a performance.) These athletes know perfectly well when they have achieved the desired results and are experts at technically evaluating their performance. They only require prompting to initiate quite significant changes in what they think or do. They are like Formula One racing cars—highly specialized, very highly tuned machines that require only the smallest adjustment to effect a major change in the performance.

For these athletes, good feedback comes immediately after the performance: Your jump could have been a bit earlier. The best feedback comes before the performance happens: This time, jump sooner.

Pegging a Performance

As the competency of an athlete improves and she moves on from needing knowledge of results to needing knowledge of quality, this seriously challenges the coach's technical knowledge. Without it, there will

Table 7.1 **What Feedback to Give and When**

Skill level	Characteristics	Training regime	Feedback
Beginner (rudimentary skills)	BIG mistakes. Lacks concentration, fitness, and tension management skills.	Blocks of uninterrupted practice	Needs knowledge of results. *Do not interrupt!*
Intermediate (skill not yet confirmed)	Technical mistakes. Significant others can cause difficulties. May fray under pressure.	Skills segmented, then chained.	Needs knowledge of results and quality. *Give feedback immediately after effort.*
Advanced (skills automated)	Timing mistakes. Mistakes in use of mental skills. Only occasional faults in technique.	Specific practice of part or whole skill.	Needs knowledge of quality only. *Can prompt before or during effort.*

be no further improvement. If you find yourself in a situation in which your athlete needs a higher standard of coaching than you can provide *at the moment*, it's time to let this athlete go and get out there and train that eye. If you continue to give her only knowledge of results at this point, this will peg her performance and ultimately frustrate her ambitions to improve. That's unfortunate if she has the capacity to do better. It will also cost you a friend.

Teaching or Coaching

Not understanding the difference between teaching and coaching is another very successful way to peg a performance. If you coach when you need to teach, you are assuming the athlete has knowledge or skills that he does not have. Coaching at such times is about as useful as asking a child who doesn't know the alphabet to read better. If you assume he knows it, that's a bit rash unless you've actually taught it to him. Even if he has learned the skill from you, you may still need to prove his current knowledge of it before moving on. Only then should you begin coaching.

The flip side of that coin is that if you teach when you should coach, you'll bore the socks off even the best student in town, whether your student is trying to learn the alphabet or athletics. So now it's easy to work out—teaching is helping others *to learn new skills*. Coaching is helping others *to get better at something they already know.*

By definition, you are teaching all beginners. Also by definition, you are coaching all intermediate and advanced learners. But hang on a minute. Didn't we say that we're all a mishmash of skills at different stages of learning? Yes. Herein lies the skill of a coach. Knowing which skill to teach, which skill to coach, when to teach a little less and coach a little more, when to stop teaching altogether, when to reteach, when never to teach, and when to coach your heart out. This is what it takes.

Enough of a Good Thing

When is enough coaching too much? Ask most coaches and they complain that most athletes don't use their coaches enough. Ask most athletes and they'll tell you they wish their coach would back off sometimes. Good coaching is steering and facilitating so that athletes discover *for themselves* their best performances. This style of coaching creates highly motivated, independent athletes who revel in exploring the possibilities of their sport. The coach is not indispensable to their efforts; she is merely a catalyst for them. This point of view may be more than the egos of some coaches can stand, but it is useful to be reminded that the athlete is the one who must pump the iron, run the miles, and practice the skills, and it is the athlete whose name is entered in the draw or etched on the winner's plaque. Coaching is a backseat game. Better get used to that.

Vocabulary

To maximize the impact of your feedback, make sure that the vocabulary you're using is suited to your athlete's stage of learning. It's of little value to use more advanced terms than a person is familiar with or can be expected to understand. Such comments will go straight over athletes' heads. Neither of you may realize that this is happening until progress grinds to a halt and mistakes prove heartily resistant to correction. Being aware of this unwelcome consequence of your attentions should alert you to keeping feedback within the scope of your athlete's sporting education. Conversely, you will find that advanced learners will tune out beginner feedback, and rightly so. To avoid this situation, you need to keep moving with your athletes' times! In doing so, pick up on ideas they may flag as being particularly helpful, and use any words or imagery that you discover work for them. Use these when addressing individual athletes since this will customize your coaching and accelerate their positive responses. If you are a team coach, developing a team vocabulary will improve cohesiveness and contribute to a healthy team spirit. This could include "in" words, jokes, sayings, phrases, or quotes that become associated with the team style of play or with particular team activities. Team songs are also useful here, with or without small adaptations to the lyrics.

When it comes to coaching, swearing is about on the same plane as sarcasm. They are both little more than vocabulary that has gotten misfiled and should have made it to the trash can. Even a mild expletive signals that your fuse is burning short, which is not a useful message to convey; it tells the world you're running out of options. Good coaches, by definition, never run out of options. Top coaches create them.

Summary

For the Athlete . . .

- Learn to learn well through your preferred style of learning.
- Learn to perform well.

It's *your* learning; only *you* can make it happen.

For the Coach . . .

- Listen as your athletes identify their learning styles through their speech.
- Learn to deliver the same material in auditory, visual, and kinesthetic modes.
- Learn to teach well.
- Learn to coach well.
- Learn the difference between teaching and coaching.
- Know the difference between knowledge of results and knowledge of quality and learn to use them appropriately. Train your eye.

8

Controlling Repeated Mistakes

Good learners, successful competitors, and generally talented people see to it that they learn from their efforts in life. That leaves the rest of us finding that few things are more depressing or more exasperating than making the same mistake . . . *again.* We also discover that either ignoring a mistake or hoping it will go away will not keep us from repeating it. We *love* to repeat our mistakes. Let's confess . . . in the course of their shopping career, many people will buy clothes that don't suit them and shoes that are too small—not just once, but enough times to fill a wardrobe. And how many people have bought cars that are lemons or tools they don't need and will never use? Some of us continue to make these unfortunate mistakes, often out of habit, and usually by accident. But is it *really* an accident? Maybe it is a faithful repetition of well-learned behavior or a marvelously consistent way of making choices. The fact that we don't like the outcome is almost incidental! If we are to improve over time, we must recognize what's going on and develop some preventative strategies that will moderate our behavior and improve our choices. This will rein in our mistakes and lead to a more productive lifestyle.

If this is happening to you in your sporting life, take a look at the choices you are making and set about breaking the cycle. To do this, first consider the following idea:

■ Prevention is *always* better than correction.

Knowing this will already bolster your confidence. It will also give your mind and body less chance to learn what you don't want them to know, and less time to practice it.

Having said that, you need to accept that as surely as night follows day, some mistakes, by their nature, will recur. These are . . .

- Mistakes that are a product of your inexperience. You will eventually outgrow these.
- Mistakes made as you are moving from one level of competition to another. Once on the top rung of the competitive ladder, you can safely say you've bypassed these too.
- Mistakes that you practice (and so become very good at making). In this case you have a choice whether to pack these in your baggage.
- Any mistake that you ignore, do not explore, or leave uncorrected. Watch out for a few of these that may recur from time to time. Get to the bottom of them.
- Mistakes that stem from a weakness in your performance (technical, physical, mental, or emotional). These are any homegrown specials that you can't bear to part with. Be brave. Put your signature on something else.

Serial Mistakes

Even in the best circles there are times when you go on making a series of mistakes, regardless of the fact that your coach is giving you corrections that should change the world. You just don't seem to take the instructions on board. This is usually not a consciously anticoach activity, but from the coach's point of view it can feel that way. Few situations are more frustrating. It's in the interest of everybody to challenge and to change this destructive scenario. Here's how to go about it. When giving a correction (presuming, of course, that it is the right one), let's establish some ground rules for the coach. It is reasonable to expect these results:

- Your correction will elicit a response.
- The response will resemble your correction.
- The performance will then change for the better.

By the same token, it is unreasonable if these results occur:

- Your correction is ignored.
- The response bears no relation to your correction.
- The performance remains unchanged.

When the athlete's performance remains compromised by the same, ongoing mistakes, you have what we call "serial mistakes." Every coach encounters these from time to time. They are not a reflection on your coaching; they are a communication problem. Most communication problems would tax the patience of a saint. Not being saints, this is where we need the **Rule of Three**.

In the interest of preserving your sanity, *never* give the same correction more than three times in succession. Having given feedback about a mistake, you must *expect change*. If you do not get it immediately, your antennae should start to twitch. If you find yourself giving the same feedback a second time, move into seriously watchful mode. If there is still no progress, move into red alert mode and discontinue further feedback. It's time to ask why you're not getting the desired result.

1. In response to a first mistake . . .
   - Give normal feedback and expect an attempt at correction.
2. In response to a second occurrence of the same mistake . . .
   - Move into seriously watchful mode and ask yourself, "Was I heard?"
   - Give the *same feedback* in the *same way,* but more clearly.
3. In response to a third occurrence of the same mistake . . .
   - Move into red alert and ask yourself, "Was I understood?"
   - Give the *same,* and *final,* feedback in *a new way.*
4. If this does not elicit a satisfactory response from the athlete . . .
   - *Stop* and *explore* the reasons.

You will find the Rule of Three immensely refreshing. It puts an end to those soul-destroying repeat corrections that elicit no change and nibble away at your self-esteem, quietly corroding both the athlete's confidence and your own.

The Rule of Three will help you work out the reasons the situation is arising in the first place. Be sure to do this quite mercilessly *the first time it arises* because if you don't address it then, as sure as God made little green apples, it will happen again. And *again!* Be sure to explain to your athlete what you're doing. Once he understands, he too will soon realize the value of this strategy and before long will recognize any similar situations almost faster than you will. At that point you'll only need to ask him whether you were heard or understood to both be able to streamline this process, to your mutual advantage.

If you establish that (1) you were heard and (2) you were understood, and there's *still* no change in the action, then clearly the communication channels are blocked in some other way. What do you do next? Here is where you hit the hard stuff because, right or wrong, wittingly or more probably unwittingly, *you are being second-guessed by the athlete.* This can be caused by a number of things.

• Sometimes the athlete thinks she knows better than you do how to perform the skill in question. This usually follows poor-quality coaching in the past that overlooked basic faults. When you return (quite appropriately) to reteaching the technique, she resents it. The result is noncompliance on a moderately grand scale. This needs a convincing demonstration of the skill. A little dazzling is in order here, by a very bright light. You can either demonstrate the skill yourself (which is most effective, but not always practical for the older coach involved in the more vigorous sports), or you can use video examples or demonstrations by another player. The secret here is to be *quick.* The longer you tolerate the noncompliance, the more difficult it will be to get the athlete on your side.

• Occasionally the athlete assumes that because he has *thought* about your corrections, he is already *doing* it or has actually *done* it, when in reality nothing has happened. This is innocent inactivity, and one of the best solutions is video. When the athlete sees for himself that absolutely nothing is changing, he will realize that it's all only been happening in his head. One snip of video is enough, however, as you don't want to cement those old images in his mind for future viewing.

• Fear can often cause serial mistakes. In high-risk sports this may be quite a significant factor and can successfully override your instructions indefinitely. There's only one way out of this one and that is to temporarily retreat to safer ground, build confidence, and return to the skill later.

• Previous instruction can also be the culprit—whether yours or somebody else's—and may have laid the foundations for later communication problems. There are many ways to teach and coach most things. Sometimes, right or wrong, your way may just be different from the athlete's past experiences. Expect some reluctance to abandon previous practices and march forth into no-man's-land at your bidding. This response is fairly benign; because it lacks the arrogant edge of the presumptive pupil, a little TLC will usually do the trick.

Outdated Ideas

Sometimes we are introduced to a young athlete and in the same breath told to accept the fact that she's always been weaker off the left leg or her coordination has always been a problem or some such other damning comment. Often the athlete herself has actually bought into it and will say, "I am always . . ." There is no reprieve from *always*. The only other word that goes with *always* is *never*. If the athlete has been exposed to long-term correction of a fault that has been the product of an underlying technical flaw, then of course she will "always" have delivered mistakes in her performance. And of course she will "never" improve as long as the technique remains uncorrected. Sadly, she will also long since have tuned out any corrections you want to give her that she sees as associated with this fault.

In such cases extreme stealth is the order of your day. The secret here is to stalk that mistake with all the cunning of a leopard on the trail of its lunch. You will need imagination to burn. You are going to make changes *without saying one single word about the resistant mistake.* You are going to attack the root cause and leave the worn-to-death details out of your day. You are going to effect spectacular change without a word of explanation—until later. Then, in the presence of the athlete, but not *to* the athlete, disclose your rationale to her significant others. If in the past they have been enthusiastic on behalf of the athlete but baffled by these mistakes, they will now redouble their support. If they have been critical and censorious, they will now fade into the wallpaper. This always works, and it comes with a cast-iron guarantee—you will never see these mistakes again.

Previous Unfortunate Results

History is at once hard to remember and hard to forget. Unfortunately, what we remember best are events with emotional price tags. Any unpleasant surprises of the past that may have been associated with pain, fear, or any kind of humiliation, embarrassment, or dents in the pride following unsuccessful efforts will be hard to beat. First you must clear the decks. Send *all* significant others packing. Set the scene casually for a number of consecutive efforts. Plan to repeat these over a number of sessions. Plan to achieve a successful result by the end of, say, four or five sessions. (You will make much better progress than this and probably get a good result in the first session, but what this does is to reduce pressure on the athlete and move back the boundaries to give him space to get it wrong.) Settle for some shaping here, where you applaud an approximation of the end result. *Be sure to stop short of achieving the result you are ultimately looking for even though you know the athlete is capable of producing it.* Leaving it as a carrot out there will do marvelous things for the next session.

Other Intruding Information

This one is a quiet little worm in the apple. Yes, your athlete is busy following instructions, but the only snag is they're not yours. Somewhere along the line she read that (or heard that or was told that) . . . and the result is that *that's* exactly what she's busy doing now. These are the athletes who can't bear to look like beginners at *anything.* So here they are very busy doing what you're very busy wishing they wouldn't. It's tiresome and tedious and terribly time consuming, but you'd better let them down gently if you want to come out on the winning side of this. You need to steer them out of trouble, not cut their motor. If you're having difficulty, call up your mentor. Lack of patience here is not a sin, but understanding *why* things are not working will be a big help.

Some athletes simply misread the present situation and not only use arbitrary information in the hope it will work wonders, but also *mis*apply that information to the present task. This is more common in sports that have many variables that impinge on performance. For instance, the young football player who has read the magical "page 32" and is busy trying to do just that now ignores the fact that there's a nice northwesterly cross breeze to accommodate. So the technical mistakes are compounded by errors of judgment here. As their coach, where does that leave you—warming up for another demo of magnificent proportions? Reaching for the video camera? Take care here. These athletes are often the supergood students who think about what's going on and are highly contributive proactive learners. What they are trying to do is bring their previous experience to bear on the present challenge. So tread most competently, but gently, on their sporting toes.

It may surprise you how resistant your athletes are to your efforts here. You may have to be very firm to get them to let go of their ideas, attitudes, or suppositions. The very best convincer, of course, is competence—yours and others'. Use film of others if necessary, or as a very last resort, show the athlete a film of his own *in*competence (in which case, stay kind, and always follow up with the contrasting film of him achieving the successful result).

■ It can be hard to reach a headstrong athlete—especially if he's had success doing what he's doing.

By now you may be thinking that it seems a bit unrealistic to expect to be able to sort all this out in the middle of your average training session, in the middle or your average day, but you will, especially now that you're wise to the more usual glitches and have a few new options up your sleeve. Just keep your eyes and ears open and let your intuition do the rest. You'll hear the Little Voice in your head yell loud and clear. All you have to do is listen to it.

Caveat

Of course this all rests on that one massive presumption that you gave the right feedback in response to the first mistake. If you are an experienced coach, confident in your technical knowledge and skilled in your communication, this will not present a challenge to you. If you are less experienced or less knowledgeable, then perhaps for the time being you could best learn how to unravel these problems by watching a mentor at work while you are safely on the sidelines. This is not the stuff of novice coaching. As always, at any level, know your own boundaries and work within them.

Chronic Mistakes

Chronic mistakes are the skeletons in the athlete's closet. These are the ghosts on their stair. Every so often they come back to haunt their keeper, and you'd better believe they can scare the wits out of the bravest performer. Chronic mistakes apparently occur at random over what can be very long time spans indeed, with the added bonus that they are *progressive.* This means that you get just a little better at making them over time, so the result gets just a little worse every time you do it. You will make them in the same situations but at different standards. You will make them in response to the same hair triggers but at different times. And over time those triggers become *progressively* more sensitive. Chronic mistakes may happen once a month or once a year. Some have been known to wait five years between occurrences. When you make them, however, console yourself that these are the *pièces de résistance* of repeated mistakes! They are murderously predictable, appear in a quite mind-bending way, are heartrendingly simple to repeat but horribly complicated to unravel, and the bottom line is you just can't seem to deprogram them. They seem to be utterly resistant to all the usual curative measures until you feel like resorting to swallowing weed killer to make them shrivel up and die.

What causes chronic mistakes? They have their roots in early sporting experiences. Very often they are the result of facing a task that seems overwhelming. They can also be the result of working with bad gear in the formative stages of skill development. These experiences leave an indelible mark, usually a scar on your confidence. When the particular mix of triggers is activated again, they produce a perfect repeat of the original mistake. The most unnerving aspect of these mistakes is the suddenness with which they appear. Like a bad dream they seem to emerge out of nowhere; then you wake up shaking and trying to remember if you ate cheese before you went to bed.

See table 8.1 for a summary of serial mistakes and chronic mistakes.

Table 8.1 Mistake Comparisons

	Serial mistakes	Chronic mistakes
Characteristics	• Appear regularly and frequently • Are well practiced • Products of communication blocks • Erode confidence • Stall motivation	• The same mistake appears occasionally, very suddenly, and over long time spans • Products of misunderstanding of technique • On a hair trigger • Progressively get worse • Complex to correct
Causes	• Miscorrected or overlooked errors in current training	• Faulty fundamental techniques in the original skill base of early training
Corrections	• Rule of Three • Improved mistakes management • Better quality practice	• Retraining original technique • Extensive use of imagery • Ongoing care

Coaches' Corner

The land of chronic mistakes is rocky country and no place for young players. Coaches do indeed go where angels fear to tread! The only way to approach these mistakes successfully is *gently*. You are going to have to tiptoe your way through the wreckage of your athlete's pride and expectations if you are to slay this ghost. You need to try to establish where and when the mistake first happened, preferably in the context of what instructions the athlete was trying to follow at the time. To best help her, you also need to know how it felt to make the mistake at that time, and also how it feels to make it now.

Intermittent choking is a good example of this kind of mistake. And it is a wrecker! Intermittent choking is far worse for everyone to deal with than regular choking because it always comes as a shock. When it doesn't happen, everyone thinks it's a thing of the past. Confidence builds, expectations rise; then suddenly the horror story is part of the present, *again,* or more correctly, *still.* For each incident, there will be a trigger, or triggers. Your first job is to find out what they are. Your second job is to teach the athlete other options that effectively "throw the switch" before she arrives at the triggers, which results in her taking a different track. It's difficult, but possible.

The main thing to realize about chronic mistakes is that they are *always* beginners' mistakes. That immediately gives us the clue to their correction. *Teach* the athlete out of trouble—*don't coach.* Remember, coaching is guiding the practice of something an athlete already knows how to do well, with the object of getting her to do it better. That's the very last thing we want here! We want to initiate new skills, and that requires teaching.

It may seem a tad obvious, but let's also remember that you can only find the right answer if you first ask the right question. To establish exactly what it is that you need to teach, try asking these questions:

- What is the last thing you think of before it happens? (This establishes the athlete's mental place at the time of the mistake.)

- What is the last thing you see, or hear, before it happens? (This establishes the athlete's kinesthetic place at the time of the mistake.)

- What do you feel just before it happens? (This establishes the athlete's emotional place at the time of the mistake.)

These questions will help you see the background patterns of the athlete's mistake. Often, athletes will return to the same mental, kinesthetic, or emotional place to make mistakes. If you know that, you can teach athletes to become aware of and stay out of those places and stop creating the catalyst for their mistakes.

Do not ask the athlete why he makes the mistake; if he knew, he wouldn't make the mistake in the first place. You are trying to empower him, and asking questions for which he has no answer does not help.

Do not even ask what happens. Usually the athlete doesn't know that either. A curious characteristic of these mistakes seems to be that the athlete enters into a momentary vacuum from which he emerges slightly dazed and not really knowing what hit him because these mistakes happen so catastrophically *fast*. Perhaps this is because the first time the mistake occurs makes such a huge impression that it is subsequently rehearsed by reliving it a thousand times, thus making it an extremely well-practiced skill that verges upon being a reflex action. Maybe it's the emotional clout these mistakes carry that gives them such massive power to derail a performance. That's not to say that they can't be beaten. They can. It will, however, take extremely diligent practice on an ongoing basis to keep these skeletons securely confined in their cupboard, and the door firmly locked. It may never be possible to throw away the key.

For some athletes, confronting chronic-mistake demons is more than they can manage. If these demons stand to sabotage an elite-level career, serious thought should be given to the viability of such a career since these ghouls are very likely to flourish under the pressures of the high-performance environment. For the coach, such a situation calls for tact and as much compassion as possible. No athletes would wish these demons on themselves. By moving from a coaching role to a mentor role, a coach can help immensely here as athletes struggle to reroute their lives. We do not always measure up to the image we have of who we want to be. At some point we all have to face up to being the person, and sportsperson, we are, ghouls and all. If we are wise, in the light of that knowledge, we live our lives accordingly.

Summary

One rule of thumb is crucial in avoiding repeat mistakes: Prevention is better than correction.

There are two main types of repeated mistakes:

- **Serial mistakes:** These are repeated mistakes that coaching doesn't seem to cure.
- **Chronic mistakes:** These are horrors that come back to haunt you when it matters most.

Coaches should remember the **Rule of Three:** Establish that you've been heard, establish that you've been understood, and if there's still no action, call a halt to coaching and find out what's happening to the communication.

9

Managing Your Mistakes

Correcting your mistakes starts with proactive situational management of your training environment as it is expressed through the quality of your gear, your practice, and your coach. Later it will also include your degree of competition exposure, the quality of your opposition, and many other aspects of your sporting life over which you have direct influence and for which you can be directly responsible.

Let's start by thinking of mistakes as uninvited visitors. You may see them coming up the driveway, but you don't have to ask them in. You're also free to decide whether to greet them with a hug or a handshake or bolt and bar the door. If you don't like visitors at all, maybe you've already put a lock on the front gate! Mistakes will appear on your doorstep equally unannounced and unexpected. They need not derail your day if you know what to expect and have practiced strategies to deal with them. You can *choose* how your mistakes will affect you—if at all. A proactive, educated stance in the face of approaching mistakes will greatly reduce the frequency of them and their potential for damage. Enjoy the challenge of gaining control of your mistakes, and take the threat of them out of your sporting life.

This chapter gives you general recovery strategies for use after *any* mistake you make in a situation in which you don't want to get embroiled in corrections, such as competition. Rather than correcting it, your job is to *manage* it. This means you need to recover well, and fast, to get on with the action.

The following strategic plan gives you new control over your mistakes and a fistful of real tools with which to address them.

Principles of Mistakes Management

1.   The first principle of mistakes management is to never ignore a mistake. It does no good to hope it won't happen again. It will. We must take responsibility for our mistakes and accept that they are of our own making. In doing this, we also have to forgive ourselves for creating them. We are not perfect, and we don't behave in perfect ways. We often don't know quite what to do or how to do it, and at such times we experiment by doing the best we can and hoping it will be enough. It often isn't. It often also falls short of what we thought we could do. We need to get off the recrimination trolley and buy into our mistakes with as much enthusiasm as we embrace our successes and to own them as entirely and unconditionally as we own the color of our eyes.

2.   The second principle of mistakes management is to plan for excellence, not perfection. Revisit chapter 1 if you've forgotten how we rewrote the ideas of perfection and excellence. We can take the shock value out of making mistakes by remembering that there will be variations in our miniperformances. At the same time we can feel confident that through mistakes management we have already taken significant steps to limit what those variations will be. This results in a reassuring sense of control and empowerment. (Flip back to chapter 2 if you doubt this.)

3.   The third principle of mistakes management is to always own your mistakes. Every mistake ever made has something good embedded in it. If you don't know what that is, keep looking until you find it. It may be an opportunity to improve your skill, practice your mistakes management, or get to know yourself better. Once a mistake has happened, it's part of history. Your history. Looking forward from that point on and putting a positive spin on your mistakes will make it easier to get away from blaming yourself or anyone else or from feeling guilty or frustrated about your performance.

4. The fourth principle of mistakes management is to give your mistakes management a new role and value in your life. Include it in your training; bring it into your competitions and find out more about it every day. Vow to do this.

5. The fifth principle of mistakes management is to develop a bank of mistakes-management resources and skills with which to manage your mistakes, and thereby make the most of them. You should know why you're making mistakes, the different sorts of mistakes you are likely to make, serious options for dealing effectively with their fallout, and ways to minimize or even prevent their recurrence.

6. The sixth and final principle of mistakes management is to develop immediate recovery strategies for use in any action situation. It is to these strategies that we now turn.

Proactive Strategies for Mistakes Recovery

Having made a mistake—any kind of mistake—your immediate task is to get back on track. To do so, you need to apply *the three Rs: Recover, Refocus*, and *Retry.*

Recover: Catch yourself by the scruff and get a grip on the situation.

Refocus: Get your mind back on the job . . . *now.*

Retry: Do it differently this time.

All this needs to happen within a few seconds. Naturally, if you haven't done it before, you'll . . . er . . . make mistakes. Press on regardless, practice as though it's going out of fashion, and start thinking of this as just another small piece of your sport jigsaw. By that time, you'll have made a few more mistakes, which should have given you the opportunity to get the three Rs right.

Recover

In the wake of making a mistake, the first thing to do is recover composure and avoid falling into any of the emotional potholes. Easier said than done! Knowledge is the key here because if you understand what just happened, it's a small step to take to get your brain busy talking about it. This will most effectively make you look where you are going, and even in a quite drastic situation you will find you can talk your way out of trouble.

This is perhaps the most difficult of the three phases. It's difficult to duck the emotional clout of a mistake, even when you know it's coming, be it disappointment, anger, embarrassment, excitement, or anxiety. The best way to do this is to develop a sense of history. This is the ability to categorically and comprehensively put the mistake into the past. It happened, it was a mistake, it had consequences. Stick with the past tense as you acknowledge that the mistake happened and take ownership of it. The moment you've done that, however, move on into action and from there *never* look over your shoulder. Save that for the debriefing. *Always look forward to refocusing.* Consign the mistake to history and leave it there, at least until the debriefing.

The ability to turn your back temporarily on a mistake in the middle of the action is a real skill. Instead of getting stuck in the consequences of it, or analyzing it to death, just get on with the job at hand. Use the mistake as a springboard for a bigger, better, higher, wider, faster, and generally more glorious effort. There will be time enough to tear it apart in the debriefing, or in front of your postperformance video. Now is *not* the time. Now is the time to look forward, start again, try differently, try harder. Anyway, you're too busy to stop here. It's time to refocus.

Refocus

Refocusing is a little more demanding than recovering. You can't take refuge in the technicalities of what's happening to you; instead you must rally your resources to concentrate on your next task, whether it be your second serve or the next 50 meters of track. The more effectively you can wrap your attention around a single point, the more successfully you will reinstate your concentration. As with most other things, this takes practice.

Having steadied the ship in the recovery phase, you now set a new course. The challenge is to crowd out the distraction and concentrate on the *process* of your job. Here's where you focus on the fundamentals of your technique, and give yourself extremely stern instructions to follow. Give yourself a job!

The other thing to do here is to give yourself time. Consider the way tennis players refocus before a second serve. They bounce that ball, twirl that racket, and take up that pose as often as they need to before they unleash another missile. Sometimes, to gain time, they summon a

ball boy, squint at the sun, or wipe their wristband across their fore-
head. Whatever it takes.

During this time of refocusing, the more successfully you can bring
your concentration back to your technique, the higher your chance will
be of producing a good technical result that will effectively demolish
your opponent. All you have ever learned about centering, breathing,

■ Wrap your attention around a single point.

tension control, positive self-talk, attentional focus, and mental rehearsal must be used now. The busier you are, the better. Remember that the technique will have to be different from what you've just done, unless you want the same result, that is, a repeat of the mistake. So be merciless with yourself in focusing on exactly what you are going to do and ruthlessly running through how you are going to do it.

If negative thoughts barge in, consign them to a garbage can, hurl them over a mental cliff, refuse to hear them, see them, or let them into your moment. Stay busy with this moment. Stay in what is happening now. That also means not letting your mind jump forward to what is about to happen. You are in the planning, not the action—yet. This is all about being grounded in the Now. The future must have no more interest or place in your thoughts than the past. You must become consumed by this dress rehearsal. You need to drive this mental process as surely as you will shortly drive the physical process. The more you have to think about, the less you will dwell on the mistake. It's history. Live now. Step into the driver's seat of your life.

When you know with unshakable certainty what has to be done, you have arrived at The Moment. You are calm, you are organized—you are ready to retry.

When you are *ready*, it's the most natural thing in the world to move into the retrying phase. If you start too early, you will feel hassled and stressed. If you start too late, both your concentration and your confidence may desert you. Different mistakes have different recovery times, and you will need to give yourself that time depending on the kind of mistake you made and the circumstances in which you made it. There is no such thing as too little time, or too much; there is only *your* time. That is the time it takes you to get yourself organized and to choose when to unleash your next effort.

Retry

Viewing every retry as another opportunity to show your skill level, or even to practice at a submaximal level, will help you to muster the necessary confidence to try again. If you have the option of taking quite a different course of action, do so, because you will then be less likely to repeat your mistake. But that is not always an option. To take another swing on the uneven bars when you've just missed the last big one is a major task. That takes tons of courage and skill. If you find yourself trying too hard and feeling tense and tight, remind yourself of excellence and dismiss even the smallest thought of perfection.

But you really don't have time to think about that. Now that it's "all systems go!" your mind is too busy looking for the opportunity to show that you have refocused well to wonder whether you have the guts to see it through. Anyway, we're talking championship material here, so of course you do! There's only one thing to do, and that is: Commit yourself to the action. Anyway, once you've jumped on the end of the springboard, it's too late not to dive so you might as well make it a good one. Better to decide that before you jumped at all.

Like any of your skills, the more you can practice this regime in training, the easier it will become to do it under the pressure of competition. At first you will make beginners' mistakes by asking the wrong questions or taking forever to ask any questions at all. But you'll quickly move on to becoming an intermediate learner and your mistakes management will become more effective, more efficient, and much more fun. As an advanced practitioner, all this will be consigned to automatic pilot and interruptions to your performance will be minimal as you smoothly use your mistakes as minitrampolines from which to bounce to better and better performances. It won't take long before your mistakes will no longer be the unpredictable, destructive force they once were.

■ If you can stand the pace, here's another freebie for the fridge: When you manage your mistakes, you manage your life.

And here's something else that will pay good dividends if it's managed well. Your learning. Maybe you thought your coach was in charge of that. After all, isn't that her job? No. Her job is to teach you what you don't know and show you how to do the rest a whole lot better. Unless she's on some sort of power trip, the rest is up to you. So how about you take charge of it?

Managing Your Learning

We are wonderful learners. We learn so easily and so quickly. We learn from good teachers and bad. We learn in all manner of circumstances and in every possible way in school, at work, at home, in society, in life, in sport. When things don't go quite according to plan, our mistakes are often not at all in what we have learned but in what we have arranged for ourselves to be taught.

Note: This in no way lobs the responsibility for your mistakes into your coach's lap. They are still *your* mistakes, and *you* made them.

If you can proactively manage your learning by arranging to be taught what you need to know, you can be confident that you will learn it extremely well. This means surrounding yourself with the most knowledgeable and caring people you can find; getting exposure to the best and most positive experiences you can find, share, or create; making the most of the negative ones; and ensuring that the whole story is *relevant* to who you want to be and what you want to achieve. If it's not, don't go there.

Merely learning from your mistakes with no effort to control *what* you are learning always puts you in the catch-up situation of trying to unlearn what you didn't need to be taught in the first place! Indiscriminate learning from your mistakes is no more useful to you than indiscriminate learning from anything else in your life.

You should *only* try to learn from mistakes that are relevant to your goals. If your mistakes are not relevant to your goals, move on and find opportunities for learning what you really want to know.

So we're back on the goal-setting track, and getting better at it all the time. The more clearly you identify your goals, short-, medium-, and long-term, the easier it is to measure and manage your progress toward them and to know whether you are on course and learning what you need to know. The results of your efforts will speak for themselves. Just make sure you are listening! This adds up to *managing* your learning and *taking responsibility* for your progress. Do this:

1. Set your goals; then *decide what you need to learn to achieve them.* Remember that to fail to plan is to plan to fail.

2. Plan your learning. Choose your coach with care; then together establish short-term landmarks in your progress. Use them to review your efforts and those of your coach

   - at the end of *every* training session,
   - weekly,
   - monthly,
   - at the end of every season, and
   - at the end of every year.

3. Know that you will learn well. It's up to you. If you want to practice the same mistakes, go ahead and give yourself access to the same lessons. If you don't, then choose to move on to new lessons and new opportunities for learning different things that are more relevant to your goals.

If you are used to setting goals in your sporting life, you'll have no problem with this. (Anyone who's unsure should flip back to chapter 5 for a quick tour of the goal-setting process.) Goal setting is always the place to start. You'll get very good at it, and although at first it may seem a bit laborious, this learning to drive your life is no worse than learning to drive your car, and it's a good deal more useful. You'll also get very quick at making decisions, just as you do when deciding how fast is too fast to take a turn on your way into town. Yes, accidents happen when we make misjudgments. Or are they just well-practiced judgments in unfamiliar circumstances?

Remember that we can never unlearn an experience—good, bad, or ugly. Whatever we learn will be with us for the rest of our natural lives. Our aim then is *not* merely to learn better from our mistakes (we already do that extremely well) but *to manage our learning better* and so make fewer, less destructive mistakes.

Coaches' Corner

Be warned: Athletes learn these self-management techniques very quickly. They will adopt them into their thinking very fast because they are easy to understand, easy to apply, and they work. The bonus is that this makes athletes feel good. If you're not prepared for such a rapid rate of progress, it can catch you quite unawares. Before you know it, your athletes are halfway around the track and you're still tying your shoelaces.

■ Hey Coach! Keep up or lose out!

Summary

Follow the principles of successful mistakes management:

1. Never ignore your mistakes.
2. Plan for excellence, not perfection.
3. Own your mistakes.
4. Give mistakes management a new role and value in your life.
5. Develop a bank of mistakes-management resources and skills.
6. Develop recovery strategies for immediate use.

Manage your mistakes using *proactive* strategies. Adopt the three Rs:

- Recover
- Refocus
- Retry

Manage your learning:

- Decide what your goals are and what you need to learn to achieve them.
- Plan how you're going to do that.
- Know that you will learn brilliantly.

PART III

Turning Mistakes Into a Competitive Advantage

10

Reasons for Mistakes in Competition

Now that you're brave enough to strut your stuff in competition, it's time to learn about the traps that exist for young players out there in front of the world. It's often a rude shock to discover *in public* that the mistakes made in competition are a breed apart from those made in training. Since you can only encounter these mistakes in the heat of competition, you may find yourself ill prepared for them. To learn about competition errors, we need to first examine how and where the dynamics of competition differ from the dynamics of training. Only with that information will you understand competition mistakes and be able to manage them.

To compete well, you need to have all aspects of your performance in good running order. Naturally, the first of these, and the one that gets all the press, is your sport-specific skill. But it's not enough to just be good at what you play; being a maestro with a tennis racket won't win you Wimbledon. There are *two* major contributors to a successful sport performance. The first is high-quality skills. The second and equally important one is the caliber of your competition skills. These will decide your fate on the day. If it's a toss-up between technical skills and competition skills, the player with the latter will win every time. So let's take a closer look at what they're all about. Your competition skills include being good at the following:

- **Performing under pressure:** It's one thing to excel in training and quite another to do it in the glare of competition.
- **Performing to a deadline:** In training you can always do it again if it isn't right, but in competition it's do it *now* or die!
- **Performing in front of an audience:** This will lift the game of some and devastate the efforts of others.
- **Repeating or restarting an interrupted performance:** Few things are more difficult than this. In some sports it goes with the territory. It takes great courage, and how!
- **"Selling" your performance:** This is where sportsmanship ends and showmanship begins!
- **Keeping your cool:** There is never time to lose your composure in competition.
- **Staying focused:** "If you can keep your head when all about you are losing theirs . . ."
- **Managing your time:** If you can't organize your life, your sport will never happen.
- **Planning:** Quite simply, if you fail to plan, you plan to fail!

These skills are very different from the technical skills of your sport, which at the elite level are taken for granted, because if your sport-specific skills aren't up and running, neither are you. That means that the competition skills are what will sort the men from the boys and the women from the girls. Had you thought of that?

Example

Many people assume that world-class swimmers are successful because they're built like torpedoes. Well that's certainly part of it, but more important is whether they can fire like torpedoes *when it really matters*. Doing so is not about swimming—it's about competition skills.

The flaw in us as athletes is that underneath it all we are people. In fact, we're people first and athletes second with all the perceptions, sensitivities, emotions, and general baggage of your average human being. Put us in a competition environment and we're bound to suffer.

Being good at competition just means being good at putting the lid on suffering. To do that you need to know yourself well, teach yourself well, *and manage yourself better than anyone else who might want to try.* Ensuring that these competition skills are firmly embedded in your skill base will make the difference between having potential and realizing it.

Self-Management

Everything that you do requires that you generate or sustain a level of tension and stress. Both are normal and healthy in the right amounts; in fact, if you didn't have them, you'd keel over and kick the bucket. When you have too much of either, however, the lights start flashing and you start to experience distress and anxiety. Competition is a magnificent vehicle for generating both tension and stress in extremely large quantities out of all proportion to the sorts of jobs you're trying to do out on a field or down on the track. Or maybe it *is* the job. Maybe the job is not to produce the best long jump in history, but to cope with the stress and do the best jump of the day. Thinking of it that way puts coping with the stress squarely in the picture as *part* of your job. And it's not the easy part.

Tension gets the best of everybody at some point. We all snap after a hard day at the office, whether the "office" is a service counter, a boardroom, or a pitcher's mound. Tension makes us irritable, jumpy, shaky, and sometimes sick. We are constantly being told how to handle it better. Despite this we should forgive ourselves if we are not 100% successful. Tension also winds up our timing and distorts our judgment, which is not useful in many high-precision sports. Add to this the general distractions of a busy competition environment, and it's no wonder we sometimes do less than our stunning best. All we can try to do is our best *at that time.* If it doesn't measure up, then maybe next time we'll get things together in a more productive way.

At some point in your sporting career it would be surprising if you did not commit mistakes as a result of carrying excess tension. You need to take steps to regulate that tension and to learn to carry only as much tension as you need for the job. Too much is an unnecessary burden, and too little will leave you at the starting gate. There are lots of techniques around, and good athletes will choose the ones that work best for them, and then get supergood at using them fast and effectively. These include breathing and pulse rate control, centering, mental rehearsal, and others. One of the most effective is to use body and mind scans, which we'll explore later. Once upon a time, relaxation meant being stretched out on the floor in a classic yoga position, taking half an hour out to destress. Nowadays athletes must flip a switch that releases the tension in less than one breath! They must do it on the blocks, on a bike, or astride a horse, and in the middle of the action if need be. Although your training sessions are the place to learn these techniques, no preparation in the world is a substitute for real competition stress.

The trick is to do the following:

- Keep your presence of mind as the tension rises.
- *Use* the tools you have developed in training.
- Have enough free brain space to keep thinking what to do next.

The first step, keeping your presence of mind, is the biggest one to take. After that it gets easier. Focusing on the rhythm and depth of your breathing is one of the most useful techniques here. As a tool, it takes up no space, it's always there when you need it, and in the general craziness of competition preparation, you can't leave it behind.

Wrong Time, Wrong Place

Lapses in concentration account for a great number of mistakes in competition. Basically, you just don't have your mind on the job. It's extraordinary really that when you're finally in a situation that you've thought about nonstop for months, at the moment of truth you're thinking about something else! It's sort of like thinking you have to walk the dog as you're taking your wedding vows! But our minds often play curious tricks on us when they get stressed or fatigued, leaping around in all sorts of nonstandard ways and leaving us wondering how on earth we could let it happen. See table 10.1 for common lapses in attention during competition and what to do about them.

Attentional Choices

It's important at this point to check that you are using the right *kind* of concentration. You'll no doubt be familiar with the four different sorts of attentional focus, but just in case they've slipped your mind, we'll just jog the ol' gray matter.

You have a choice of four places to be. Your attention can be broad and free ranging or narrow and very focused. In addition you can be

Attentional Disorders During Competition

Table 10.1

Attentional mistake	Characteristics	Training remedies
Inappropriate type of focus	• Wrong time, wrong place syndrome • Can't read game, opponent, or self	• Practice using appropriate focus • Hold focus with distractions • Simulation training • Imagery training • Develop concentration over longer periods
Loss of focus	• Easily distracted especially at beginning of performance	• Improve mistakes management • Focus on technique • Reinstate routines
Distracted by winning or losing	• Occurs right at end of game or performance	• Practice holding focus under distracting circumstances • Hold focus until very last seconds of performance • Win more often
Distracted by opponent	• Occurs during game	• Stay focused on your own task • Hold your rhythm • Hold your pace • Stay in your routines
Distracted by crowds or presence of significant others	• Uncharacteristically poor performance	• Develop "glass dome"

concentrating on things that are external to your body or you can be thinking of things from the inside. You'll probably have done tons of this in your mental skills training (and if you haven't, then see to it quickly!), and you should already be familiar with the different types of attentional focus that are best suited to your various sporting tasks. This is about as important as knowing which lane you have to run or swim in or which position you are to play on the court or the field. In other words, you can't be in the right place if you don't know where to go.

Example

If you want to read the play on a basketball court and assess the general situation, you need to have a *broad,* external focus. If, however, your immediate job is to shoot from the edge of the circle, you will need to prepare yourself using a *narrow,* external focus (if you're still busy reading the play, you're going to miss your shot). On the other hand, if your tennis shots aren't working and you're trying to pull your backhand into order, you'll need a narrow, *internal* focus, which targets exactly what your stroke is doing and allows you to analyze various ways you might improve it. If you're doing a whole-body movement such as an ice skater's spin or a gymnast's somersault on the beam, you'll need a *broad,* internal focus to track the whole of what your body is doing.

Different sports typically require their own predominant type of attentional focus. Nonetheless, since you will probably use all of these different sorts of focus in the course of a performance, you must be able to move smoothly and quickly among them.

Also, bear in mind that we all have our individual preference in this matter. Some of us are more comfortable with an external focus, whereas others naturally prefer an internal one. Similarly, some of us are more at home with the big picture (a broad attentional focus), whereas others prefer the details (a narrow focus). When under stress we all tend to return to our preferred mode. That's fine as long as it's appropriate to the task, but not so fine if we need to be in a different mode.

Nerves also play a part here. Take that basketball player again who needs to connect with the basket from the edge of the circle. It's his first big game. The result hangs on his shot. He's very nervous—and nerves tend to make us adopt a narrow, *internal* focus of attention. Yet what he needs here is a narrow, *external* focus. Unless he's aware of what's happening and deliberately changes his focus, that shot could miss by a mile.

Much of concentration training is often done in quiet circumstances, which is very different from the hurly-burly of competition. If you are to learn *appropriate* concentration skills, however, then you must learn to concentrate in surroundings as similar as possible to those in which you compete. Consequently, though your early concentration training should be in a quiet place with as little distraction as possible, you will progressively need to desensitize yourself to increasing amounts of noise and interruption.

Training Progression

If you wish to improve your attentional skills . . .

- Begin by practicing narrow, external focusing. A good way to do this is to focus on a mark on a windowpane. Narrow your focus to pinpoint accuracy. Do not close your eyes; just be still and quiet—and *pay attention.*

- Hold your focus for as long as you can (which at first may be only a few seconds) and *do not let your attention wander to other marks on the pane.*

- Once you become accustomed to the discipline of doing this, practice moving from this narrow, external focus to a *broad,* external focus. To do this, just look through the pane and spread your attention across the view outside. *Do not let your eyes rest on any particular part of it or allow your attention to dwell on any one thing that you see.*

- Then practice moving between the two, alternately bringing your focus back to the original mark on the windowpane, then taking in the view beyond. Using your eyes to train your mind like this is quite a useful device. Remember to do the same thing when competition stress distracts you from your task.

- When this is starting to feel easy, practice a narrow, internal focus by turning your attention to an internal "object" such as your breathing. Use your ears to help you this time, and listen to the rhythm of your breaths. Be sure to totally ignore the outside world. *Do not let your attention wander to any other bodily sensation.*

- Practice this until you can hold your concentration effortlessly for several minutes. Then, to move to a *broad,* internal focus, just concentrate on any general whole-body feeling, such as the feeling of well-being.

- When this feels easy, move from one internal mode to the other, as you did with the external focus. If you've already done some mental skills training, then you're probably familiar with these modes because they're the ones you use to practice your imagery.

- Finally, mix them all up and move deliberately among all four modes. In doing so, you may be able to identify your natural preference. It will be the mode in which you feel most comfortable and into which you find it easiest to move.

- As soon as you've got all this working, you need to progressively turn up the distractions until you can hold your concentration without a blink with the radio blaring, doors slamming, and people coming in and out of the room. This eventually means practicing in the local shopping center, on a bus, walking down the street, and anywhere else that is noisy, busy, and visually distracting. Dismiss any curious onlookers from your space—they're just leading ordinary lives. When you can hold unbroken concentration in these circumstances, you have concentration worth having! That's all that concentration is—being able to hold your focus. In so doing you learn to effectively shut out the rest of the world, which leaves you free to concentrate on the piece of your choice.

- Practice when you feel tired, angry, excited, or nervous, or any other mood that taxes your concentration skills.

- You will have gained advanced status when you can hold your attentional focus while carrying on a sensible conversation!

The competition environment presents a megachallenge to your ability to concentrate. Add up the unfamiliarity of the venue and facilities, the disruption of your usual routines, the changes in food, sleep patterns, and other personal habits, the presence of so many people, and all the general excitement and hype, and it's no wonder this lands on you like a ton of bricks. You need to shield your skills from this onslaught of unwelcome distractions to continue to function well.

■ You need to think *about what you are doing.*

The rest of the world must slide off you like the proverbial water off a duck's back. Only when you have developed this quality of cast-iron concentration that absolutely refuses to become distracted from the job at hand will you have the kind of focus that will withstand the rigors of the competition environment.

You will probably find some of your imagery devices useful here. Operating in a bubble or under a glass dome are well-known ways of setting up a barrier between yourself and the outside world, thereby cutting out distractions and transporting a familiar, personalized, user-friendly environment into the midst of every competition. Any such device can be extremely helpful because visual stimuli are so powerful. It doesn't matter whether you're "seeing" imaginary things or out-there bricks and mortar stuff because both will seem equally real to your brain, which is not at all fussy and does not distinguish between them. Don't believe that one? Consider your dreams—they can seem real enough, and you're not even awake.

The Cost of Winning

Winning can easily be a trigger for the disintegration of concentration. Especially powerful is the anticipation of winning. This masterful distraction can lure even the most steadfast competitor off course. A moment's thought about the potential trophy on the mantle, or the size of the winner's check, and that last stroke or shot turns a dream into a disaster. No competition is won until you are over the finish line, past the last whistle, or through the final flags. Holding your focus right to that moment is always a bigger task if you're leading the field than if you have the heels of an opponent in your sights. But either way, the key is to stay focused to the very last millisecond. If you tend to make competition mistakes when a win is imminent, you need to examine your competition campaign and make sure you are not jumping up the ranks too quickly in your quest for glory. Maybe taking a breather and competing at a slightly lower level for a time will relieve the stress associated with your wins and restore a more balanced approach.

The Cost of Losing

Losing is no less a distraction than winning. The drama and disaster contingent on a mistake in the final moments of a competition can sometimes invade your mind, and a negative thought or image can cut across your concentration with devastating results. This can happen either as a response to the heightened tension of being in the lead, or as a desperate "I can't beat him" as you see your hopes of victory vanishing with the dying moments of the competition. Either way, it's very difficult not to let such intrusive thoughts derail your performance and sabotage your skills. If you catch yourself doing this, you need practice at holding your skills together in more threatening training environments. By boosting your confidence in your skill base, you will find yourself better able to forestall the challenge with an attack of your own when losing threatens your concentration.

It may be helpful here to sort out exactly what happens when you lose concentration. Well, let's get this straight: You don't actually *lose* it at all. It's not a matter of even misplacing it. Rest assured, even in moments when your brain feels like cotton candy, you have just as much capacity for concentration as you ever did. So where does it go? It goes wherever you have chosen to put it. That's the reason you can always refocus on what you *really* want to do. Think of yourself as being in charge of a spotlight on a very dark night. You can choose anything within the range of that spotlight—anything at all! So too you can swing your concentration across anything in your sights until it picks out what you want to focus on. When it's lighting up something you don't want, just move on.

Exercise

Practice swinging your eyes around a room and concentrating on a whole series of different objects. Now, keeping your eyes *open,* let them go out of focus as you *imagine* the same objects and practice swinging your concentration from one to another. Then practice concentrating on tasks instead (make them easy, well-practiced ones to start with, such as a familiar drill or a favorite shot). Finally, practice concentrating on those same tasks walking down the street, in a roomful of people, or anywhere else equally challenging. If you've successfully completed the earlier attentional focus exercises, this one will soon feel easy. If it doesn't, then repeat the earlier exercises to give yourself more preliminary training, then return to this one.

Eyes of the Crowd

Few things intimidate us more in life than the eyes of others. Some eyes will matter more than others, but bet on it—there will be somebody whose gaze will make you feel uncomfortable, for any of a thousand reasons. Competition gives everybody the perfect opportunity to scrutinize, criticize, demonize, or deify what they see. Hold on to your hat if what they see is you. As one of a crowd, the spectator is anonymous, which makes it very easy for him to be judgmental and officious. We all know this because we've all sat in the spectator's seat at some time or other, and yes, we've all been guilty of scrutinizing someone else. Of course, it's also a wonderful chance to yell and cheer and generally regress to a level of excitement few of us have felt since childhood. But there are also expectations of being entertained, of being associated with a winning team, or of being a fan of a successful individual. Those issues, and the general atmosphere of the competition, create stress and tension for the spectator too, and many people's favorite way to dissipate this tension is to off-load it onto the athletes.

Most of these watching eyes will probably be unknown to you. These are the easier ones to deal with. When the eyes belong to significant others, however, the stakes of the game get markedly higher. Here you have a lot more than sporting success on the line—now things like pride, status, and other much-treasured personal artifacts. Further down the scale, somewhere between the well-known significant other and the unknown fan, are your peers. It's hard to say which are the most influential sometimes, those of your own side or those of the opposition. Either way, they pack a decent punch that can make an impressive dent in your performance with no trouble at all if you let them

■ Performing in front of a crowd adds another layer of tension to competing.

distract you from your task. This is where all that practice in noisy, busy places will come into play.

Lack of Experience

Rest assured, nobody was born experienced. In the rough and tumble of life that means that we're all going to make mistakes through lack of experience—to gain it. The next and much more important thing to realize is that you can choose to be in the box seat for the majority of the time to determine exactly *what* experience you want.

When it comes to sporting competition, no one competes just for the experience. Not on your sporting life! Not unless you want to gather a long and ultimately dismal list of dramas and disasters that you will look back on as your sporting career. If you are to enjoy positive and constructive experiences, you need to plan them. Failing to plan them is planning to fail . . . again.

To do this successfully, you need to name the experiences you think will benefit you. Then you can choose the time and place to make them happen. This is easier in sport than in many other arenas of life because sport events are graded and scheduled, which makes for straight-forward planning and allows you to progress at your own pace.

In the interests of building and maintaining confidence (of which much more will be said in chapter 19), your sport experiences need to be *positive*. To get very good at turning apparent disasters into must-have successes, practice remorselessly both on and off the field. It's a whole attitude to life. It doesn't matter whether you forgot to put the cat out or just lost everything you ever owned; you must be able to turn it into a positive experience of success and benefit to you. Wise athletes try to think this way. Wise people make it a mission.

Competition Campaigns

Experience is only a result. When you look at your competition sched-ule, try looking at it in terms of the results you expect it to yield. By all means, give yourself a margin either way, which means being reason-ably flexible in your expectations.

Begin with your goals. It doesn't have to be the Big One—any medium-term goal will do, but it should be big enough to support a season's competition. Working back from the date of that competition, draw up a schedule of all the lead-up events. Include any qualifying competitions and any run-up or introductory events. Include early experimental forays at new levels of competition. Include any simulation events you are using to become accustomed to a particular venue, which you will attend for a major event later. Include a couple of reserve competitions that you will probably not attend but will need to have on your calendar in case you miss others as a result of accident, injury, or other unforeseen circumstances. Then add a little extra time to the overall plan to cover delays in training for things you haven't thought of or events beyond your control. This will give you a competition schedule.

Now that you've had your sessions on goal setting, drawn up your grand plans A, B, C, and made it all process based, you go to competition *to compete.* If you didn't want to do that, you might as well stay home! Implicit in competition is a result that will categorically tell the world that you were better than some or all who were there that day, or maybe worse or shouldn't have been there at all. Let's bite the bullet and, while keeping a steady gaze on your goals, agree with Lombardi that *of course* winning is the only thing. Because the only other option is losing. How many sportspeople can you find who will state clearly and confidently that they are competing to lose!

Whether you like it or not, you are not an island of your own effort—you exist in a cultural setting that imposes its own values that may be very different from your personal values. While you set your personal goals and drive your own efforts to meet them, you cannot—and must not—ignore the social interpretations of what you are doing. Taking the sporting high ground on this whole winning issue is not helpful. It will not contribute to a robust response to your competition results, especially when, despite achieving your private goals, they appear publicly disappointing. So let's stop pretending that winning doesn't matter. Let's agree that it matters *enormously.* Especially to you. Let's address the issue, but let's do it in realistic terms that in no way compromise your commitment to your personal goals.

It *is* realistic to go into competition with some expectations of success. They may be grand or they may be very modest, but they will be there somewhere. Better admit to that now.

Exercise

On a clean sheet of paper write out *a range* of results for each competition that would allow you to go home happy. We will call these your *competition expectations.* It is particularly necessary to do this if you are contemplating qualifying rounds of any kind, want to amass a particular number of points on any sort of leader board, or have to finish within a certain quota of the field to reach your goal. To pretend that this is not important when your heart and soul know perfectly well that it is absolutely vital is only another way to store up worry and create a sense of inner conflict that will contribute nicely to raising your stress levels.

So clearly it is unrealistic to expect any normal sporting mortal not to want to win, especially when the whole of the rest of the world appears to think it's an OK thing to do and roars its approval when you do. You just have to take a little care in how you go about it, that's all. You may also have to tinker slightly with the terminology to reconcile—but not confuse—your competition expectations with everything you've ever learned about goal setting.

To do this, do not extend your wish list to winning. That is a nonnegotiable absolute state of affairs that will depend on a lot of things you can't control, including the quality of the opposition on the day. Do, however, write in some socially acceptable expectations of success, such as making the quarterfinals, finishing in the top six, or even ending up on the rostrum. These are *outcome-based* statements and are quite different from your performance goals, which are all *process-based*. They are merely admissions that you are a social creature in a social world, and furthermore that you like it that way.

This whole sporting show rests on the results because they are the reason for the show in the first place. Sorting out these matters will make your sporting career sit more easily with your cultural values. You may not have thought that you had any cultural values, but unless you grew up in outer space, it's a pretty sure bet that you've had a family of some sort, an education of some kind, and a social life of some description. Even so, you may still think that none of this matters at all. It doesn't, except for the spin-off. Like it or not, unresolved conflict creates stress, and you carry that stress whether you are aware of it or not. Sorting this to your own satisfaction will be enough to dissipate that stress, which will mean you can put that energy to better use kicking harder, jumping farther, or running faster.

Smart people figure out that what they want privately and what others want for them publicly are not necessarily the same thing. Neither do they have to be. And this will not be the first time we've had to run our personal lives with an eye on the social values of the society in which we live.

We begin to see how very different is this approach to competition from either of the more usual positions on the sporting continuum. At one end where we compete to "win at all costs" and where winning is unsubstantiated by any other meaningful goals or at the other end where we compete "just for the experience." Watch out, because when you stand up to the competition for no better reason than that your Saturday just happens to be free, your sporting career might just fall in a heap. It is better perhaps to settle for the middle ground here. Acknowledge the social pressure to believe that winning is the only worthwhile result. But let other people own these *outcome-based* goals. Meanwhile, you can quietly enjoy owning the *process-based* goal that you can measure, achieve, and control. If your standards are high enough, this will mean that you win anyway! This is the place to be. This is where the real winners hang out.

Real winners also know that sometimes they win privately, sometimes publicly, and occasionally on both fronts. That's a buzz.

Trying Your Best

Trying your best very much goes with competition territory in a way that even the most exacting training does not squeeze out of you. Undoubtedly, you will strive to do well in competition. Sometimes you'll strive too hard. This makes a mess of your timing, fitness, and physique. The results are always disappointing, so it makes a mess of your fun too. Here's where you must try very hard not to outperform yourself but to restate exactly, precisely, and without any embellishments whatsoever what you have been doing in training. If your trying is misdirected into struggling to do something you've never done before, then this is neither the time nor the place for entrepreneurial effort. This is the place for well-practiced, thoroughly rehearsed, and utterly familiar productions of well-learned skills. Let the competition itself do its job of putting a little icing on your cake, but you should leave that icing alone! This is rather the same as letting your training exercises contribute to your improvement—you don't have to make *everything* happen because good exercises will contribute their own ingredients to your success if you are well prepared and they are the right exercises at the right time. You hope of course that a similar enhancement of your performances will happen in competition, but you should not in any way try to contribute to it. Just look forward to it every time, and then enjoy it.

Coaches' Corner

There's nothing quite like competition to see how cool a head you can keep. There you are—all your coaching on the line—there's no kick, pull, or throw you can make which will help or hinder the result, and not even your shadow on the dais when it's all over. It's time to remember that you volunteered for this spot. It's also time to remember that sport is for the athletes. It's their day now. It's also their goals that they are striving for. Be sure of that. Your goals must be equally clear, but equally yours. Sad scenes sometimes happen at competition, which result from somebody moving the goalposts when other parties weren't looking. Suddenly winning is important after all. Or it's much more important than the cozy little chat in the locker room had everybody believe. For a comfortable day put the following protocol into practice:

- Make sure the goals of the day are clear in your mind and in the minds of your athletes.
- Decide who owns which goals.
- *Do not change any goals from those set in training.*

You will also need a disaster strategy just in case things go seriously wrong. You need to at least give the possibility a passing thought so that you can give hope and cheer where needed. The bottom line is that win, lose, draw, disgrace, or disaster, the buck stops with *you*. And the worse it goes, the bigger that buck gets.

All coaches need hard-to-ruffle feathers that shed unwanted comments well, and a small streak of steel through their backbones. Sometimes the steel must show. When a disaster stops neatly at your feet, use the spring in the steel to bounce back. Knowing you have that capacity is sometimes enough to save your day—even if you can't salvage that of your athlete.

Summary

By its very nature, competition challenges both coach and athlete in many ways.

For the Athlete . . .
- Learn to *perform* well.
- Learn to *compete* well.
- Learn the difference.

For the Coach . . .
You need broad shoulders to carry the responsibilities of winning and for everyone else to cry on when they lose.

11

Typical Competition Mistakes

Competition mistakes are a breed all their own. What makes them so peculiarly tricky to deal with is that since they occur only in competition, we have no way of rehearsing for them other than out in open company, where there are so many different variables that it is hard to find a pattern in the mistakes. But perhaps if we look at the dynamics of competition, these will give us the clues we need to rally a strategy to sort them out.

In competition, performing the skills we've learned in training rests on being able to do them in some pretty extraordinary circumstances, including the following:

- At call, which may not be exactly when we're ready
- In front of a crowd, which may include significant others, knowledgeable onlookers, critical others, and fans
- Under competition pressure on our own account or on account of our team, state, or country, where others hold expectations of our performance

- In situations over which we have little or no control such as crowded or noisy warm-up conditions, delayed or rescheduled events, bad weather conditions, and so on
- In unfamiliar venues organized by unfamiliar officials and competition personnel

It is easy to see from this list that any of these factors or any combination of these factors could contribute to making mistakes. The best way to isolate which ones are doing the damage is to keep a log of the things that happen and how you feel about them. You probably won't have time to do this during the competition itself, nor be in the mood to try, but after it's all over, this can be a very useful part of your debriefing. It will give you the key to finding the triggers for your mistakes. Look for patterns of behavior in the day or from one day to another, or repeat situations that seemed to trigger both the good and the not-so-good performance. You can then work to either repeat or desensitize those triggers in training. Ask your coach how to go about it if you're short on ideas. Table 11.1 summarizes common mistakes made during competition.

Increment and Decrement Mistakes

Tailoring your training to your upcoming competitions is an art form. Not only do you need to cover all the skills your competition demands, but you also need to have them confirmed and at call before you leave home. For the very technical, open sports with many variables outside of your control such as the equestrian disciplines or team sports, success in competition will require you to train to the standard of the competition *plus some*. Here is where the *10% Decrement Rule* comes in. When you compete, you can expect to lose as much as 10% off the standard of what you are producing in training. Sometimes losing only 10% is very good indeed (if, for instance, you're performing in bad weather conditions). Losing only 5% may be absolutely brilliant. In doing this, you are not making any significant mistakes because this drop in performance is normal and to be expected. It is a response to performing in an unfamiliar environment, in less than ideal conditions, and under the usual pressures of competition.

To come out ahead of the pack in competition, therefore, means you need to train to at least 115% of the demands of the competition. Competitors who are not expecting to confront this scenario, and who

Table 11.1 Mistakes During Competition

Mistakes	Characteristics	Training remedies
Increment mistakes	• Unexpectedly energize performance • Can cause misjudgments and inaccuracies	• Do not rely on them • Better self-management • Consistent training • More competition mistakes exposure • Repair your performances after each outing
Decrement mistakes	• Expect some loss of performance, especially in early competition	
Primacy-recency mistakes	• Last thing learned is first thing forgotten	• Train new skills over and beyond those you need at your current level of competition
Pressure mistakes	• Too high levels of tension • Uncomfortable stress • Feeling "pressured" • Errors of judgment or timing • Inappropriate mental or physical energy levels • Getting too excited	• Read chapter 14 • Practice relaxation techniques • Improve breathing control • Centering exercises • Focus on tasks • Know the energy needs of your sport
Emotional mistakes	• Being rattled by other mistakes • Being "on the run" from the opposition • Losing your temper	• Read chapter 2 • Develop behavioral options • Make better choices • Practice under a range of circumstances
Nervous mistakes	• Any one of 100 ways you may tell the world you're in a knot	• Read chapter 14 • Improve tension management • Compete more often • Win more often!

consequently do not train to reach the standard of the competition *plus an allowance for the performance decrement*, are often surprised and left wondering what went wrong. Suddenly the standard of the competition seems to have skyrocketed. They're in with no showing and little hope of having any fun. When this oversight also clash with a misjudgment of the *actual* standard of the competition, it produces disasters by the truckload. But take heart. It's all thoroughly avoidable if you just take the 10% Decrement Rule into account in your training and plan your competition campaigns with care.

Another way you can tackle this performance decrement is to improve your mistakes management. Remember we said it would lift your game by 10%? Add that to lifting your training standards, and you're a winner! Tennis players, for example, assume that only a percentage of their shots will be effective. You can do the same and simply try to increase the percentage of your own performance that is effective. Raising the bar like this helps you generally work to a higher standard and make higher-quality mistakes. This will be enough for you to outperform the opposition!

Some sports, usually the ones that attract large crowds, may actually encourage a performance *increment* during competition. The presence of the crowd affords enough hype to actually lift the performance beyond what the athletes achieved in training. This is common in football and swim meets. It would not be wise, however, to rely on this increment to achieve a win. That would be a naïve mistake. For one thing, you'd have forgotten that it lifts the opposition's performance too.

Primacy-Recency Mistakes

This one is a snake in the grass that you step on only when you least expect it. There you are, slaving away in training, perfecting just exactly the right skill that will win you the next competition. Out you go to meet the world and *bang!* your nice new skill evaporates. Well, join the ranks of the also-disillusioned. This is the primacy-recency principle at work, which means that under pressure, the first thing you forget is the last thing you learned. Of course, competition provides just enough pressure to ensure that this principle holds true, and there you are bereft of your newest and most glittering weapon at the hour of your greatest need.

Don't you just hate these theoreticians? The trouble is that at least this time around, they are right. You can absolutely bank on this rule working every time. The positive side of *this* shiny little coin is that you always know what's coming. Without fail, the rule will hold true in all circumstances and at all stages of learning. There are no exceptions, no variations, and nothing to remember about it—except that it works. Consequently, there is really *no excuse whatsoever* for ever making a primacy-recency mistake. The only known antidote is to practice the new skill until it feels old before you use it to dazzle the world.

Self-Management Mistakes

By this stage in your game you will surely be entirely familiar with the idea that different skills in different sports require quite specific levels of energy control, both physical and mental. You know that gross motor skills such as weightlifting or explosive sprints are best achieved with very high levels of energy and mental readiness, while those at the fine end of the scale such as golf or gymnastics require lower levels of readiness and a more discreet use of energy.

Generally speaking, anything that requires a lot of judgment or superaccurate timing, such as motor racing or a tennis serve, is compromised by too high a level of mental energy. We've all heard the wail "there's no time to think," and that's exactly what's happening if you have high levels of mental energy burning a hole in your brain. If you have a simple explosive task, then maybe your brain doesn't *need* time to think. If, on the other hand, you've just asked it to mastermind a highly complex operation possibly involving visual input and maybe judging speed or distance, or if it's being asked to decide between a number of alternative courses of action, then your brain certainly *does* need a bit of uncluttered airspace to be able to come up with the right answers. Magical and marvelous as the brain may be, it is as subject to overload, fatigue, distraction, and stress as the rest of your body. It's a mistake to think it can operate effectively in all conditions. Flood your brain with energy, and it will operate about as well as your car does when you flood the carburetor with fuel. Like cars, we choke too!

Competition is, of course, the sportsperson's greatest energy trigger, be it in the form of excitement or anxiety. Now you begin to get the picture. The challenge is how best to regulate your energy levels to be appropriate to these various tasks. Clearly, in the high-energy sports, competition will be inclined to facilitate successful performances. In lower-energy sports, however, competitors are faced with a very different scenario. Here they must battle to contain their mental energy to keep it from interfering with their fine motor skills and their judgment of speed, distance, and timing. Although it may be said that the different sports tend by their very nature to attract people whose temperaments and trait anxiety levels are compatible with the sports, no matter how laid back you may be, you can easily be stirred by a few flags, the scratchy rasp of a PA system, or the sight of opposition colors. Managing your physical and mental energy levels is no easy task at the best of times, but in the heat of competition it becomes a major skill that can make or break the result. Harboring energy levels that are inappropriate to your sport accounts for many mistakes. The trick is not to focus on the mistakes, but to adjust the energy level that produces them. If you can correct that, then you can head off further mistakes and any similar mistakes in the future.

Pressure Mistakes

Pressure mistakes are all in the head. There is no "pressure"—competition or otherwise—beyond what we as individuals perceive it to be. What a hard pill to swallow that one is! However, it does explain why some people experience extreme pressure while others appear to be enjoying or at least surviving the same experience. We'll talk about how to positively manage pressure in chapter 18, but for the moment, all we need to know is that pressure is very much what we make it, and competition can generate a whole volcano's worth if we let it.

The results of feeling pressured can be pretty disastrous, as we all know. Vital gear gets forgotten, strategies come unraveled, skills desert you, and everything moves into crisis mode. No sooner do you sort out one drama than you seem to be up to your ears in the next one. Not a happy place to be. So what is the solution?

Perhaps the worst feeling associated with being under pressure is the loss of control. Somehow you no longer feel at the helm, and whoever is driving the show seems to be doing it at breakneck speed. You run out of time, you run out of skill, you run out of options. And therein lies the clue to all this.

■ Slow . . . the . . . whole . . . thing . . . down.

If you can create some time for your brain to get a grip, it will soon start to function more normally. A bit of quiet time will do wonders. The tension will subside, a sense of order will return, and as your skills reappear, so will your confidence. This is, of course, a Big Ask in the middle of a major panic attack. Unfortunately, there are no soft options. Learn to make the Ask happen, or die young. No contest, eh.

Attentional Mistakes

Sometimes it's not only difficult to get into the right mental gear for the job at hand, but your attentional gears seem to get stuck too. You adopt one particular focus and just can't seem to move out of it. When this is an inappropriate focus for what you're doing, then you're right in the middle of a major attentional mistake. If you skipped chapter 10, now is the time to read it because if this happens to you on a regular basis, you need to do some exercises to help you become more aware of the different attentional places to be and to practice moving in and out of them. It all sounds very complicated on the page, but out in the action it's much easier to understand. Your friendly coach will undoubtedly help to steer you past the worst of the pitfalls.

Now comes the bad news. You know that by nature we all have one type of focus that we prefer and that we'll gravitate to that one, especially in times of stress *and irrespective of the task we're trying to accomplish.* This is especially relevant to competition, where the high levels of stress may skew or narrow your focus. There's a strong possibility that the sort of attentional focus you need for competitive success may not be the one you are most inclined to adopt in competition. Naturally, this is not helpful. This is a serious attentional mistake and is likely to be your most common one. It's not just what you're paying attention to, it's *how* you're paying attention. Catch up on some background knowledge here if you're a bit rusty, or reread chapter 10 and refresh your knowledge of the four main possibilities at your disposal: internal broad and narrow focus, and external broad and narrow focus. Be in the *wrong* quarter, and you may as well have gone to the wrong grounds or turned up on the wrong day for your competition. Be in the *right* quarter and think about the *right* things, and you've got a fighting chance. Get to know your own preferences and be sure to practice your *least* favorite sorts of focus.

Strangeness Mistakes

Strangeness has a curious and insidious effect on us. When we meet new people, we are never quite our usual selves at least for the first few minutes, and sometimes for very much longer. When we move into a

■ Strange environments can bring strange performances.

new house, it's a while before it feels like home. Even when we sleep in a strange bed, our bodies often register their disapproval in the quality of that sleep for the first night or so. The ancients called this response "misoneism" (dislike of the new or unknown), and it's been with us since the beginning of time. It's small wonder, then, that moving even temporarily to a strange environment to perform our skills in a new and unfamiliar space has a peculiar, sometimes unidentified, and often underrated effect on our performance.

Competition environments are usually quite different from training environments. They are frequently on a much grander scale and have facilities such as spectator seating, which you may not be used to seeing on a daily basis. For major meets, they may even be in different areas of the country with different light, air, colors, and smells. And that's before anyone goes overseas or takes into account such things as climate or altitude. All this has a subtle and profound impact on you that you must make certain allowances for if it is not to be to your cost.

Strangeness has its own effect on attentional focus. It tends to turn it inwards and to narrow it. Recent research suggests that our well-known fight-or-flight response is not triggered by external circumstances at all but is our body's reply to feelings of fear, nervousness, or anxiety. If you narrow in too early on arrival at a competition venue, you'll find yourself much more nervous than you would have been if you had maintained a broader focus. This is because you generate, and then concentrate on, these nervous feelings. Also, your narrow focus will keep you from paying attention to the venue, which will result in it feeling stranger for longer. By narrowing your focus too early, you will have put yourself in an altogether more stressful situation than other competitors who manage themselves better. Be sure to discipline yourself here because this may be critical if your favorite place to be is in the narrow half of the attentional whole.

Underestimating the effects that strangeness has on your performance is a significant mistake. Simulation training will help, hence the common practice of training to background crowd noise. Taking as much as you can of your original environment with you will help too (your own pillow, special or favorite foods, etc.). However, there's no substitute for the real thing, and until you have actually experienced competing at a particular venue, this is going to be a determining factor in the quality of your performance and in the production of various mistakes that are responses to the strangeness around you.

Appearance Mistakes

No one doubts that as a way of life you normally move heaven and earth to take up your spot in the team or to line up with the best for your event. But there are circumstances that will defeat even the toughest competitor, and times in every athlete's career when competition is just not possible. Some of these circumstances will include . . .

- Carrying injuries that are not properly healed
- Having your preparation interrupted to the extent that your fitness or your skill development has been compromised
- Difficult personal circumstances that may make it practically impossible to play well, such as many athletes experienced after September 11

- Compromised confidence as a result of not having recovered from an accident or other major trauma

These are times to continue training, but you may want to temporarily stay away from competition until you are able to muster *all* your resources and address the task in a manner that will do you and your supporters credit.

Misjudgments of Standards

This is a hazard that attends any competitive event. How good will the opposition *really* be? There is no way of knowing until you actually get out on the paddock or the track or into the pool or onto the court, and it's too late by then if you've misjudged them. As sure as night follows day, this will happen. Oops! You're hard into damage control and wishing you were somewhere else on the planet! This competition variable is bound to trip you up sooner or later. Better get used to making this mistake because you are not privy to the opposition's training regime, or rate of improvement since you last saw them, and you don't know what their new coach has been up to or how they're feeling that day. In the light of this it's reasonable to forgive yourself ignorance of the state of their game—but it's not always that easy. Far from forgiveness, what most of us feel in such a situation is frustration, anger, and a quite irrational sensation of having been shortchanged. Hang in there! There is always tomorrow (or at least talk yourself into temporarily believing that there might be). Failing that, make the best of today by sticking to your performance goals and rewrite your public image sometime later.

Overload and Fatigue Mistakes

Yes, we know all about overload and fatigue in training, but that's different. In training, if gasp comes to heave, you can stop. Anyway there's nobody watching you sweat and shake at home. Losing your last ounce of everything when it really matters and in front of all those eyes is another matter altogether. So why does it feel so different in competition? First, you must ask yourself, Have I *really* trained for this competition? If you are on deck with heat after heat or playing a whole 40-minute halfmatch, have you really trained to be able to do that? If your training stopped short at 20 minutes, then it's no wonder you've had it at the 30-minute mark. And if you don't ever do more in training than you might do in half of the real thing, then of course you're out of everything before your competition day is done.

Bear in mind also that carrying the emotional hype of competition takes its toll. Then there's all the general coming and going that is an inevitable part of being in an unfamiliar venue where most of what you want to do next is somehow happening at the far end of the grounds. If you add this all up, you'll find that in terms of effort, one competition day probably adds up to about three days' worth of training. This needs to be factored into your training. So you don't just train for the event—you train for *the competition.*

Opponents' Mistakes

Opponents' mistakes are a bit of a wild card. So often they come out of the blue and you are taken very much off guard, which from our opponent's point of view hugely enhances the value of their mistake *for them* because it often precipitates a mistake of your own. Try to absorb an opponent's mistakes into your game with as little disruption to the rhythm of your own play as possible. Also, quietly peel the emotion off the mistakes and try *not* to feel glad when your opponent blows set point or his goal strike hits the bar. Leave the emotional fallout for him to deal with. That way, his mistakes will have minimal clout and maximal value *for you.*

Comic Mistakes

A word now about a rather special sort of mistake. This is one we've practiced since childhood. All of us can remember mistakes that have been the cause of laughter. But things change as we grow older and things such as peer pressure, social standing, and that extraordinarily anonymous quality called "face" begin to matter. As adults we often become peculiarly sensitive to being the object of other peoples' mirth. Our mistakes are generally not something to be laughed at. *We* are not to be laughed at! A spectacular mis-hit may relieve the immediate tension of competition, but our own comic errors are usually enjoyed more in hindsight than they ever are at the time because these mistakes deliver a double whammy.

First, like any other mistake, comic mistakes are an unexpected disruption to the rhythm of your performance. Second, they deliver a seriously out-of-context result: comedy. This does not fit at all comfortably into the business of competitive sports where at almost every level the scene is ferocious concentration, exhaustive effort, and sometimes superhigh personal, social, or financial stakes.

Comedy is not to be confused with fun. The fact that we laugh at both is incidental. What—or more precisely who—we laugh at, and what sentiments that laughter expresses, are the important issues here. Not many people can carry on when a cast of thousands bursts out laughing—not with them, but *at* them. The laughter may be as embarrassed as it is embarrassing.

Comic errors are not for the fainthearted. They can be very difficult to recover from. Joining in the laughter is not an option. Anyway, that may be more than you can do if the mistake has just cost you the championship, a year's work, or your superannuation.

So where do you go when you suddenly find yourself on very shaky ground? Back into safer territory. Back into your well-known, well-practiced, predictable routines. Make yourself repeat your preserve, prereceive, prejump, prerun, pre-whatever routines. Do them several times if necessary while the hubbub dies down. *The hubbub is your saving grace because it buys you time.* Use that time to recover. Use it well.

■ Keep moving, keep busy—stay focused.

Example

- Championship point. An ace is all you need. You wield your racket with gusto and aggression, all set to scorch the center line. But when you serve, you nearly take the nose off the ball boy. Howls of laughter. A moment of horror. Not what you planned. Wish it wasn't happening . . .

Training Strategies

- Focus! Focus! FOCUS!!
- If you haven't created a glass dome in which to play, you had better create it right now. Learn to shut out the outside world together with its destructive potential. Do it quickly and completely and stay in your dome until further notice.

- Compare this with your response to the feel-good laughter, where you joined in. Join in this one and you're dead.

Biggest Risk

- Not taking comic mistakes seriously.

Coaches' Corner

Comic errors will really test the mettle of your athletes. They will also really test you. This is the time to remember that you are a significant other to the athlete. Being laughed at by the general populace is one thing. Being laughed at by her resident significant other is altogether another matter. It may be difficult to contain your laughter since it's probably almost as spontaneous as the original mistake was, but awareness of your huge potential to hurt your athlete may be a moderator here.

Action Pact

- Kindness is the order of the day. Appreciating the athlete's feelings and understanding the true cost of the mistake will soon put a gentler spin on your response.
- Practical help may be difficult in public circumstances, but later training should glue together the glass bubble if cracks have appeared under stress.

Summary

Competition mistakes include the following:

- **Increment and decrement mistakes:** These are misjudgments of how much the competition will lift or lower your performance.
- **Primacy-recency mistakes:** The last thing learned in training will be the first to go in competition.
- **Self-management mistakes:** Getting the energy level right can be a tricky business.
- **Pressure mistakes:** Pressure may be all in the mind, but it's the body that has to let off the steam.

- **Attentional mistakes:** Being in the wrong place at the wrong time is not helpful.

- **Strangeness mistakes:** Misjudging the impact of a strange environment, strange food, different climates, and so forth, can wreak havoc with the best-laid plans.

- **Appearance mistakes:** Knowing when to compete and when to stay at home is critical to long-term success.

- **Misjudgments of standards:** You don't always get it right; sometimes opponents really *are* that good.

- **Overload and fatigue mistakes:** Many mistakes are prompted by these factors; we often underestimate the increased fatigue that is a product of competition.

- **Opponents' mistakes:** Let them deal with it and keep your mind on your job.

- **Comic mistakes:** Everybody laughs, except you. Take these mistakes seriously and train your refocusing abilities.

12

Minimizing Competition Mistakes

No competitor ever born hasn't regretted a mistake or three in the course of his or her career. (Review table 12.1 [pp. 166-167] for a summary of mistakes made during competition.) Mistakes pretty much go with the territory, although they're a bumpy part of the territory. We *have* made them and we *will* make them, but if we can cut down on the numbers, at least we won't have as much to regret. *Minimization* is our new buzzword.

Routines

Nothing—*nothing*—is more important to the dyed-in-the-wool competitor than routines: precompetition routines; intracompetition routines; routines of eating, sleeping, warming up, and warming down; routines of thinking, rehearsing, practicing, and practically anything else you can think of that is connected with your performance. Running in the same shoes, playing in the same strip—add a dash of superstition such as wearing any sort of charm or pulling on your right sock first for luck, and you're right in there. We are such creatures of habit. We like familiar people, places, ideas, activities . . . you name it, and we feel better if we've done it before and know what's around the next corner. Some of us need to know *so* much that we consult cards, stars, and soothsayers in efforts to find out. We all perform better too in familiar circumstances. While the nature of competition does not usually permit this, we can do our very best to surround ourselves as much as possible with familiar objects, people, and *well-used, thoroughly comfortable routines.*

Perhaps the most immediate advantage of using routines is that they free up our brain space to be better able to concentrate on activities of our choice. We no longer have to think about what might happen next— we know! This lets us focus much more easily on the things that really matter in competition—such as our technique. Routines allow us to "lock in" to a predetermined pattern of thinking and behavior, which makes us far less easily distracted. They also allow us to feel more se-cure and generally more relaxed and less uptight. This frees up energy that we can put to good use elsewhere!

When you have practiced your routines often enough, like any learned skill you'll do them automatically and not have to consciously think of the process at all. This is when you'll really gain the maximum benefits from them. Routines *are* your competition preparation. The higher the quality of your preparation, the greater the potential for giving a magical performance. We know that there is no accident about a good performance. It doesn't happen to unfit, unskilled, underprepared athletes. No athlete can just pull a magical performance out of the hat. They don't make those kinds of hats. A good performance at any level is created only by fit, skilled athletes who rely on water-tight routines to prepare themselves well for their task. Time for another refrigerator sticker, and let's make it a biggie:

■ Your *performance* is only as good as your *preparation.*

Put that one anywhere that you'll see it at least three times a day.
Preparation makes good sense. You can't suddenly have strength in unfit muscles or produce skills in competition that you haven't learned and practiced in training. So if you want to be a champion, you have to prepare like one. That means heaps of effort, masses of mistakes, too many early mornings, and probably a lost youth. But you do get to keep the glory. If that thought doesn't fire you into your next training session, nothing will!

Routines are a highly personal matter. They will include everything from what you eat for breakfast to whom you pray to as you let fly down the track. Some people like to isolate themselves before their event, others like to fraternize, especially in a team situation. You will need routines of every size and shape, and you need to stick by whatever works for you. If you *must* twirl your racket twice counterclockwise before your serve, then that's the way it is! Routines are the oil that makes your competition wheels turn smoothly.

Should you abandon your precompetition routines, you will immediately start making mistakes. This is because your preparation is not what you usually do, and you are trying to produce skills from a new and unknown base. This is beginners' country. You will therefore make gross mistakes because they are beginners' mistakes. Imagine training to high jump off a hard surface, and then going to a competition and being told you have to jump off soft sand. Suddenly nothing works because nothing works *suddenly*; everything takes practice. It's all a lesson in matching your routines to your competition demands in order that you prepare for a winning performance.

Training Routines

Training routines are the first of your routines to put in place. Establishing a rhythm to your training is extremely important for it will allow you to develop patterns of effort, of motivation, of confidence, and of skill acquisition. If you usually train on a Sunday morning, then *do not* let your social life rewrite that. If you like a pepper-hot shower when you come in from a session, then get your elbows out and be at the front of the line *every time* before the hot water runs out. Look to your preferences, honor your sport—but stick to your guns like a bandit! Before long you'll find you become very sensitive to any disturbance of these patterns, which will be the first signs of trouble brewing and may signal over- or undertraining, motivational problems, or any of a number of other issues that need attention. If you miss these signs, you may unwittingly carry your problems into competition. This is an unnecessary and avoidable mistake, which naturally will be reflected in your results.

Tapering Routines

Tapering routines will evolve over time if you keep an eye out for what suits you as you approach each competition. These may start a week or even a month before an event and might include things such as a special diet or having not less than eight hours' sleep a night. They will

Table 12.1   Competition Mistakes Summary

Mistakes	Results	Remedies
Competition stage fright	• Misjudge standard of competition • All seems too difficult • Intimidated by opposition	• Improve planning • Train to higher standard before competing at a lower one • More competition exposure
Strangeness mistakes	• Feelings of "exposure" • Lack of confidence • Anxiousness	• Simulation training • Arrive early at venues
Appearance mistakes	• Overwhelming • Feelings of isolation • Lack of confidence in skills	• Not ready for competition—should have stayed at home! • Better competition scheduling
Misjudgment of opposition	• Feelings of inadequacy • Want to be somewhere else	• Better planning • Easier contests • Stick to your own game plan
Comic mistakes	• Crowd laughs at you, not with you • Disrupts your rhythm • Disturbs your focus • Generates embarassment	• Keep moving • Keep busy • Stay focused
Follow-up errors	• Irritating after your own mistake but exasperating after your opponent's	• Focus, focus, focus!
Overload or fatigue	• Fade during performance • Exhaustion	• Train for all the competition

Table 12.1 *(continued)*

Mistakes	Results	Remedies
Attentional mistakes	• Inappropriate focus • Loss of focus • Distraction	• See table 10.1, page 137
Skill-learning mistakes	• Primacy/recency • Increment/decrement	• See table 11.1, page 151
Self-management Mistakes	• Buckling under pressure • Emotional mistakes • Nerves	• See table 11.1, page 151

certainly include tapered physical and skill-learning programs. Some athletes even include a spell of "nerves" to get them over and done with before the event! You'll know how long to make these routines because you'll feel the point at which you "engage" with the event. From that point on, it's alive and very much in your psyche and will drive your life. As you lose interest in many of your usual activities, this is a sure sign that you have logged in to your competition mindset.

Precompetition Routines

Depending on your sport, precompetition routines will probably start with your precomp briefing and end with your warm-up, and they'll certainly include everything you do in the last half hour or so before you perform. They will culminate in you using imagery of your actual performance, and in sports that have very precise technical requirements, such as gymnastics or diving, you will be "seeing" and "feeling" every last detail of what you are about to do. It's during these routines that you'll also bring into play all the other mental skills that normally facilitate your performance. You will probably be using everything you own.

A typical precomp routine will include . . .

- Working through your physical warm-up procedures
- Swinging your self-management into gear to regulate your energy levels

- Using your imagery skills to create a quiet space and run through your techniques
- Continually adjusting your attentional focus
- Continually adjusting your tension levels to suit the job ahead
- Last checks on your gear
- A final mental rehearsal of what you're about to do

Some athletes like to isolate themselves as they work through this process. Team athletes may include some bonding activities.

Postcompetition Routines

Postcompetition routines come hard on the heels of finishing your event. They're the poor relations of the rest of the routines, but you'd better knit them into your system if you want to put success in your rights. After all your efforts out there, it's easy to forget that this is the point at which you are most vulnerable, both physically and mentally, to any *adverse* consequences of the competition. This is where your body needs its warm-down if it is to avoid injury and be ready to perform again quickly and in good order. You need to dissipate excess lactic acid in your muscles, restore your normal resting heart and respiration rates, and rein in your adrenaline levels. It's also the time to check in on your attitude toward the result. Good days are easy; others take more effort.

Like the other routines, postcompetition routines take practice, but the time you put into them will be well worth it. Deciding to make the best of a bad day can influence every event for the next six months. You need to do this yourself before *anyone* else imposes *their* interpretations on what happened. Not your coach, your fans, your family, your teammates, or your opponents! What they think about things right now doesn't matter a bit. It's *your* spin on *your* effort, and *you* need to feel good about it. It's a mistake not to set aside just a few minutes for this. Anyway, it rounds out your competition nicely.

Recovery Routines

Recovery routines are a very important part of your big picture. After all the excitement and anticipation of a competition, you may be tempted when it's all over to just "veg out." Don't forget that until you've done the recovery routine, the competition is still running—that is, if you want to get the maximum mileage out of it. There are still debriefings to do and de*griefings* to get through (see chapter 13) and maybe injuries to mend, and by the time you've gotten through all that, you'd better get started on the strategies and tactics for your *next* competition.

Routines are not something you can sit down and learn. They will evolve over time. You'll edit them and alter them and wish you had and hadn't changed them. Above all they must be what works *for you*. The more you compete, the more sophisticated and increasingly personalized your routines will become. There is no better way to minimize your competition mistakes than to install a fistful of routines into your sporting life. If you need confirmation of this, just watch any high-performance athlete in action and you'll see that right down to the last little detail he lives a perfectly ordered and utterly repeatable life during the

■ Make it routine and make for success.

last few minutes before each event. You'll see seasoned players going through *exactly* the same set of actions before every game. With those actions go very particular, well-organized, well-practiced thoughts. And as we know, winning is very much a mind game.

If the idea of developing these routines is new for you, there's no time like the present to adopt them into your sport life! Begin with short, general things that you have to do anyway, but do them in the same order from now on. When you have the skeleton of a routine in place, begin to build on it. Gradually create a block of specific, predictable, repeatable behavior. This will soon become automatic, which means you won't have to think too hard about it other than to kick it into gear. You have just created a brand new habit.

Here are some mistakes you might make in your routines:

- Making them too complicated
- Making them too long
- Changing them without good reason
- Letting other people interrupt them
- Interrupting them yourself

Cement your routines into your training. They are now *part* of your performance. Now transfer them lock, stock, and detail to your competitions. The adoption of them will instantly abolish a fistful of your old competition mistakes.

Imagery

As part of your routines either precompetition or pre-event, few things are more effective than imagery. The clearer and more positive you can make your imagery, the better. No one can do things right all the time, but everyone can do everything right in imagery! Of course you can make mistakes here too (what's new?) if you let negative or destructive images intrude into your head.

Practice imagining yourself producing gloriously competent skills and playing wonderfully complete games every day of the year. Get so you can feel the air or snow or water on your skin, hear the squeal of a winch or the clink of a bridle, taste the salt on your lips and smell the sweat of your effort—in short, live your sport. The more brilliantly you can do this, the more successful your imagery will be as a catalyst to your actual performance.

Developing your own scenarios and putting your very own spin on the production is a luxury you *can* afford, and the more customized your imagery is, the better it will work for you. You can replay favorite scenes endlessly without boring the socks off anyone else. The only thing you need to do is to run this personalized "video" in the shower, after breakfast, before lunch, over coffee. Amuse yourself with this slice of your favorite action when you're running for a train or waiting for a bus, and as part of *every single one* of your routines. This mental warm-up is *at least* as important as your physical one. You wouldn't dream of tampering with that once it's right, so don't be tempted to mess with your routines either. Cut them short at your own risk, and cut them out at your peril.

Dress Rehearsals

Dress rehearsals are neither practical nor necessary in all sports (no one can run a marathon on Monday as a dress rehearsal for the Saturday effort!), but as far as you can, make sure that you do cover all your competition bases. Train in *all* gear you will use in competition, break in new boots or shoes, and review all older gear for wear and tear. *Never* use gear in competition that you haven't already used in training. It's an absolute sure bet that you'll find at the utter last moment that it doesn't fit, is too hot, is too heavy, or rubs you in unmentionable places. By then it will be too late to change it, and you've trashed your performance.

A word here about weights. It used to be quite common practice to train using bigger or heavier equipment than what you'd use in competition. The rationale for this was that you'd be bigger and stronger and therefore find the lighter gear a breeze to use. Wrong! Your muscles and nerve pathways learn specific patterns of timing and effort. If, for instance, you train them to play with one weight of bat, they won't be at all prepared to do it with another. If you doubt this, try playing badminton hot on the heels of a game of tennis. You'll find it's as much as you can do even to make contact with the shuttlecock. Play it the other way around and you'll find you're trying to connect a sledgehammer with a cannon ball.

The Boring Part

Make sure any paperwork for which you are responsible is in order and at hand before any competition. All entry passes, tickets, vouchers, visas—whatever they might be—are no less vital to your sporting success than any of your sport gear. There's no way you're going to win if you can't get onto the grounds, and—you'd better believe it—it's happened! *It is a monolithic mistake to duck out on this paperwork.*

There's more. If you're operating in unfamiliar territory, make sure that you have all the maps and timetables you will need to cover your journey from where you are staying to the venue. It is essential that you know where you're going and how you're going to get there. Only then can you work out travel times. These should have at least a 100% contingency, remembering to make this extra allowance for rush hour, traffic delays, parking, getting lost, and finding your way around the venue once you do actually arrive. Many of the big stadiums of the world are in central-city locations. Often athletes are billeted in more residential areas, and there may be a considerable journey between the two. How about those Olympic athletes who got stuck in Sydney's commuter traffic while the clock ticked past their event time and their years of training went down the tube. It doesn't bear thinking about.

Damage Control

Sooner or later, with all the preparation in the world, competition stress will probably get the better of you. No one is invincible, so there's no need to be embarrassed about this. Anyway, it's good to be reminded that you're human! You will always get warnings when your world is about to fall apart, but if you're too busy trying to keep it stitched together, you may not recognize them. Here are some of the most common signs:

- You may become suddenly bad tempered and snap at those around you. That's a response to stress and the fact that you're not enjoying it.
- You may shake—at the knees, in your stomach, with your hands, or in your head.
- You may mentally "freeze" and be unable to think what to do next.
- You may lose your way, your gear, the thread of a conversation, or your cool!

Regard this uncomfortable state of affairs as a cue to move into damage control. Pull yourself back into your most appropriate routine, refocus on the job at hand, and do your utmost to blot out external distractions. The more you can retreat into the familiar, comfortable world of your routines—*your* world—the better you will feel and the more quickly you will regain control.

Lessons in Self-Preservation

As you climb the competition ladder and the stakes get progressively higher, it's only realistic to accept that a number of your opponents might not have your best interests at heart. We've all heard of competitors being "psyched out," and there have been many physical incidents over the years ranging from inconveniences to assaults. Sometimes the pressures of the moment just get the better of people, and from that point on *anything* goes. It is prudent to recognize this and not just to assume it will happen to somebody else. You may be winning, you may be about to win, you may be a new kid on the block and therefore a threat to those already there. Perhaps you are a scapegoat, you might be receiving hate mail, you could be a worst enemy. In any case you're probably an altogether innocent party. Ask Monica Seles, whose dreadful assault certainly gave new meaning to the phrase "Watch your back."

Potentially threatening situations *not* to be entered into include . . .

- Any social activities that collide with your competition routines
- Anything that disturbs your pre-event isolation, if you need it
- Any unusual proximity to other competitors, spectators, or officials
- Any situation that exposes you to negative, destructive, or manipulative gamesmanship on the part of your opponents, which may range from efforts to change a draw to their advantage (and your *dis*advantage), attempts to influence judges or officials against you, directly or indirectly involving you in conflict through personal confrontation, or perhaps lodging protests against you

Beware, because the list goes on! Any or all of these situations may compromise your competition, so steer clear of them all and guard your preparation with your life.

Gearing Up for Success

Never—*ever*—leave your gear unattended, unsupervised, or in any place where it could be tampered with or waylaid. Its value to you is second to none, and right on the brink of competition it's *priceless!* Have you ever seen how frantic a runner gets when one shoe seems to have disappeared? Bad mistake. *Her* mistake. Her second one was not having spare shoes.

As you get more into the high-performance end of your sport, you will become progressively more particular about exactly what gear you have and how it's set up for you. You will also become increasingly aware of the need for security. In the early stages this will primarily revolve around your gear, but in time you will probably extend it to include information about your training regimes, access to training sessions, and personal contacts during competition. Apart from the fact that most sport gear is expensive, you cannot afford the disruption it causes to your whole performance if your gear is not 100% operational as a result of being misplaced or damaged in any way. It's bad enough if it's your own fault, but it's a whole lot worse if you suspect others may have had a hand in it. Not only does it throw your physical efforts out of kilter, but it also most thoroughly throws you mentally off your game. No matter how OK any makeshift, borrowed, or mended gear may be, it's not *your* gear. That psychological hiccup will be quite enough to give the opposition a clear advantage—which of course they know—and you will pay dearly for your naivete.

In equestrian circles, some of the less scrupulous competitors extend the old adage "If you can't get the ball, get the player" to include the opposition's horse. Now you really are busy because not only do you have to watch your gear, but you also need to mount a guard over your horse! Yes, you can laugh, but it's true. And no, this is *not* melodrama. People have been caught trying to dope, poison, or injure the opposition's horses since the dawn of time! By comparison, rackets, skis, skates, and boots are easy targets, but there's no doubt these tactics can be extended to include cars, motorbikes, boats, bicycles, and most of the other sporting goodies that are so essential to competition. A serious part of becoming a seasoned competitor is learning how to safeguard your gear and protect yourself from attempts, either mental or physical, to sabotage your performance. Make no mistakes on this one.

Dangerous People

Without sowing distrust and discontent, it is in your own interest to realize that not *all* the world will want you to win. Your opponents may already be seasoned competitors. Some of them may be a great deal more seasoned than you are. They may also be clever. Don't make the mistake of underestimating their cleverness. They may use it to engineer your downfall—a word at the wrong time in your nervous ear, half a conversation just long enough to destroy your focus—sometimes just a look will do the job. The classic one is the swimmer who murmurs to the next guy as they step up onto the blocks, "I just peed in your lane." Good one!

We are people first and athletes second, and people have emotions and weaknesses to be exploited under the hard spotlight of competition. Have no doubt, the killer instinct is alive and well at all levels of sport today. So stay away from your opponents, other coaches, any less-than-positive members of your team, your connections, and even your family as you lock into the final stages of your preparations.

Coaches' Corner

This one has been for your athlete. There are times to coach and times to step out of the limelight. Remember, competition venues are no place to be coaching. If you and your athletes haven't done your homework by now, it's too late anyway. You will certainly notice mistakes in your athletes' preparations, but you need to be circumspect in correcting them, remembering the 10% Decrement Rule and not expecting them to turn out 100% of what they have done in training. At this stage, your attention needs to be focused less on the technical aspects of their performance and more on their competition skills. These may need to be buffed up in training using simulation, desensitization, stress management, or other mental skills training.

Here are things to watch for:

- How nervous your athletes get
- How well they cope with it
- Whether their routines stand up
- How they handle the results of their event
- Which systems of their skill base worked well (physical, mental, technical, emotional)
- Which systems didn't work well
- What sorts of mistakes they made
- What triggered those mistakes

Armed with this information, you will be able to make sure that future training covers the areas that need attention or improvement. You have an active role to play in steering your athletes well clear of dangerous situations, in warding off dangerous people, and in denying any other nonproductive, inappropriate, or stray bodies access to your athletes.

Summary

Routines, routines, *routines! They are a matter of style and preference, and they matter a very great deal.*

Athletes should develop these routines:

- Training routines
- Tapering routines (including all aspects of preparation)
- Precompetition routines (including briefings and warm-ups)
- Postcompetition routines (including warm-downs, debriefings, and degriefings)
- Recovery routines (including injury regimens)

Coaches should respect the athlete's routines and develop their own complementary routines.

Dress rehearsals are vital for you too. The more familiar you are with exactly what you're going to do out there on the big day, the better you'll do it. Remember to rehearse *everything.*

Learn about security issues before it's too late.

- Watch your gear
- Watch your back
- If you're a rider, watch your horse!

Lessons in Self-Preservation

Protect yourself and your performance from the following:

- **Dangerous situations:** These are anything that threatens to intrude on your normal competition preparation or that might interfere with your competition routines.
- **Dangerous people:** These are anyone with a vested interest in your downfall, and there are plenty of them out there!
- Remember—all's fair in love, war . . . and sport.

13

Blueprints for Competition Success

Little did you guess when you started out on the campaign trail that you would bump into the business world. But there's lots you can learn from good business practice, including how to manage your workload and your productivity.

To start with, we'll borrow one of their maxims: *You can only manage what you can measure.* So see to it that you measure your sports career to within an inch of its life.

Your sporting life begins with a plan. Hopefully, it's your plan. You dream and scheme, and wish and wonder . . . and end up with a plan. Some of us make very good plans, and others seem to get caught in their own webs. Plans vary in size and complexity, and while most can be constructed in a week, some may take months or even years to put into practice. Good ones are an art form. Then comes the easy part:

- *Measure* your success by comparing what you actually achieve with what you had planned to achieve.
- *Manage* your progress on the basis of your success. This means keep doing what's working for you, and change what isn't!

To do this you will need to take notice of the nuts and bolts of every facet of your preparation and your competition events, regardless of their outcomes. The resulting tools of the trade will be the series of blueprints that you will develop to help you effectively manage your sporting life. They will include protocols for briefings, debriefings, degriefings, and lists of just about everything!

Briefings

Briefings are the first of these blueprints for your success. A large, ambitious plan may have many briefings embedded in it, each of which should leave you feeling well informed, in control, and thoroughly well prepared for the action ahead. You'll feel more confident and generally happier if you know what's going to happen next, or even if you *think* you know! So whether a briefing is an informal half hour over coffee with your coach or a large gathering of all concerned (as is the procedure in some sports before a major event), the objective is the same: to give you information that is relevant to your smooth and successful participation in the event. This will vary greatly depending on your sport, but it should range across all topics and may include information on the following:

- Administrative issues, such as opening hours of the secretary's office, where to get lunch vouchers, where to buy souvenirs or programs of the event, where to get spare copies of the rules, your race or heat numbers, and so on
- Logistical information, such as maps, distances from your accommodation to the venue, local transportation facilities, and parking arrangements
- Life-support information, such as the location of good eateries and the addresses of the nearest drugstore, doctor, and so on
- Recent rule changes, changes of course, or change of location of an event
- Peculiarities of the venue, siting of the course, local track conditions, and so on
- Expected weather conditions for the event
- Organizational information, such as start times, any revised timetables, cancellations, or rescheduling of events

- Communications information, emergency procedures, and the availability of competition staff, organizers, paramedics, and first aid stations
- Information specific to the event, such as attendance of selectors, new sponsors, and so on
- Incidental information, such as local entertainment venues, places of interest for visitors, and details of social events running in conjunction with the sports event
- Housekeeping information such as where to get laundry done, hire a car, access the Internet, send a fax, or call home

Then of course there's all the information on the opposition! This may include . . .

- Knowledge of specific game plans or play they may use
- Their strengths and weaknesses
- Team or coaching changes they may have experienced
- Recent results of their team
- Any other information relevant to the way they are likely to play

Last but not at all least, you must consider issues relevant to your own performance. Your plan of action will include:

- Strategies you or the team will adopt
- Tactics you will use
- Adjustments to your gear or equipment
- Changes brought about by weather conditions
- Anything else that might impact performance, such as a last-minute withdrawal of a team member due to injury

Put all of this together and you have your blueprint for success.

Being well briefed is easy: Just leave no stone unturned until you know all about your opposition and exactly how you're going to tackle them. Being badly briefed is the same as handing your opposition an advantage on a plate, all for the sake of soaking up a little information. Compare different briefings that you have had in the course of your career and take a look at what they do to your stress levels. You'll soon realize their value to you. You may find them to be boring, exciting, tedious, or tacky. If your response is less than enthusiastic, just imagine your opponents as they mop up, chew on, stash away, or otherwise file every morsel of information they can find about *you*.

Debriefings

A good debriefing not only *always* gets the best out of a situation, regardless of whether it was a triumph or disaster, but also is the springboard for your next performance. So it *has* to be good! If in a debriefing you address only the positive aspects of a performance, you've only done half the job. You also need to address the negatives *and what caused them.* If this isn't done, then those reasons aren't recognized the next time they appear and consequently are neither avoided nor fixed.

Your confidence will respond quite spectacularly to good debriefings. If the experiences were good, you will go out next time baying for more. If they were less than wonderful, you'll go out with a resolve of steel not to repeat them. Either way your confidence will soar. Use debriefings well because they are an easy and available tool for constantly repairing your confidence.

New Visions of an Old Image

For some, debriefing can be a vague and rather negative idea that often does no more than conjure up pictures of a lackluster team gathered at the feet of an irate coach who berates them for all the things they didn't do in a match or game that might have won it. Unfortunately, debriefing is usually associated with losing, not winning. That's a pity because a good debriefing after a strong win can go a long way toward the next win. In the face of this somewhat gloomy image, we need a good, positive working definition. So we will write our own, and we will decide the content and our attitude toward it on the basis of a new and far more powerful image. How about this?

■ Debriefing is *managing what went right in order to repeat it, while understanding what went wrong in order to repair it.*

If things went well in the competition, you want to be able to repeat that. There's no point in reinventing your competitive wheel with each event. You need to know what makes it run smoothly and what works well for you so that you can include those things in your next competition preparation. If sausages for breakfast proves to be the ideal start to

■ To make the most of a performance, debrief it afterward.

your competition day, then for whatever reason (probably none of them gastronomic), you need to make sure that sausages are on the menu for your next event. You may have to bring along your own if they are very particular sausages or the supply is in doubt. Sounds silly, doesn't it? But just wait and see what curried noodles do for you when there's not a sausage in sight.

■ **Debriefing is also a hunt for the positives.**

For your debriefing to be complete, you will want to know and list the following:
- All the good things you did
- Anything you did well
- Anything different that was helpful

- Anything that made you feel better, stronger, more in control
- Anything that made you feel less nervous
- Anything that boosted your confidence

You can include anything prior to, during, or immediately after your event that contributed to your performance. While some things may have detracted from producing your best-ever result, if you did anything that made your effort *feel* better, now is the time to see that it gets onto the list.

If you learn well from your debriefings, your planning will improve like any other aspect of your performance. A better plan next time could mean the difference between winning and losing.

If you debrief thoroughly, covering every aspect of your competition, and do it while it is all fresh in your mind, the process is a breeze. It needs to be done while you can recall the details of your event. Remember it's only *your* impressions and feelings that matter. So if you were as grumpy as a bear with a toothache, that's just fine as long as you're *happy* being grumpy! The motto of the day is: If it suits you—do it.

For team players, sharing your feelings on the game is great, but be sure to give your coach some airtime to discuss the technicalities first as sometimes group emotion can get in the way of an objective view of the game. The team may even need a cooling-off period before it can sensibly listen to or contribute to a productive debriefing.

And by the way, debriefing a week after your event is no use to anybody. Neither is wading through anecdotes or chewing the ear off a long-suffering friend! Debriefings are serious stuff. They deserve your best attention and are entirely in the interests of your success.

The Running Debriefing

If you are involved in multiple events, keep a running debriefing after every event if you can. This may require no more than a sheet of paper and a pencil kept somewhere you can guarantee to find it, ready for you to jot down a few words as you go that will prompt your memory so you can fill it out in more detail later. You will be quite astonished at how much you will forget by the end of a meet or a tournament if you sit down to debrief only when the whole show is over. There's so much you can do to tighten up your performance on the way, that keeping a running debriefing can actually improve your results as you work your way through the competition. In this way each debriefing becomes a springboard for the next event. If you can look on a debriefing not so much as related to the *last* event but as the beginning of the *next* event, you will then accord it the value it deserves.

Lists to Live By

One way to get the best out of debriefings is to keep a running list, or lists, of all the things you packed, used, did or didn't need, of what you did, which routines you used, and so on. Afterwards, cross off all the things you took but didn't use (excluding necessities such as first aid gear, of course) and add all the things you needed but didn't have. Rewrite routines that didn't work, and document those that did. If you liked them but they didn't work, put them in a box marked Not Yet Useful. If you just can't bear to part with them, file them under the bed. Before you have many outings to your credit, you will have developed an excellent, highly personalized set of lists.

Blueprints to Die For

These lists—refined, reworked, edited, and put into action—will form the blueprints for your competitive career. Many things will contribute to your success, but few will prove more useful. As it turns out, your mother was right: Never leave home without your lists.

Lists minimize the potential stress of such incidents as trying to find your favorite toothpaste at a drugstore you can't locate when there isn't a bus in sight and you can't take a taxi because you don't have the fare, and even if you did, your event's about to start! Don't think there's anything automatic about remembering your toothpaste next time either. Putting it on your list is an easier option.

Apart from purely practical considerations, lists are great because they free up brain space for other things. Who wants to be thinking of toothpaste anyway when there's the championship of your career in the immediate future?

Degriefing

Now here's a new idea. Let's agree that there are times when your emotions get the better of you. To not cast dark shadows over our bright and sparkling new image of debriefing, we will consign dealing with uncomfortable issues to a de*griefing* session.

Again we need a working definition. Degriefing is *managing emotional issues so that they don't interfere with your performance.* We're still on the positive track, but this time we're looking to identify the points at which things came unglued in order to glue them together more strongly or differently next time. Just knowing that there is to be a degriefing session after a game can cool an incident between opposing players that might otherwise erupt into unpleasantness or even violence. You don't have to "cool it"; on the contrary, you can keep as much heat in it as you like and boil over like never before or since. Just do it *later!* The degriefing session gives you a place to express negative, destructive, nonproductive feelings without having to deny them or even control them. They are just postponed. Invariably it is unsatisfactory on the field or court to express anger or frustration. Officials penalize you, and crowds don't like it. Even your fans take exception to a show of temper, and the opposition chuckles all the way back to the dressing room. Generally, it's only possible to shut such emotions in a box if you know it's a large box and you can sit on the lid! How much better to really let rip in a good degriefing session than to compromise your game or create your very own disastrously well-tailored distraction that will derail any further good performance.

Mopping Up

There will be some outings the results of which we regret. Seeing our dreams in tatters and our hopes down the tube, either temporarily or permanently, is nobody's idea of fun. Sooner or later, everybody ends up astride *that* piece of barbed wire. The smart thing is to ensure that it never happens again by facing up to the emotional impact of the situation. At such times, normal mortals get angry, sad, frustrated, or miserable and are generally very poor company. Our behavior is not endearing and may be irrational, dysfunctional, violent, or otherwise antisocial. A good degriefing session is just the place to have those feelings, shed those tears, punch the stuffing out of anything large, soft, and inanimate, and rant, rage, yell, or howl if that's what it takes to blow a gasket or three. This is where all your mistakes management really comes into its own. The more successfully you can *defer* negative outbursts and counterproductive behavior from your performance to the degriefing session, the less you will disrupt your performance. *You* are the one who stands to lose if you lose your cool. Better have a good degriefing *later*. If you can work out why the wheels fell off your performance, that's the next best thing to a guarantee that it doesn't happen next time.

YOUR READY RECKONER FOR
INSTANT MISTAKES-MANAGEMENT

The ones best to avoid are	• all mega-mistakes • most maxi-mistakes • survival mistakes
The ones to move on from are	• comic mistakes
The ones to get to the bottom of are	• deliberate mistakes • serial mistakes • chronic mistakes
The ones to be tolerant of are	• skill-learning mistakes • other people's mistakes
The ones to sort ouf if you want to win more often are	• follow-up mistakes • all competition mistakes • all self-management mistakes
The ones to enjoy are	• feel-good mistakes • successful mistakes • useful mistakes
The ones to celebrate are	• mistakes worth making!

This all comes for free and you end up owning a knowledge base that empowers you not only to understand your mistakes but also to manage them in a positive, proactive way. Degriefings are there for you to put your sports trash in, so clean up your performance, and hose down your emotional outbursts. Do it, and do it well. Dump those negative feelings there, park the behaviors that go with them right there too, and move on.

Progress in the Bag

Even if you're not yet very good at managing your competition, you're on your way to becoming masterful! Just keep trying, talk about it, and try some more, and you *will* succeed. There's no magic in making it work—only practice. You will make mistakes in your management, just as in everything else, and it's no big deal. The greatest mistake out there is to not manage your competition in the first place, so you've already got that one by the ear!

Kind Words and Courtesies

Some moments in sport bring out the very best in us, and it's from such moments that much of our sports lore arises. We *can* be altruistic, we *are* thoughtful New Age people, and sometimes winning *isn't* quite everything. That's when you hit the next shot out to even the score after a bad line call for your opponent, or help him to his feet after a particularly hard tackle. This brief acknowledgment that not *all* mistakes are *entirely* manageable, that luck—good or bad—may just play a small part in the scheme of things adds a human touch to the game and saves us all from becoming slaves to the urge to win.

Social Note

A much neglected part of your self-management is the contribution that your social skills can make to your sporting success. When it comes to taking your sporting cause to the world, you need to be on a mission. No one can promote you as well as you can. It's called image management, and it doesn't happen sitting at home and wondering why nobody knows who you are. It is a mistake not to attend social functions associated with your sport, however much you may think they are not your scene. These occasions offer great networking opportunities, and they are where you can get your name and your face known to potential scouts, selectors, fans, sponsors, and others who are vital in administering, promoting, or supporting your sport. As you remember from our previous discussion, we all prefer to stick with the familiar, but don't let that keep you from making sure the people that matter are familiar with your face. If that means you have to get a new haircut or brush up on your social skills, then do so.

Bridge Building, Fence Mending, and Other Engineering Skills

In defense of your image (and with an eye to sponsors, teammates, and others you may be associated with) never be afraid to bury the hatchet, eat humble pie, or otherwise graciously bow out backwards if it's that or a public brawl. It's seldom to your credit to have the media eat you for breakfast, and sometimes it's better to say almost anything—or nothing—rather than get drawn into a fight. The fallout may take a good deal longer to get over than the black eye or the bruised ego, and there *are* more important things than your pride. It *doesn't* always matter who was right. Let common sense prevail. Any sort of brawl is always a mistake and casts a very long shadow.

Coaches' Corner

Support has various connotations, but it is the name of this game. Whether you are coaching professional athletes and must manage the competition schedule, or coaching recreational players who just want some fun, you are expected to be at the helm steering the team through a series of successful encounters. There is no better tool for adjusting your team's performance as you progress through the season than informative, interactive briefing sessions. Your thorough preparations for the briefings, your attention to detail in the debriefings, and your cool perspective in the de*griefings* will yield rich rewards.

Summary

In managing competitive success, learn the importance of . . .

- A thorough briefing
- Productive debriefings
- Lists to live by
- Blueprints to die for
- Running debriefings
- De*griefings*
- Social skills and a little common sense

14

Excelling Under Pressure

Let's get the terminology right. You have barrow-loads of courage and a bucketful of nerves. It's just that now and then the bucket gets a little more awkward to handle than the barrow. If you find yourself unable to park the bucket when you wish, it's time to take a look at your options. Putting a lid on the nerves in your bucket, and deciding what exactly they are all *about*, are the first things you need to sort out.

The best thing about being nervous is knowing that whether you think you're ready or not, your body is telling you it's all wired up for action. This is good. Well, take a look at the alternatives. Your body could be telling you that it's done for the day and ready for some time on the beach, or that it's sick, or that it wants to sleep, none of which would be at all useful for what you have in mind. So by contrast, when it signals that it's reporting for duty, this is a most helpful state of affairs. What remains is for you to get your head around the business of the day. To do that you must first decide exactly what that is. Your immediate task is not winning the upcoming 200-meter race or surviving the first quarter; *it is organizing your resources.*

There are many ways to do this. Right now the important thing to do is to recognize that *your nervousness is also a resource.* If you weren't nervous, you'd be a nonstarter. So give that bucket a rattle. All athletes get nervous; they have to be or they wouldn't be ready for the action. It follows that every competitor either beside you or against you is also nervous, no matter how big, wide, and high they may appear to the outside world. It can be comforting to remember this when your bucket gets in the way.

Redefining Nerves

We're getting good at creating new definitions now. We've had a crack at perfection, we've sorted out success, and we've reinvented mistakes. Tinkering with nerves is a breeze.

To restore a measure of calmness and peace of mind, from this point on we will redefine being nervous as a normal, healthy, inevitable, and above all *necessary* thing to do! Usually we only think of ourselves as being nervous when the butterflies start to flutter in our stomachs. Well, we will now reinvent our interpretation of being nervous and think of it in terms of being ready. In fact, we need to be ready for anything and everything beyond brushing our teeth.

In no time you will become extraordinarily good at assessing exactly how ready you are, and at regulating precisely how ready it is appropriate to be. You will then program, or *re*program, your brain to issue your body readiness instructions that *match* your upcoming task. Remember—these days you are hardwired to win. Don't have your software let you down.

Labels

Many people have studied nerves in dozens of different ways. Nerves have had many different labels, which from a practical point of view, as you're lined up on the blocks, all add up to the same knot in your stomach and a strong desire to be somewhere else. What about arousal? Well, what *about* arousal? We know all about the theories, and that doesn't help at all. How about anxiety? Somehow that makes us feel inadequate. We could call it tension, but then we don't feel in control. The newest word of course is *stress*—buzzword of our age. And then they tell us to relax. *Relax?!* Who wants to do *that* when everything you've ever cared about is on the brink of making megaheadlines and you're looking down the barrel of immortality!

Don't get caught up in the language here. Does it really matter whether it's nerves, readiness, anxiety, tension, or arousal? As far as your body's concerned, *it all feels the same!* So think of it however you like because it's all only a matter of degree. What ultimately matters the most is how it feels *to you.* So get comfortable. Get used to getting comfortable. You're about to enjoy the feelings of competency and being in control that come with knowing *how* to get comfortable. Simply pick up your bucket, then just top it off—or tip it out.

Physical Signs

What exactly are the telltale signs of these nerves anyway? Let's try to quantify them. When it comes to your own nervousness, the physical signs are some of the easiest symptoms to identify. They will undoubtedly include these:

Dry mouth	Feeling shaky
"Weak" muscles	Butterflies in the stomach
Feeling nauseous	High resting pulse rate
Shallow breathing	High resting respiration rate
Pale complexion	Fumbling or clumsiness
Excessive or inappropriate sweating	

These are not especially pleasant, and each is a sure sign that your body is reacting in an anxious way to the incoming information. If these responses are not appropriate to your upcoming task, then your brain is clearly overresponding to this information. Before it directs your body to become thoroughly overready for action, it needs reprogramming to generate more useful responses. Some signs may be more critical to your performance than others. For instance, if you were about to give a speech, then finding your tongue stuck to your teeth would be more incapacitating than feeling your ticker working overtime. If you actually feel unwell, you may have to take emergency measures and engineer a rapid retreat. But try to talk your brain out of such an inconvenient response to what is generally not the end of your world.

Mental Signs

Mental signs of anxiety might be less obvious . . . at least to you. They may include any or all of the following:

Poor concentration	Inability to get the timing right
Inability to focus	Negative self-talk
Negative imagery	Poor time management
Feelings of being distracted	

It's most disconcerting that in your absolute hour of need you are incapacitated not only in relation to the job you want to do, but also in terms of sorting out why you can't do it. This is a very hard place from which to recover your bearings. As the Irishman said to the tourist, "Sure, I can tell y' the way t' go home, but if I were you I'd not be startin' from here." Given your limited choice of where to start from, it's perhaps best not to set your expectations too high until you really develop a game plan to get out of trouble. We will do this very shortly in the calm and ordered environment of a typical nonstressed day, but let's first just complete your inventory of giveaways.

Emotional Signs

Emotional signs, such as the following, are likely to be the first ones other people complain about and the last ones *you* notice:

Irritability	Impatience
Lethargy	Anger
Lack of humor	"Nervous" laugh
Rudeness	Brusqueness
Forgetfulness	

This is where you lose friends and fail to influence people according to your grand plan. Before you know it, you've been an absolute bear all morning and have kicked the cat and snapped at your mom before you finished your first coffee. Not only do nerves take their toll on you, there are probably a dozen close folks in your life who could write the rest of this chapter on you and your nerves, and you'd probably be quite shocked at what they had to say.

Changes in your speech are typical at such times and may well draw unhelpful replies as you exhibit:

Babbling	Silence
Stammering	Repeating yourself
Tangling your words	Sarcasm
Self-denigration	Negative comments

These signs of nervousness in speech make conversation difficult. They also successfully scramble instructions, erode goodwill, carve large holes in your self-confidence, and gain you an impressive reputation for bitching, backbiting, or slander. Trying not to go there is more than tricky since you seem programmed to spit out words that are about as friendly as porcupine quills despite your best efforts to do otherwise. Don't panic . . . yet. With a little practice you will soon learn to regain your equilibrium and behave in a more socially acceptable way.

Behavioral Changes

Behavioral changes are not difficult to enact if you have well-established training and precompetition routines (which, of course, is just another good reason for having them). You will soon catch yourself doing atypical things that disrupt the normal rhythm of your preparation. This will set your alarm bells ringing and before long may also alert those around you. From there it's only a matter of taking things by the scruff of the neck to swing them back on course. Look for things such as . . .

- Unplanned changes in routines
- Hurrying through routines
- Reluctance to begin preparing for training/competition
- Making excuses for mistakes
- Refusing to take responsibility for gear, travel, etc.
- Unpunctuality
- Social withdrawal (not to be confused with isolation)
- Seeking distraction from the task at hand

This time *you* are the most likely person to pick up these indications early. This is because no one else is quite as carefully tuned to the normal pattern of your preparation, and therefore no one else is so sensitive to its disruption. Be sure to take the long view here and really try to cast an objective outside eye on your precompetition patterns of behavior. It's difficult, but possible.

Performance Indicators

Performance indicators are the most obvious signs of excessive nerves, but if these are the first ones you notice, then you need to sharpen your self-observation. Easy indicators to find are . . .

Mis-hits	Miscues
Misjudgments	Poor mistakes management
Early mistakes	Uncharacteristic mistakes
Lack of "flow"	Inability to get into the rhythm

Does that about cover it? You can now make your own list and add your own idiosyncrasies, but clearly it's time to off-load some of the contents of your bucket until you can firmly and efficiently put a lid on it. Before you do so, ask your coach to amend your list, and stand by for a few surprises. This amended version will now be the basis for the size, shape, and design of your new, personalized *bucket extraordinaire.*

Why So Nervous?

The next thing to do is to identify exactly what you are nervous *about.* You can then add these items to your bucket. You might choose from among the following:

Skill level	Image
Reputation	Possibility of winning
Chances of losing	Consequences of succeeding
Cost of failing	Glare of publicity
Fear of anonymity	Competition
Opposition	

You may think of other things you'd rather be nervous about. That's fine as long as you identify precisely what they are. Make sure to be specific about the causes of your nervousness because you cannot possibly be satisfactorily nervous about *everything.* Anyway, it's no fun to be just generally anxious. That just allows the list of anxiety-provoking factors a license to grow of its own accord. Before you know it, you're upset because it's a clear day and the sun's too hot and your potted plants are probably dying in your absence! Keep a handle on things. Make a list; then decide to be anxious *only* about the things that are on it. At least that way you can exert a little damage control. Even if you can't stop the war, you can at least limit the number of battles you have to fight.

Oh, and don't forget the great unknowns, which include any random things you like to worry about, such as . . .

- Being overwhelmed by the "great occasion" atmosphere of your competition
- Being intimidated by the possibilities of injury, terminal or otherwise
- Your results, especially if they're less than wonderful (that's a nice open-ended one!)
- The opposition and all the things they might know that you don't
- Your luck and whether it's going to be good, bad, or absent when needed

These are all very broad generalities, so don't settle for any of them. If they are on your list, you need to tease them out until you have worked out *precisely* what the issue is that is bugging you.

Once you have all this information (which takes five pages to write about and less than two minutes to gather in your brain), you are in an *invincible* position. You can now set out to control your nerves and plan your way past squandering all that energy. You can now harness it and use it instead to add zest to your performance. Good move!

Having done all this, it begins to put a fence around what you want to be nervous about. You should already feel better knowing you have plenty of choice and that you don't have to be nervous about *everything* after all. This will be liberating and invigorating, and in no time you'll find you have tons of energy to address the next piece, which is all about deciding exactly *how* nervous you are prepared to be.

How Nervous Will You Get?

In deciding how nervous it is appropriate to be, consider . . .

- How will being nervous benefit your performance?
- What if you're not nervous enough?

- What if you're *too* nervous?
- Do you have other or better things to be thinking about?
- Could you use the energy for anything else, such as winning?

If your answer to any of these questions is *"I don't know,"* go back to the beginning of this chapter. Otherwise, read on.

Positively Nervous

This is where you really want to be. You want to be just nervous enough to be ready for war, but still able to enjoy the fight. You want your body to be fired up but not fizzing over, and your brain to be active but not in overdrive. This is a delightful state. You are full to the brim with anticipation and excitement but effortlessly in control, bursting to get in on the action, but cruising up to the line. You are hero material.

Negatively Nervous

This is other people. In particular, this is your opponent. They are squeamish and jittery and their bucket's too big. They will make poor decisions and bad mistakes and trip over their bucket. You will do better.

If, however, you are the negatively nervous one, regard it as an entirely temporary state of affairs. You are about to change as radically as if your hair had gone from black to blonde or you'd just won a Porsche. Read on.

Reprogramming Your Software

Fact: Feeling nervous is just a physiological response. It's not something you can prevent from happening any more than you can prevent yourself from shivering when you get cold. That's just how bodies work. You're quite unfazed by shivering because you are familiar with it, and anyway it isn't usually life threatening. Neither does being cold stop you from listening to your body's message. There is nothing different in the nerves department. Nobody ever died of nerves either, and a few butterflies never stopped anybody from listening to their mind or their matter—provided they want to hear what it has to say.

If your brain has targeted a task, it's hopefully going to kick the body into the appropriate gear. But don't be blinded by the multitalented, megacompetent image of your brain—*it doesn't always get this right*. If you're dozing in a hammock, your brain may refuse to send action information to your body to heave it out of the hammock to mow the lawn. And no doubt sometimes it goes the other way: it wakes you up at 3:00 A.M. saying it's far too busy to carry on sleeping so will you kindly get out of bed and start the day. And what about the times it makes your body fidget or blush or itch or burp!

Next time work your way through your competition routines, and make sure your brain gets it right. Listen to your body, and on the strength of what it tells you, feel free to agree or disagree with your brain and reprogram it if necessary. If you need *more* nerves to be ready enough to do the job, stir yourself up more by telling your brain to get up and get on with it. If you need *less* nerves, then take the pressure off and tell your brain to settle down and no, you don't have to be ready for a moon mission at noon or a trip to the dentist. Get used to the idea that nerves can be managed in exactly the same way that you manage the other physical, mental, and emotional aspects of daily living.

You no longer need to feel at the mercy of your nerves. Anyway, you'll be glad to know that even in the best sporting circles, excessive nerves are as much a normal part of life as the common cold. This gives rise to a very comforting thought: You are not alone. Armed with this new information that everybody has a bucket, it's time to learn how and when to tip it out, or top it off. Either way, you'd better get used to its being around.

So using a small spoonful of your courage, confront your bucket, give it a sharp rattle, and decide how full or empty you need it to be for it to hold just the right amount of readiness for your upcoming task. For tasks with high levels of explosive effort, such as a 100-meter sprint, your readiness needs to be at a high level. For anything in which your judgment is important or in which fine motor skills are needed, as in golf, you need much lower levels of readiness. When your nerves are driving your readiness levels way beyond what you need for your job, then empty some *out* of your bucket. If you're a bit too flat and in need of a bigger spring in your step, then get busy and pour some more readiness *into* your bucket. Use your imagery skills to help you "see" the levels in your bucket and just keep practicing until you can adjust them at will. Don't forget to use lots of color too. *See* your readiness as red paint if it makes it more real for you. It really is that easy. Now, having taken firm control of your bucket, enjoy your day.

Surviving Under Pressure

When the deadlines are looming and your prep has been less than wonderful and none of it's fun anymore, stop trying to rebuild the clubhouse and instead just start rearranging the furniture. At such times, even giving that monster locker a nudge is a breeze compared with relocating the locker room.

This is the kind of thinking that will help to make you pressure-proof. Because so much of feeling nervous is tied directly to how much pressure we perceive ourselves to be under, the better we can cope with pressure, the better we will be able to manage our nerves. Also, many of our mistakes happen when we feel we are under pressure, so less pressure immediately means we're going to make fewer mistakes.

What's the difference between an athlete and a volcano?
Athletes blow their tops more often.

The Enemy Within

Hateful though it may be to admit it, you are your very own best enemy. For one thing, even if someone else knows how to tread on your corns, no one else this side of eternity knows how that *feels*. Let's call it the ouch factor. You even know exactly how tight to lace up the shoe to create that ouch factor in the first place! Similarly the pressure that you feel in competition is also absolutely and *entirely* of your own making.

Myth: Pressure comes from the outside.
Fact: We manufacture it on the inside.

This explains why different people can experience the same situation as either exciting or nerve-wracking. It's not the situation that creates the pressure; it's our interpretation of it.

Myth: Pressure is part of competition
Fact: Pressure is our response to competition.

But how can we *possibly* manufacture our own pressure, and how can it possibly be *our response* to anything? Anyway, has the rest of the world gotten it all wrong? Yes! So wrong, in fact, that we've tied ourselves in knots trying to fix it. Yet again it's time we refused to toe the

■ Pressure comes from the *inside*.

party line. Clearly we need to poke our heads outside this homemade pressure-packed square and come up with some new ideas. Let's start with who we are.

Living History

This is us. We are living history. We are our past experiences right down to our bootstraps, and it is quite futile to pretend it's any other way. As we claw our way up the sporting ladder and become steadily more successful, our experiences are assumed to be ever more glittering and glamorous. Hmm. We all know that ain't necessarily so. Past experiences are not always quite what they're cracked up to be, despite the fact that they often make a good story, with a lot of laughs that weren't in the original script. Sometimes that experience gets in our way and it becomes difficult to get past it in subsequent moments of crisis.

For the stars among us, previous experience will always be seen as an asset to be drawn on, or against, when crisis looms. For these lustrous beings, their experience will save the day. Think of the numerous times you've seen any of the world's top sportspeople in a tight spot and how very often they just seem to inhale a barrel of aviation-gas and motor right over the top of the opposition like a jet-propelled bulldozer. Having done it once, it becomes a resource to be used again. Such players are the class acts on the circuit. Less gifted mortals have to resort to the mundane business of limiting the amount of pressure they generate and coping valiantly in the face of the mistakes they make before the pressure gauge implodes.

Mistakes under pressure fall into one of three categories:

- Pre-pressure mistakes—those you *anticipate* you will make under pressure
- Mid-pressure mistakes—those you make *while* under pressure
- Post-pressure mistakes—those you make *after* you have been under pressure

Deflecting Pre-Pressure Mistakes

Mistakes you *anticipate* you will make under pressure are hard to identify. You are shadowboxing with what might—or might not—happen. To prove yourself right (and who doesn't need to do that now and then?), you will find yourself carefully engineering these mistakes just as you planned. Do you recognize these beasts yet?

They're called *self-fulfilling prophesies.* They lurk in every preparation ever made. They are the scourge of your unguarded moments. Well, at least admit they exist. If you have ever said, "I always" in a negative context, then consider yourself the creator of a self-fulfilling prophesy. Anticipating pressure in a negative way by whipping up an emotion such as doubt will actually induce a microresponse in your muscular and nervous systems as your body braces itself for trouble. It works the other way around too: You can give yourself a rehearsal of negative feelings by creating a worried expression or nervous body language. As if you need the practice. Before long just a passing thought will be enough to trigger your well-practiced responses, and the negative connotations will just come along for the ride. Be careful here. The process is so fast and you become so slick at operating this very smooth button that you may find it quite difficult at first to identify exactly what is happening.

The answer is to slow down. Then you have to listen a lot more carefully to your Little Voice, which may have become accustomed to being drowned out in the general hype. When you do finally hear it, make sure you get a handle on exactly what it's saying. If it's moved into negative territory, then now is the time to call *Foul!* and stop the game right there. By this time you should be so busy getting your Little Voice back on your side that you will have been totally distracted from the "pressure situation" that was causing all the drama. All that remains is for you to learn this lesson well and to umpire the game more tightly next time out.

Surviving Mid-Pressure Mistakes

If you've moved through the barriers and onto the field of play and *then* find that the pressure's too much, that's a different ball game altogether. Here you are in the midst of the action and you find the ground caving in beneath your feet. Suddenly you'd rather be somewhere else—in fact, just about *anywhere* else would do.

It's time to ignore all symptoms of stress. Forget all the theory you ever learned about performing under pressure—immediately—*and focus on the job you are there to do.* Nothing else on the planet will put your performance back on the rails if you don't, won't, or can't *think about what you are doing.* To do this you will need to follow a designated order of action:

1. Pay attention to your *job.*
2. Recite *out loud* the technicalities of your *job.*
3. *Do* your *job.*

Nine times out of ten your attentional focus will be out of whack: either it will be too broad and you'll be mopping up a million messages from every corner of the compass, or it will be too narrow and you won't get past the churning of your stomach. Either way, that leaves you too busy to pay attention to your *job.* Get a handle on this one, and *as a matter of discipline,* focus on what you have to do next. There is nothing quite like having a job in life to put the rest of the world in its place. Once you have restored your sense of perspective, your game will reflect this masterly effort and your performance will shine, as usual.

Avoiding Post-Pressure Mistakes

Mistakes that happen *after* you have emerged apparently unscathed from a pressure situation are more difficult to deal with. They seem to occur just when you start to relax a little, having decided that the world is not out to get you after all and then, blow me down, it does! These mistakes are most common in the last few minutes, meters, or even moments of a race or a game, usually just when you thought the day was won. The motto of such a day, of course, is that no game or play is ever won until the finish line is crossed, the last shot is made, or the final whistle is blown. Never, *ever* assume that you have won so much as a raffle ticket—never mind the raffle—until your number is actually called. Then check your ticket. *Then* smooth your hair, straighten your tie, and rise from your seat to the deafening applause of the multitude. Then don't trip on your way to the podium.

Inside Information

When it comes to getting the truth, the whole truth, and nothing but the truth on how nervous you *really* feel, just listen to your Little Voice and you will be told the absolute undiluted state of affairs. But of course, therein lies the problem. We *don't* listen to ourselves! Or, if we do, we often listen indiscriminately, taking all the advice of the Little Voice— good and bad, right and very wrong!

It's time to live by an unbreakable rule. Never let Little Voice wind you up, break you up, or run you down! And don't let it taunt you, tease you, or tempt you either!

Remind yourself too *that you've heard it all before!* It may startle you to realize that Little Voice and Co. are not very creative. You will recognize key players who reappear over and over, with their predictable remarks and their mind-flattening vocabularies. Rewriting their scripts is not going to be that difficult after all.

The chances are that some of the Little Voice's accomplices are either significant others you already know well or critics—friendly or otherwise. So as not to be taken by surprise, get busy now and write out a list of who these tormentors are. *Put a name to them all.* Significant others may or may not be friendly. Critics may or may not be kind. Crash on, hero. Identify these people who are tramping—uninvited—through your head. It's high time they got a life of their own!

From here on you are master of your own destiny. Pressure will now bring out the best in you, and buckling under the weight of it will become a thing of the past.

How Not to Blow a Fuse

Blowing a fuse is without a doubt the most spectacular mistake to make under pressure. Generally, the more pressure you have manufactured, the more of a show you make of letting go. Somehow things that on a normal day wouldn't even rate a mention take on all kinds of horrendous proportions. Innocent events such as misplacing your towel suddenly become pivotal points in history. And there's never any *time*.

The secret here is to create time. Turning your watch ahead 10 minutes will give you time to find your towel. Bringing your start time forward another 15 minutes will give you time to lose it—and find it—again. By slowing down the rate at which you invent disasters, you will have more time to cope with the ones you actually invent. You might like to re-read the section on anger in chapter 3 and refresh the ideas on de-griefing in chapter 13. And try a little ice on the back of your neck. It's quite soothing even if you don't yet have a nosebleed.

Disarming the Opposition

This one is only for the experts. It's not a bluff. It's a double bluff. You look like you're a basket case and you act like you've lost it, but you think like you've got it all together and you feel like you've been made a king! This is strictly for sophisticates. It has been done with success, as when the Olympic runner created mayhem in the dressing rooms prior to the race by faking a near-hysterical episode. But you must be very well rehearsed, and it must be an entirely normal part of your competition routine for it to work to your advantage. Don't try this one unless you're supersure of staying supercool.

There are lots of other less dramatic options that serve to keep your mind on your job and therefore your pressure levels down and your mistakes to a minimum. Everyone's heard of psyching out the opposition. There are a number of very straightforward ways to do this:

- Being seen doing your signature move
- Taking over the warm-up area

- "Owning" a bigger than normal personal space
- Looking—and feeling—confident to the point of indestructibility
- Having a lot of supporters
- Having any kind of novel gear, clothing, or equipment
- Having a strong team image, mantra, or mission
- Having the track record to go with any of the above

Using a carefully thought-out strategy to create an invincible image may be at least half your battle. After all, competitors have a great deal longer to contemplate playing, racing, or matching you than they ever have actually doing it. You can take advantage of the time they spend thinking about you. You can quickly create a competitive persona with its own reputation that will precede you to your next competition. If that image is one of a tough and intimidating competitor, the chances are your opposition is already on the back foot before you've hit the first shot or run the first heat.

If that's not your style, then consider the Olympic runner who, just as everyone was lining up to settle into the blocks, walked across the line, looked each competitor in the eye, and offered to shake hands. Why was this such a clever tactic? Because it interrupted their last-moment routines, it violated the convention of not looking at your opponent but keeping your eyes to the ground, it invaded their personal space and "burst" their isolation bubble, it took control of their focus and moved it from internal to external, and it initiated personal physical contact at a time of physical withdrawal. Add to all that a friendly greeting at a time when they were wishing he was dead—not to mention the surprise factor—and it is hard to think of a more innocent, intrusive, and effective way to derail even the most seasoned competitor. The only person it didn't disturb at all was the guy who did it because it was his normal precomp routine.

The motto of this story is, if it works for you, do it. As long as whatever tactics you adopt are within the rules of the competition, ethical, and productive for you, it's everyone for him- or herself out there, and may the best athlete win! Of course you'll try things that don't work before you discover those that do, but regard them as developmental. See them as mere sketches of the final design, and expect to fill a waste basket or two before you resolve the issue. The more imaginative you can be, the better, and the more cleverly you can find a persona that you can wear with a body suit of confidence, the more successfully you will pressure-proof yourself and maximize your opportunities to win.

Coaches' Corner

Although athletes' pressure management is by its very nature very much their own affair, you can often help them kick-start the process. It will do no harm here to remind them of the rewards for their efforts. You can dangle the odd carrot in front of the athlete who hungers after the more tangible, extrinsic rewards, and reinforce intrinsic rewards for those who put job satisfaction at the top of their list. As long as you understand what they're doing *and don't get in their way,* skilled athletes are going to work all this stuff out for themselves. Facilitating it without casting a shadow is clever coaching.

■ Thought for the day: Pressure makes diamonds.

When you make mistakes (by putting forward strategies your athletes don't like or they can't make work), just wake up to them *early.* That way at least you won't have wasted too much time, and your credibility will have taken only a minimal hiding. If you can keep all this working under the pressure of a major competition, then you should get a medal too.

Be patient and observe your athletes most minutely so you can help them to fill in the gaps in their self-assessment. It may take a little while before they can successfully adopt a positive nervous stance. If they are not already in the habit of being positive, feel free to help catapult them into their new hemisphere! Maybe sit down and reread this chapter together and give them some tips and prompts to aid their self-awareness as they draw up their lists. Not all of them will have heard of the Johari Window (and if you haven't either, go find a library in a hurry!) nor recognize that they have a blind side, and it may come as something of a shock to find that others know them rather better than they know themselves! Observe yourself most minutely too. You are still their *role model extraordinaire.*

If your previous attitude toward nerves has been unhelpful, cynical, dismissive, or all of the above, then it's time to arrive at a new working definition that will be less of an encumbrance both to you and to those you coach. Perhaps it's time you got *really* nervous yourself. Try doing something new at the front line. No matter how nervous you get from the safety of the sidelines, it's not the same as when your name is pinned to the action. A quick refresher on just how it feels to be "alone with God out there" won't be wasted.

Summary

Nerves are a necessary part of living that can be managed as successfully as any other part of you. You have a choice of . . .

- How nervous you get
- What you get nervous about
- Whether to get positively or negatively nervous
- How to manage your nerves
- How to reprogram yourself, if necessary

Get to know your own indications of how nervous your body is. Learn to read the following signs:

- Physical
- Mental
- Emotional
- Behavioral
- Performance

We can believe that . . .

- We are hard-wired to win
- We don't need to perform well under pressure because we're not going to create it in the first place!

We can control blowing a fuse by . . .

- creating time,
- rereading the chapter 3 section on anger, and
- revisiting the chapter 13 section on degriefing.

We can disarm the opposition

- legally,
- ethically, and
- totally!

PART IV

Laying the Foundation of Your Sporting Future

15

Motivation in Spite of Mistakes

Knowing how to maintain motivation after making mistakes is a skill in the palm of the hand of every seasoned competitor. If this leaves you currently baffled, read on. Should you already consider yourself very seasoned, a few freshly ground ideas may add a new flavor to your day, so you're encouraged to read on anyway.

Let's start on good, solid, familiar ground before we move on to new and more challenging territory. Everybody knows that goals are the key to motivation. Everybody's been there, done *that*. It's old news, and goals have been "done" to *death*. That does not, however, detract from their importance in life. Neither does it change the fact that every goal starts with a dream. It's not possible to make goals before you have had the dream. And we're not talking about a nighttime dream here. We're talking about a wide-awake, daytime, walking, humming, strumming, *living* dream. We're talking about being on a mission in life, about wanting to do something so much that it burns holes in the soles of your shoes, sets fire to the hairs in your nose, and hijacks the mainframe of your brain! Nobody knows why or how this happens. Nobody cares—except you, but then passion has always been a very personal thing.

It's not very fashionable to discuss dreams in the serious motivational literature; it sounds a little like psychobabble with much scope for being vague. But can anyone explain how to live without them? Some things defy the best, most rational brains of science, and dreams are currently among dreams. That doesn't stop every human being on the planet from dreaming their heads off for a third of their lives. And that's just the after dark effort! How many times have you been accused of dreaming while very much awake? Was it at school, through your least favorite lecture, on the bus, or in the bath? Or maybe it was

■ Passion fuels your dreams and goals.

at one of the other half dozen junctures in your day when you took time out to muse on how you'd really like your life to be.

Perhaps there is no more famous dreamer than Martin Luther King Jr. His words rang out like a clarion call and echoed across a nation, "I have a dream!" So saying, he struck a chord in a million souls. We have all had a dream about something special in our lives, even if it's tucked away in a dusty old drawer somewhere. Dreams are the first things we have and the last things we lose. Dare to dream or grow old early because dreams are dear to our hearts like nothing else. They are the source of our hopes for all we wish to be, do, or have in life—the fountainhead of our motivation. Just as a great river begins with a small spring, so our motivation begins with a dream. These dreams grow until we are carried forward by the current of them streaming through our lives.

To talk of motivation without acknowledging our dreams is to trudge to the top of the mountain and forget to admire the view. It is equally fanciful to suggest that setting goals without first addressing the dream that drives them will determine, define, or in any way satisfactorily regulate that motivation. It won't. The goals will somehow fail to deliver the satisfaction we expected. Our step will falter. Our motivation will wither. So we must set our goals only *after* we have done some serious dreaming. Only then can we put a name to our passion and know our most private ambitions to be burning with a flame bright enough to light up the rest of our lives.

Navigational Mistakes

Along the way, there will be many goals you do not or cannot meet. You will become temporarily lost. Do not feel you must immediately carry on from where you are. Until you actually find where you are, it is quite hard to orient yourself. Anyway, you might find you're somewhere you don't want to be. So "take five" and locate yourself by moving squarely into the central role of your best and favorite dream. Dream well! Then take a bearing on your life and decide what you want to do next. This may change over a series of dreams so be ready to adapt to new wants and wishes, and don't be afraid to own them all. *Then* you can reset your goals with a clear view of how to make them happen and a brand new road map of how to get there. Motivation? Alive and well, thank you, restored to excellent health by appropriate dreaming!

The secret to maintaining your motivation when your goals lie in a shambles around your feet or are persistently beyond the reach of your already-outstretched arm is to go back to your original dream. Relive its early magic! Recapture the energy and anticipation until you kick-start the adventure all over again! Take your courage in both hands and dream your way out of trouble, dream your way forward, dream your goals back into life, dream your yesterdays, and dream your to-morrows. You'll find that today will take care of itself. Your goals will be easy to reset. They will be the right goals because they will relate to your dream. Your motivation will be legend.

Dreaming Your Way Out of Trouble

Did you know that dreams are one of the most potent antidotes to the aftermath of almost any major mistake? If you've just shot an old dream to pieces, don't wander about among the pieces looking for some glue—call up a new dream! If you can patch the pieces together, be aware that a mended dream is never quite the same as the unmended original. Most personal relationships will attest to that.

Wear and tear on a dream inevitably takes its toll too, and as the dream grows progressively more threadbare, it does lose some of its early appeal. This is the time to refurbish it, add new colors, put it in a new setting, or decide it has served its purpose. Sometimes you can modify an old favorite if you just need to update it, don't need to ditch it, or can't bear to part with it, but most times it's more satisfactory to have a new dream altogether.

When you are recovering from a mistake, you will find that a five-second dream will transform feelings of frustration and exasperation into feelings of empowerment, tolerance, and calm. Your mistake will cease to be larger than life and will assume the proportions of a mouse, over which you have all the control you'll ever need. If you do not experience this relief, dream again until you do. If you have to do this more than twice, you need to seriously improve your dreaming skills. Take an intensive dreaming course, and dream five times a day for a week. This is a useful strategy to employ any time your mistakes feel as though they are getting away from you. Just substitute your five-second dream for the recovery phase in your mistakes management (see chapter 9); then follow it with the usual refocusing and retrying phases.

Dreaming for the Skeptics

Not everyone takes dreaming seriously. In fact, it's quite probable that *you* don't. It's quite likely that you think it's all a spoof.

Here are a few facts, some of which may be relevant to daytime dreaming:

- We sleep for about a quarter of a century during our lives.
- We spend at least 15 years nighttime dreaming.
- That amounts to just over 130,000 hours of dreamtime.
- From memory, we need to do 10,000 hours of most things to get good at them.
- Conclusion: we must be *very* good at dreaming.
- Why do we dream? Nobody knows.
- Common sense tells us dreaming must have some use (like breathing?).
- If we daytime dream *only 10% of the time we spend nighttime dreaming*, that's 13,000 hours of wishing.
- That's a truckful of practice and barrow-loads of hope.
- That's *got* to be the start of something useful!

To prove the value of daytime dreaming to yourself:

1. Pick an area of your life in which you are likely to make a moderately significant mistake. (This may be in your sport, at home, at work . . . whatever.)

2. Choose a five-second dream relevant to that area of your life. It may be one you have held for years (such as winning the club tournament or restoring an old car), or it can be a brand new dream such as seeing your name on the selection list for next week's game or riding a camel through Cairo.

3. Find a trigger to start your dream (it may be a word or a piece of gear or clothing such as a camel-colored coat). Keep your trigger in mind while you dream your dream several times until you are familiar with it.

4. In due course, when you make a mistake, *immediately* use your trigger and dream your dream.

5. Dream often and dream well. Then see how you feel.

Continuing skeptics are reminded here that all of this is free. Try it—you've got nothing to lose. There is always the hope that you might discover that it actually *works.* Alexander Pope wrote, "Hope springs eternal." He obviously knew all about dreams.

Living without a dream is as sad and empty as existing without a name. So do dream, because every dream is a new beginning. In the unlikely event that you did not feel that your dreaming achieved a useful result, you may need more information on effective dreaming. Check out the next section.

Daytime Dreams and Other Delights

Dreaming is perhaps the only occupation that we can indulge in absolutely endlessly without any barriers or boundaries whatsoever, and that we can customize to suit our every whim with no effort at all. While much has been written, if little understood, on the merits of nighttime dreaming, we have little information on daytime dreams. That need not bother us, however, because we are already experts on the subject and have many years of experience to bring to bear. Common sense will just have to prevail.

Living with a dream is one of the great joys of life. It never gets in the way, doesn't need grooming, exercising, or feeding, is very low maintenance, takes up no storage space, and doesn't upset the neighbors. Added to that, dreams are highly transportable, repeatable, shareable, interchangeable, and free. They also keep well (some have an almost indefinite shelf life), and while a few are gender or age specific, many will suit all sizes and shapes of dreamer. Their only drawback is that they sometimes get forgotten. Most of us have a dream or two that has gathered cobwebs in the dark recesses of our past. That's OK . It's not necessary to achieve all, or even *any,* of them. If it were, that would create intolerable pressures that would ultimately spoil what dreaming is all about. We need to dream. We need to believe that in some part of our life we can be successful, indulge our passions, perform wonderful feats, and enjoy every moment of living.

Since we all do it, it seems a bit of a waste of our talents not to use dreaming in a slightly more organized way. We can do better than ignore this amazing capacity to give our lives focus and purpose. It is a necessary and marvelously productive pastime from which we can benefit endlessly. Enrich *your* life. Enhance *your* motivation. Do a little dreaming every day.

How to Dream Well

There are a number of rules for good daytime dreaming. Like anything else, to become good at it you're going to need practice—preferably guided, high-quality practice—and lots of it (approximately 10,000 hours, to be precise!).

Training yourself to daytime dream can be done anywhere, anytime. Begin now. Just in case you are harboring any irrelevant preconceptions (otherwise know as *assumptions*!) about dreaming, let's first put all of our cards on the table.

Daytime dreaming is *not* any of the following:

- Relaxing
- Musing
- Spacing out
- A waste of time
- Passive
- Any combination of the above

So do not start your dream work in a quiet room with a comfortable chair. The object is to stay very much *awake!*

Beware of just daydreaming. This tends to be very unstructured and with arbitrary content that we often can't recall later. Most of us daydream intermittently to give our brains a brief rest from the world. Daydreaming is about disengagement. It is an escape from the present. Certainly it is a most pleasant and utterly benign state into which we may lapse from time to time, but do not make the mistake of thinking it will contribute directly to where you want to go in life. It will not. If you do more than your fair share of it, you will wake up with a jolt one day to find that life has passed you by.

From Pipe Dreams to Plans

Sometimes we also indulge in pipe dreams. These are the stuff of muse and the meandering mind. They are not to be taken at all seriously for they go one stage further from reality than daydreams in that they usually arise from highly fanciful, if not futile themes that have minimal prospects of ever being achieved.

For instance, *I wish I were a king* is not a dream for which one can immediately structure a career path. On second thought, one could create a kingdom (it has been done), marry a princess (possible but not probable), or self-appoint following a coup (might be messy). All things considered, however, it's generally a mistake to indulge in pipe dreams. They tend to be rather unreliable, especially when crowns of any kind are concerned (although there must be a satisfactory precedent because *somebody* started this king thing).

That's cleared the air. So now you can decide the approximate content of your daytime dreaming. Let's say you want to compete at the Olympics. Don't be shy about this—you don't have to tell the world until you're ready. Press on. Soften your gaze, letting your eyes go a little out of focus, and slip quietly into your favorite dream. All dreams begin with the words *I wish*, so here's where you can move shamelessly into wishing mode. Truly experienced dreamers begin with *I want*.

This initial statement is not to be confused, compared, contrasted, or in any way related to your goals, which all begin with *I will*, and thereafter itemize, quantify, or otherwise define how your life will happen. That's all very necessary, but it comes much later down the track. Dreams must not do any of that. Dreams begin with the wish and then just dwell on the continued wishing. Dreams are all about what *might* be or what *could* be. They are the ultimate What if. For those of you who've had a lot of coaching, we may be starting to press some well-trained buttons here, but take care not to get hung up on the rusty ol' goal-setting wire. Dreams are not the place to thrash out the process, they are not even the place to consider the outcomes. Dreams are all about happy endings. With this in mind, enjoy the very best of your wishings, and at this point just presume they will all come true.

Do not let your dream ramble around. In fact, if you can complete your dream in five seconds rather than ten, they'll be more useful to you. Time yourself. Five seconds is a lifetime. Ten seconds is a generation.

Commit yourself to the dream until you can readily and consistently recall it. You need to get to the stage at which you know exactly what to expect because you've dreamed it all before. No surprises please. Just create another habit.

Your daytime dreaming will work best for you when it is

- active,
- purposeful,
- passionate,
- positive, and
- fun.

Daytime dreaming will help you keep the fun in your sport better than all the training sessions ever invented. If you only dream for five seconds once a day, it will still be more than enough to refresh your spirit and send you bouncing back down to the gym or reaching for the telephone to organize your world. Those five seconds are the first major step toward the positive management of your motivation. The first mistake in that management is to spend them doing something else.

From Dreaming to Doing

While most daytime dreams inspire hope and happiness, you will have to focus your thoughts just a little more clearly if you are to dream with any more serious purpose. This will afford you endless pleasure.

First of all you must dare to dream. Ponder on the prospect of winning something wonderful. Dawdle around the idea of one day playing for your country. Contemplate the possibility of an Olympic career. Each dream must begin with a vision of splendor with you as the central figure. Never dream on anyone else's behalf—that's a mistake because the most important thing about a dream is that it's your own. The moment it belongs to somebody else, it loses its magic, so dreaming on behalf of anybody other than yourself will go nowhere.

You may want to share your dream. This helps to keep it alive if it currently seems a long way from happening. Be careful whom you choose as your confidante, however. Dreams can be fragile commodities, and in rough hands they will spoil or shatter quite easily. You need to learn to defend your dreams and protect them from people who may have scant regard for their value to you. It might be better to write a private contract with yourself and file it away somewhere safe if you suspect you are holding such company. This contract can state all the essential elements of your dream, but you know it is safe from spiteful remarks and impertinent comments. For the time being, it is also protected from sabotage, which is important because booby-trapping other people's dreams is a common practice in some circles. Alternatively, you may feel sufficiently proud of your dream to make a public declaration such as, "I'd like to learn to fly."

You'll find that dreams vary enormously in their size, shape, and complexity. A modest, unambitious dream can be toyed with on a Sunday afternoon, or run alongside your favorite CD. Since variety is the spice of your life, and your dreams too, you may have several dreams going at once (although not many committed dreamers can manage more than three or four at a time), and you may flit among them to suit your mood and moment. Old favorites can become ongoing delights to return to when the going gets rough. New dreams create their own special brand of excitement and anticipation. A major dream can run your life. Whatever kind of dream you have, each one is a most essential and wonderful *start*. What exactly it is the start *of* is up to you.

So now you've moved on from the outlandish, farfetched, and improbable pipe dreams (though perhaps we all need a little dose of fantasy now and then) to the dreams that are the beginnings of something magical, marvelous, and *real*. Such dreams give you a purpose in life, a reason for living, a challenge to meet! When dreams fire your imagination to the flashpoint, then you will cross that great divide between dreaming and doing. Without dreams, there is no doing to be done.

And that is how one day you wake up and suddenly just dreaming is not enough. Your mind clicks into gear, your brain hops into overdrive, and your body catapults into action. It is that wonderful moment when your motivation propels you out of the armchair and you roar off down to the gym to begin your 10,000 hours—*immediately!*

It no longer matters whether the dream was practical or possible, right or wrong. All you know is that your dream has turned to doing, and your sporting career now has all the motivation of a newly fired rocket on its way to join the stars.

Coaches' Corner

Many dusty volumes have been written, if not read, on motivation. Much hype has been created in its name. You are not expected to quote the dusty volumes or regurgitate the frantic marketing pitches. You just need to ask your athletes which dreams really, *really* matter most. They'll do the rest, if you don't get in their way.

Summary

Dreaming is utterly necessary to health, life, and happiness.

- Daydreams are time-out.
- Pipe dreams are luxury items.
- Night dreams are usually recreational.
- *Living* dreams are the stuff and fabric of your future.

16
Likely Sources of Misery

There are a number of ways to end up on the unhappy side of life. Most of us flirt with a few of them but find they're altogether too dismal company to stay around for long. Who hasn't gazed enviously at the car that is closer to a space shuttle than it is to any normal mortal's conveyance and moved on feeling vaguely inadequate and somehow rather sad? Perhaps you've caught yourself staring at an ad for the vacation that will never happen or have finally been defeated by one more look in the mirror at the body that will never be beautiful. Maybe you're getting worried at the unreasonable amount of effort now needed to pick yourself up, dust yourself off, and start all over again. Too bad you didn't see all this coming. Too bad no one understands.

Sometimes it's unrealistic expectations that lead us to this. Other times having inappropriate goals—or no goals at all—lands us in trouble. From time to time we can blame somebody else, which is occasionally comforting, but the relief is short-lived. This is because it's quite hard to find enough people on whom to park our misery without feeling guilty afterwards. Of course we could always lie and pretend that we're actually quite happy. That may fool most folks, but it won't fool *us.* Failing most other things, we can put our demise down to a bad lunch, bad company, or the weather. About the best thing we can do is to be practical. Not many things in life refuse to respond to a brisk appraisal and a nice clean, logical approach.

So, Stage 1 of your relocation to a more cheerful spot has to be to establish the facts. Make a start by brewing the best cup of coffee in town and making a list of what you don't like about how things are. Then flip the page over and write a list of how you'd like them to be. Then in a column down the side of both the pages add all the feelings attached to what you are doing. That makes it easy to be clear about what works or doesn't in your present life. Make sure you include all the things that generate even a small amount of misery. Include the people who irritate you, add the cat if you must, but don't drop anybody off the list who contributes even a minuscule amount of misery to your current life. It's best to do this while you're in one of your most positive moods. You should also be not more than moderately tired and only lightly stressed. There's not much point in cheating.

Let's move on to stage 2. Study your lists with care. It's then only a short step to take to changing your world. Your new clarity of perspective will make it a lot easier to stay happy. Being happy is easy when you compare it with the truckful of effort it takes to be miserable. This is the key to leaving misery alone and having lots of spare energy for being joyful.

You have arrived safely at stage 3. It's time to unlock some options. We'll explore these in detail because they represent your future life. The only thing that's more important than what you're *going* to do is what you are doing right now because there are no dress rehearsals in life. By all means plan to enjoy the future, but in the meantime make very sure to enjoy the present. To do otherwise is to sell yourself seriously short. Some people, however, like to tinker with disaster. The following section is for them.

How to Manufacture Misery

Here are a few good ways to become terminally miserable. They will ensure that your motivation never sees the bright light of day and that you remain in a gloomy torpor for most of your waking hours.

First you need to seriously compromise your motivation. There are plenty of options to choose from, but these are some of the most effective:

Options	**Antidotes**
Dithering	Doing
Procrastinating	Planning

Making assumptions	Establishing facts
Distracting yourself	Focusing on your goal
Doubting yourself	Believing in yourself
Ignoring your needs	Stopping wanting the world
Forgoing what's out there	Enjoying your share
Being too passive or aggressive	Being assertive

These antidotes to misery options are pretty fundamental to your enjoyment of life, so let's explore them.

Dithering Versus Doing

Dithering is a magnificent pastime. It ensures that you do not win, you cannot fail, and you can blame both on the rest of the world. It also absolves you from the responsibilities and consequences of making any decisions whatsoever or moving on at all in any direction from where you are now, which is securely within your comfort zone. This has a number of advantages. It means you don't have to cope with or adapt to change. This is particularly useful since it extends to people around you who would otherwise be challenged to accommodate the new moving-and-shaking you. They don't have to change either and can stay within *their* comfort zones. Life is therefore altogether more peaceful and less eventful. Some folks like it that way. The downside is that you're stuck with what you have, which you may or may not like and which might (but more probably will not) get you where you think you want to go. Only when the gap between you and your ambitions grows sufficiently uncomfortable will you want to move on. For that to happen, you have to immediately cease dithering—and *start doing*.

Naturally, the first question that springs to your newly activated mind is, Doing *what*? Therein lies the challenge. If you can decide the *what*, the *do* part is quite easy. Starting with the *what* will also help you to gather momentum for the *do*, by which time you'll be raring to go. This is motivation at its best! This is turning the motivational tractor-trailer around inside its own length and rerouting your energies in a fearfully positive and exciting direction. For all the right reasons, you are back to planning, goal setting, and the other details without which you will be neither rich nor famous. In fact, sometimes the best place to start is to decide precisely how rich and famous you actually want to be. Work back from there, and the rest is a breeze. If you're still inclined to dither, you might like to read the next section on procrastination. It could help, but then again it might not, and there are no guarantees it would be useful. You might be better off doing it tomorrow when you've got a bit more time. . .

Procrastinating Versus Planning

Just as there are potential sports stars who never shine, there are would-be winners who never plan. So they never win (well, not the big ones, anyway). Planning is just something they never quite get around to, so they never quite get around to the success they thought they deserved either! It's sad really. This is procrastination. It is not to be confused with dawdling; dawdlers at least start to do something—they just do it *very* slowly. Procrastination is in an altogether different league. It's putting off temporarily, indefinitely, permanently, or repeatedly what any other normally intelligent humanoid knows has to be done. But don't be defeatist about it. It's just a planning mistake.

The worst thing about procrastination is the paralysis. Somehow you just can't start. You don't know what to say or how to say it. That may be because you're a perfectionist and want to do it too well, or it may mean that the idea bores the pants off you and you'd rather watch a movie. Either one is a pretty negative response to the challenge of steering the rest of your life. Then again, perhaps you're just not ready to accept the facts and you feel pretty hostile toward anyone who suggests you're not on track in the first place. Anything's possible. There's even an outside chance that you actually find it more exciting not to plan at all. Some people like reeling from one crisis to the next. Others plan to fail through failing to plan (remember that one?). Recognizing procrastination for what it is—a static mistake in your planning processes—will help you want to move on.

Here are a few tips on how to break the deadlock:

- Don't feel you have to start at the beginning. It's easier to start in the middle. That might mean scribbling on the back of an envelope or doodling on the shopping list. It could happen midway through an argument or 10 minutes into the Sunday sermon. It doesn't matter where or when or how you write it or say it—*just do it!* You'll be surprised how much easier it is to amend a first draft (or doodle) than it is to face that first blank piece of paper. The moment you put something down, it gets easier from then on.

- Reward yourself for the start you have made. Buy yourself a block of chocolate, plan a vacation, or take a friend to lunch. Do anything that is special for you and that you haven't done for at least a week.

- Break up the planning task. Just set out your long-term goals. Write out only one of them—after all, you can always do the rest tomorrow.

- Nail yourself to your most *un*comfortable chair and *do not get up* until you have written 10 words on goals. This will set up triggers for future action, and the next time you sit in this chair you will galvanize your brain into the necessary action just a little more promptly. We'll take the optimistic option here—before the day is out, you will draw up goals, timetables, and periodization charts; plans B, C, and D, and lists of options, and agendas. You'll make a few mistakes, most of which you will ignore, but that won't scare you. Anyway, your procrastination has been impressive and you've chewed a satisfying amount off the end of at least three pencils. You're ready to roll.

- If by the end of the day you have made no move to break the procrastination, the less attractive option is to think about it in detail as you take a lengthy, and very cold, shower. This is called aversion therapy. If you haven't leaped into some sort of action after three showers, take sport off your wish list. It's kinder to tell yourself now that perhaps you don't quite have what it takes.

Assumptions Versus Facts

Assumptions are a way of life, but they can wreak havoc on the athlete and are dynamite for the coach! So why don't assumptions get the bad press they deserve? Well, the bottom line is, they're useful. We make assumptions on the basis of stereotypes with which we are comfortable. We make assumptions to protect ourselves from being misinformed, uninformed, or otherwise lacking. We make assumptions to put new information into familiar boxes so that we can cope with it. What we have to be careful of is where and how we use them. If they become the building blocks of our lives and we cease to question them, then assumptions get us into all kinds of trouble. Suddenly we find we're up a creek without a paddle! At this point, the bottom drops out of our motivation along with our confidence and we're out of what we thought we were in, because we assumed we were somewhere else. By the time we've worked all that out, we've usually given the whole show away and gone home.

The only way out of this maze is to establish the facts, prove the facts, and then act on the facts. That's a fair run on reality, and *that's* what you need to nail. It's quite easy to do this because the relief that comes from knowing you are on solid, factual ground is enormous and rapidly spurs you on to further effort. More motivational adjustments—and all to your advantage!

Distractions Versus Focus

Distraction is a necessary and abidingly rewarding procedure. It is marred by the fact that we usually feel guilty about doing it. This is too bad since it is an enormously self-protective device with which we can become familiar and comfortable. The bottom line is that we distract ourselves from things we are not yet ready to deal with, and that is OK. What is not quite so OK is continuing to use distraction as an ongoing coping mechanism. We then experience a peculiarly unpleasant form of frustration and irritation that we cannot define and are unable to resolve. That is not fun. Since fun is a basic component of a happy life, distraction is therefore ultimately counterproductive to happiness.

The antidote to distraction is first to become aware of when and how you distract yourself from the matter at hand. Do you get up and make a cup of coffee, phone a friend, go out, spring-clean the house, dawdle, doodle, or decide to redecorate? There are an infinite number of attractive options in the face of an unattractive task, none of which you can justify taking. Look at what you *really* want to achieve. If you don't have the courage to head on into it, then bail out now with as much dignity as you can muster, knowing you will shortly have a good deal less if you continue to dodge the issue. Either way, your motivation will blossom in the wake of your new decision and you will find considerable relief from the uncertainty and self-deception. This will free up energy for other, more constructive activities. Focus on what you really want to do, and then plan how you are really going to do it. Focus on the outcome; then focus on the process you need to put in place to achieve that outcome. Focus on yourself, on how you feel now and how you will feel when you achieve this goal. Focus on your life, right now and as it will be.

Doubts Versus Self-Belief

Doubting that you can achieve your goal—be it a sparkling and illustrious dream or a quiet achiever's modest back-room effort—is pretty much par for most courses. We all doubt ourselves sometimes. Now and then we all wonder if we can really do what we set out to achieve and whether it was such a good idea after all. What seemed so natural a course to take, or what felt so possible when we were sitting in an armchair in front of the fire, assumes a very different character out there in the rough, tough, ruthless world of endless training sessions, remorseless competition, unjust press reports, untimely injuries, unwanted setbacks, and unlucky breaks. It's enough to make even the

■ We all doubt ourselves sometimes.

most dyed-in-the-wool competitor doubt her dreams, question her self-confidence, and wonder if it isn't all just too hard sometimes.

The good thing about doubt, though, is that only you know about it. That's quite handy because it gives you grounds to talk yourself into another headspace. Often it astounds us to learn from prominent figures, especially actors or film stars who are used to being in the limelight, that they have enormous doubts as to whether they can do what the rest of the world is expecting of them. Big stars don't usually admit to their doubts before the action starts, but when the full story comes out later, we find that what looked like an impregnable armor of confidence didn't feel at all bulletproof from the inside. Dealing with your demons can be a tricky business, but at least it's a comfort to know that everyone else has to do the same.

Believing in yourself is the magic antidote to doubting. The hallmark of all great athletes is that they *do* believe in themselves—not in an arrogant way, but as a fact of life. They just know that's the way things are. For lesser mortals, however, turning around a wavering attitude to the world is not an easy matter. If this is you, try starting with some positive affirmations pasted around the house in all the places you can't avoid them in the course of your day. Prime your family and friends to chew your ear off every time you act negatively toward yourself or your life. Give yourself treats when you succeed in staving off the doubts and implanting a confident thought. Enjoy the feeling that comes with that thought. Get used to listening to your thoughts and cut out the worms in an otherwise good apple. Rewrite your self-talk to include some self-applause when you do well and some self-encouragement when you don't. Enjoy the support you are giving yourself. Better still, just enjoy being you!

Needs Versus Wants

Confusing needs and wants is such a common mistake that you'll only have to look five feet to find someone doing a pretty good job of it. So how does this happen? First you have to distinguish your needs from your wants. There may be lots of things you want in life—none of which you need. If you pursue the wants at the expense of the needs, you will end up in a muddle. For instance, you may want to own a big house some day, but in the meantime what you actually *need* is a roof over your head. It would not be sensible to take out an oversized mortgage to get the big house and in so doing put the rest of your lifestyle on the line. But neither would it be a great idea to forgo owning a roof at all just because you couldn't afford a maximortgage. What you *need* is a stepping-stone, a minimortgage for a modest roof, with potential. Later, you can then either extend the property into a palace or sell it for squillions and go shopping . . . for a palace.

Determining our needs is not easy because our comparatively affluent society envelopes us in advertising campaigns for a thousand goods and services we can actually do very well without. From all quarters of the media we are beset with tempting ways to part us from our money. In the face of this barrage, it's sometimes quite difficult to set aside what we often want quite badly and concentrate on deciding what we actually need. But this is the crux of the whole matter. Miss this bus, and you *walk* home.

Forgoing Versus Enjoying Your Share

Education is a curious thing. It stuffs us full of irrelevant facts, yet often doesn't teach us how to navigate life. Perhaps the best education wouldn't actually teach us any facts at all—it would just teach us a style of living and how to employ it in time to enjoy life. Meanwhile, passing up on what's out there is an educational error because we then fail to learn that a large chunk of it is rightfully ours! So don't think for a minute of becoming an underachiever. There's always room for new talent, so if you haven't already done so, sign up now as a high flyer. Anyway, success is the icing on life's very big cake, and there's a slice out there with your name on it.

It's also time to be gracious about coming forward to receive your dues. Take what you have earned, given that you have probably worked extremely hard for it and devoted large chunks of your life to making it happen. There is no such thing as overnight success (except perhaps in the eyes of the media who were busy looking the other way while you sweated through the obligatory 10,000 hours of training on your way toward center stage). Then it happens! You are suddenly noticed! *Terrific!* Sooner or later we all like to be noticed, so keep toiling and brace yourself for the stare of a thousand eyes! Factor in the toiling, and you'll find taking your bow to be a marvelous moment. Remember that the buzz with this one usually comes after the curtain falls on the action when you can say I did it! and start to party. Some parties should last a lifetime.

Choosing to be Assertive

Much misery can be self-generated by poor behavioral choices. Any inappropriate response will do the trick, whether you are too aggressive, too passive, or just too out of sync with those around you. Learning to be appropriately assertive will help to put out a few of the fires, and for those in the impact sports being superassertive becomes a necessary skill.

Assertiveness gets a lot of bad press because it gets mixed up with aggression. These two are quite different, however. Being assertive is about stating what you think, feel, or want, whereas being aggressive is about attacking others either verbally or physically *with the intention to cause them harm.* It's possible to be extremely assertive without being at all aggressive, and most people could easily double their assertiveness quota to their advantage.

Being superassertive requires making your point just a bit more clearly, and it is usually reserved for the more interactive sports where push does come to shove. But again, there is no need to mix it up with aggression, no matter how physical things become. For the coaches out there, do not confuse it with bullying, which is some sort of power trip that begins with inequality and ends with exploitation. Superassertive coaching can indeed get the best out of some athletes, but for others it's a disaster.

Like most other things, being effectively assertive takes practice. To further your sporting career, improve your college results, or just enhance your daily achievements, you will need to take a vow to change if you identify with any of the less productive options. That takes courage. You do have some—otherwise you would not have withstood the barrage of new ideas loosed from these pages. Nobody's going to measure it, but now is your chance to show you have *enough* of what it takes to put some of these ideas into practice. Start with a small project, such as asking someone not to do something that you've been putting up with until now. Decide on a date and time to address the matter, plan what you'll say, and give the person a number of alternatives that are acceptable to you. The assertive way to achieve your purpose is to employ some "I" statements, remaining courteous but firm. State clearly and calmly exactly what you think, what you feel, and what you need. You'll soon find that it feels great to be heard and to have your needs met. Be quick to recognize your success and give yourself praise when you get it right.

Examples

State what you think:

"I think it's only fair that . . ."

"I think it is more fun if . . ."

Share what you feel:

"I'd feel happier if . . ."

"I feel more comfortable when . . ."

Ask for what you want:

"I would like you to . . ."

"I would like to . . ."

You may need to strike a bargain and offer to do—or not do—something in return, but your imagination will supply the necessary options. You'll soon move into a new operational mode altogether and find that good things just seem to happen. As the wheels of your life start turning, don't forget that it was you who greased the axles, almost all on your own!

Coaches' Corner

Numerous sources of misery are available exclusively to coaches. Try some of these:

- Pinning your success as a person to your success as a coach
- Deciding that your coaching input is the *only* thing that will make your athlete a winner
- Living your dreams through your athletes (whatever you do, go get a dream of your own!)
- Taking too much responsibility for your athletes' success and wondering why they feel crowded
- Ignoring all the other things that contribute to their success, such as fatigue (theirs), pain (theirs), and money (theirs!)
- Taking too little responsibility for their success, then wondering why they don't want to share it
- Wishing you were doing the winning
- Wishing you were getting a bigger slice of the glory

Summary

It's not generally what happens to us in life that determines our success and happiness, it's how we choose to respond to it. Better choices will make for fewer disappointments, and choosing to avoid some of the more obvious sources of misery will be a good start. Sometimes that's a choice between a rock and a hard place, but most times we can opt for action and a positive point of view. This won't change the world, but it will change how we feel about it. For most of us, that's pretty important stuff.

Best sources of misery for athletes are . . .

- Dithering
- Procrastination
- Making assumptions
- Creating distractions
- Self-doubt
- Confusion of needs and wants
- Foregoing your glory
- Lack of assertiveness

Antidotes to all these are in your choices.

For coaches, misery is guaranteed . . .

- Anytime you don't live your own dreams

- Anytime you don't create your own glory

But happiness is always an option.

17

Measuring Your Commitment

Few matters are more fundamental to our sporting success than our commitment to make it happen. Equally surely, no other aspect of our activities more habitually frustrates our coaches since without sufficient commitment to tackle the training and withstand the disciplines and disappointments of an athletic career, even the most spectacular physical talents will remain undeveloped. Without waiting to define what commitment really is, and without any clear idea of what the practicalities of it will mean in our lives, we demand it of ourselves (and others around us), easily agreeing that the higher the goals that have been set, the more commitment we will need to achieve them. While coaches, scouts, and selectors routinely evaluate many aspects of our physical and mental capabilities to assess our performance potential, our level of commitment is not generally included among them. Neither has any successful means of identifying it or measuring it yet been found. Our capacity for it is merely assumed, until we find it isn't there!

Commitment is a sticky subject about which little has been said and less has been written. Yet we are constantly called on to be committed to one thing or another, from winning the next competition to passing exams. Nobody tells us much about how to go about *getting* committed, what it feels like to *be* committed, or how to *stay* committed in the face of drama, destitution, divorce, or other natural disasters. We will explore this uncharted territory together. This will demand much vigor and some courage, and you'll have to address a few personal motives and other tricky matters. Participating in this adventure will offer you insights into yourself that have the potential to steer you on many different courses. Take heart, take a very deep breath, and dive in the deep end in the knowledge that your life will now never be quite the same again.

Commitment Versus Motivation

In everyday language we often tend to carelessly use the terms *commitment* and *motivation* interchangeably. This is the mistake of the century because the two are far different (table 17.1). Some of the best brains in the business have been doing it for years, which is why nobody has come up with any successful answers to the commitment questions we face. As working athletes and coaches, we can challenge this in the course of any working day. Everyone has met highly committed athletes suffering a temporary slump in motivation. They are passionate about their sport but just don't seem to have their usual appetite for training. Been there, done that? We've also known highly motivated competitors who are apparently undercommitted when it comes to putting in the hard yards to achieve their goals. They're nowhere to be seen if extra training collides with a night out with the boys. While these athletes are often extremely sharp on the field, it's getting them there that poses a bit of a problem. Let's take a closer look at some possible reasons for all this, and at the risk of putting the cart before the horse, we're going to look at some of the mistakes we make before we look at why we make them. Curious? Good. Read on!

Let's start with the stuff we know—that nobody is questioning your commitment to your sport. You're still as much a deep-down, dyed-in-the-wool sportsperson as you ever were; it's just that your motivation has hit rock bottom. How come your team is still so central to your life, but you just can't seem to get out of bed in time to make it to training? That's a strange and uncomfortable combination of feelings to have toward your sport, and there doesn't seem to be any rational explanation. Worse still, none of the usual training solutions seem to work, and the best motivational hype in the world leaves you feeling about as chilly as an early winter's morning in an empty gym. What's going on here?

Well, it may not be time to hang up your boots after all. It may be nothing more than a mismatch between what you are expecting from your sport and the sort of thrills, spills, and glory the sport offers. Playing recreational sport will not satisfy the high flyer, so if that's you, you may find you're bored with the training and not enjoying the competitions any more. So it is time to move up a league. Or perhaps you're the intimidated athlete who no longer looks forward to training and may even have given up competition but who mysteriously maintains the habit and just can't seem to give up the sport. Well, being only slightly out of your depth is as good as being half a mile out to sea if you can't swim! Happily, a lifeline is at hand. Reducing your involvement to one where you feel comfortable with the level of risk, effort, and skill will soon solve the problem.

To do this, you can also move sideways by, for instance, changing a team position to provide opportunities for more, or less, offensive or defensive play. Perhaps you'd thrive on more leadership. Many a brilliant captain has shone in the leadership role despite not previously having been a particularly outstanding player. By the same token, some outstanding players have made disappointing captains.

Table 17.1 Commitment Versus Motivation

Commitment	Motivation
An expression of need	A response to incentives
Long-term involvement (shows up over years)	Short-term phenomenon (demonstrated daily)
Evidenced by sporting history	Observed in training
Measured by commitment threshold	Measured by motivational status
Linked to confidence	Linked to goals
Provides ongoing fulfillment	Gives immediate gratification

If you're still finding that there's a mismatch between your expectations and what your sport delivers, you may have made a much more spectacular mistake: You may be in the wrong sport! If you think that's farfetched, what about the leading Australian rugby player (with heaps of short-term motivation but no long-term commitment) who recently changed hats and one day calmly walked into professional boxing—at the international level! Everybody gasped, and he left a trail of devastated fans in his wake, but he was instantly successful and still maintains that it was the best thing he ever did.

Important Differences

It seems our first job is to distinguish between motivation and commitment (table 17.2). If you have a problem distinguishing between them, let's compare them with something else that you're already familiar with—focus and concentration. Just as *focus* is really a smart word for "paying attention," and concentration is the ability to sustain that attention, motivation is interest in doing something *now*, and commitment is the ability to sustain that interest over time. Having one in no way guarantees that you have the other!

This is the point at which we diverge from conventional wisdom on the matter because, as you have already discovered, commitment and motivation are usually spoken of interchangeably. You have also learned that this is a mistake. Why? Because different problems naturally demand quite different solutions. We commonly try to address commitment problems using motivational solutions, or vice versa. Since this has never worked, it's time to move outside the motivational square and create a commitment square. If there's nobody out there to help us, we'll just have to do it ourselves!

Practicalities

You are about to discover a combination of factors that are characteristic of your sport involvement. These are

- your participation pattern,
- sport inhibitors (positive and negative),
- dropout factors, and
- your sportstyle/lifestyle mix.

Table 17.2	Mismatches Between Commitment and Motivation	
Mistake	**Current outcome**	**Training remedies**
1. Confusion between commitment and motivation	Your remedies for increasing either or both aren't working.	Reread this chapter and decide which of these is the real problem.
2. Low commitment in spite of high motivation	You may feel unsettled and impatient to race on up the competitive ladder before basic skills are secure.	Settle down or prepare for mega-errors in your life. You may even need to change to a less technical sport.
3. High commitment but strangely low motivation	You may feel tense with low energy levels and may be tempted to skip training while not enjoying the competitions anymore.	May need to aim higher in your sport. Try new techniques, a new team position, or even a new coach.

Everyone has a unique combination of factors that makes up a picture that we call a *commitment portrait*. Determining your commitment portrait and comparing it with that of successful athletes who are typical competition gives you lots of very personal information. It tells you how committed you are to your sport and the sorts of things that will accelerate, inhibit, or end your sporting career. Since nobody argues that success at progressively higher levels of competition demands progressively higher levels of commitment, it's also a very useful tool in assessing your *realizable* potential.

Participation Patterns

Participation patterns are the features of different groups of athletes who are characteristically involved at different levels of competition. It's easy to distinguish them in the sporting arena, and you'll soon recognize yourself and many of your sporting peers. These patterns include not only the level and frequency of participation, but also considerations of lifestyle management and such things as the extent of personal resources that have been invested in the sport. You will soon see how these features characterize the various groups and allow us to assign individual athletes to them.

Sport Inhibitors

Sport inhibitors are any elements of your lifestyle that effectively prevent you from participating more often, or at a different level than you are currently enjoying. They may be positive or negative and are significant sometimes by their presence and often by their absence. All sorts of things will spring to mind, and together they will characterize your levels of commitment to different things.

Positive Inhibitors

Positive inhibitors are the result of achieving your performance ceiling and are generally pleasurable. They include:

- Fulfillment of commitment needs
- Winning (for some competitors)
- Social acceptance

Example

Despite the fact that the state titles are in your hometown this year, you decide not to play because it clashes with the club tournament. You explain to your friends that you are already "committed" to supporting your club. This may be true, but it may also be an excuse for not confronting the bigger challenge of the state competition. You'd rather take a shot at winning the club cup than work off a few spare pounds.Clearly you're more committed to winning a trophy than you are to climbing the competitive ladder. And it *does* come down to winning because otherwise you'd be out there and after that state title!

Winning the club cup is a positive sport inhibitor because it prevents you from playing far more dangerous tennis, which you might not win at all.

Negative Inhibitors

We are adversely affected by negative inhibitors since they are generally accompanied by feelings of frustration, impatience, overarousal, or other signs of stress. These include the following:

- Self-inflicted handicaps (such as smoking)
- Logistical problems (such as transportation difficulties or lack of parental support)

WHAT'S YOUR PARTICIPATION PATTERN?

Find out by matching your sports participation to the one in the groups below.

Sport group	Characteristics	Typical sport participation
Recreational players	"Weekend" sportspeople	Likes "messing about in boats," social tennis, and similar light-hearted sports activities. Minimal, intermittent, sport-cum-social/ fitness involvement. Looking for fun. Little or no competitive ambition.
Club competitors	The backbone of sports clubs	A few lifestyle adjustments to generate time and money for sport. Enthusiastic spectators and fans. Keen club competitors.
Open competitors	The best of amateur sports competitors	Significant lifestyle choices to facilitate sport participation. Family, education, etc. are still important. Competes up to state level.
Champion athletes	Serious sportspeople—future stars. By now they are professionals and working hard at their sport.	Seriously shapes lifestyle to sport. Resumes sport at same level after injury or other difficulties. Works toward specific goals. Specializes within their sport. Competes at state/ national level.
Elite performers	Our sports heroes, living and breathing a professional sportstyle, and loving it!	Typically lives a sportstyle without a significant "other life." All resources chan neled into sport. Totally focused on training and competition at national and international level.

- Financial constraints
- Personality-based problems (lack of confidence, fear, emotional difficulties, etc.)

Some inhibitors are fluid and can be either positive or negative or change from one to the other. These include the following:

- Socioeconomic circumstances
- Famous forebears in the sport
- Life events (e.g., marriage)

Sportstyle/Lifestyle Mix

One of the most easily identifiable differences among athletes is where they lie on the "lifestyle-with-sport to sportstyle-with-life" continuum. Recreational players typically fit their sport into their lifestyle, whereas elite athletes' lives center totally around their sport (table 17.3). Your level of commitment to your sport can be immediately identified by the lifestyle and sportstyle choices you make. You have a track record as open to scrutiny as any other aspect of your career! New idea? You'd better accept it in a hurry because none of us can erase our past. Our darkest commitment secrets are about to be revealed for every coach and selector in the world to see! As you would expect, this has vast implications for any serious sporting future.

Choices. You make them every day. You make good ones, productive ones, exciting ones, adventurous ones, big ones, boring ones . . . and bad ones. The worst that can happen here is that you fail to make *enough* choices, and so you *over*commit. You then spend your time trying to keep so many plates spinning that you don't achieve anything masterful with any of them. Spreading yourself too thin across too broad a band of the sport/life continuum is a recipe for high stress and low achievement. It leads to juggling unreasonable numbers of activities in impossibly short amounts of time. We've all overcommitted at some time or other, and it's not a comfortable place to perch. Overall, the solution is to keep your eyes firmly on a *limited* range of goals and keep an equally firm hand on the tiller to see that you stay on course to reach them. You will also have to make some decisions to live by and decide which end of the sport/life continuum really suits you for where you are in your life (table 17.4).

What Influences Your
Table 17.3 Sports Participation?

Sport group	Principal sports inhibitors	Biggest dropout factors
Recreational players	Excuses not to practice.	Pressure to improve or compete.
Club competitors	Lack of time and money. Other interests.	Lack of winning. Other interests.
Open competitors	Reached limit of motivation, money, and commitment.	Lifestyle pressures. Lack of support and resources. Demands of the sport. Lack of competitive ambition.
Champion athletes	Lifestyle factors that athlete chooses not to change.	Insufficient resources. Fear of failure. Lack of good coaching or facilities.
Elite performers	Frustration with lack of major wins. Injury. Burnout.	Injuries or retirement. Often go on as media commentators, speakers, celebrities, etc.

You may find you sit on the borders of two groups, or belong in different groups in different sports. Identifying which group is the real you will either fire up your ambitions or take unnecessary pressure off you. It will also help your coach and your family to knit together an appropriate level of support.

Dropout Factors

Dropout factors are the major potential causes of withdrawal from a sport. They are different for each athlete. Our tolerance of these factors will vary greatly, and what may affect us strongly in a sport to which we have a low commitment may be entirely bearable in another to which we have a much higher commitment. Dropout factors may be positive or negative, and they contribute to typical and predictable patterns of retirement. Positive factors include things such as reaching

Table 17.4 — Misfits Between Commitment and Lifestyle or Sportstyle

1. High commitment but too much lifestyle	Do you never seem to have enough time for your sport because too many enjoy the things get in the way?	Prune the other things out of your life (if you can't be ruthless, be patient) until it's less of a lifestyle and more of a sportstyle
2. Low commitment but too much sportstyle	Perhaps you feel resentful at how much you have to train and even dislike the pressure to perform	Ease off the sportstyle, cut down on sports involvement, and live more of a lifestyle instead
Over-commitment	Are you strung out and feel that your life is run by the clock?	Take more choices and learn to say "no" (nicely)
Under-commitment	Does your sport leave you feeling empty and vaguely disatisfied?	Find a fresh challenge and set some exciting, new goals. Perhaps go for a higher level of competition or try out for a new team.

our goals, or even growing too old. Negative factors might include injury or breakdown, burnout, or poor coaching.

Despite our best intentions, some of us just do not like letting go. We may know it's time to move on but don't know how, or where, to go. Leaving gracefully is an art form; don't wait until you've got more wrinkles than an old prune before you quit the scene. The only mistake here is *not* to drop out when the time comes.

Commitment Thresholds

We are about to establish that commitment can be measured. This is a whole new world! We will see that commitment thresholds separate groups of sportspeople in much the same way that social or cultural differences separate different groups in society. It is possible, but not usual, to cross these invisible barriers, but you need the right prerequisites and very good reasons for trying to do so.

Four major commitment thresholds give rise to five main groups of athletes. Each group has its own commitment portrait. Further, each group is clearly identifiable by its level of competition. Thus, the thresholds become benchmarks of progressive, demonstrated degrees of commitment. The longer you spend below one threshold, the less likely it is that you can move up through it. Your commitment portrait will ultimately determine whether or not you remain within your current group, or whether you move on or drop out.

The thresholds separate the various levels of sport involvement of which an athlete is potentially capable. Most important, the threshold at which you're *currently* performing is not always obviously related to the standard at which you could *potentially* perform. It could be a good deal higher than you might at first expect. Occasionally an athlete is actually better suited to competing at a lower level. Measuring an athlete's commitment will tell the smart coach whether he is dealing with an overstretched or *under*committed athlete. (Remember not to confuse commitment levels with current motivational status.)

Athletes will have as many different commitment portraits as they have sports in which they are involved. *You* will have them too. Let's take a closer look.

Recreational Players

Recreational players are the socialites on the circuit. Our commitment portrait reflects a sport involvement that is enthusiastic but relatively minimal. They like "messing about in boats" and are just not interested in the heavy end of the yachting spectrum. They occasionally get caught up in a hit or two at the squash court, but that's about the size of their competitive ambition. Most of them are recreational players in at least one sport for fun, usually with a few friends. Often their participation is intermittent, and when they're involved in multiple sports in this way, which is often the case at this level, they'll have multiple participation profiles that reflect this. They may have a very different profile in their principal sport.

Sport inhibitors for recreational players are a whole slew of reasons not to participate, which may be no more substantial than negative responses to the weather (these are commonly known as excuses). If "normal" expectations of competitive progression are attached to them, their general lack of practice and therefore of progress may be a major source of frustration to their most patient coach, who by definition has a considerably higher commitment ceiling.

While the vast number of players and coaches within this group may not be a major seedbed of elite talent, their involvement is nonetheless important to them, it and is not to be underestimated. Recognizing that you may belong to this group, at least in a part of your sporting life, will allow you to set appropriate goals and make realistic training demands in pursuit of modest results. The dropout factors for recreational players are pressure to improve at an uncomfortable rate or level. It may also be simply pressure to compete.

■ The first threshold: This divides the recreational player from the publicly declared club competitor.

Club Competitors

Club competitors are the backbone of all sport. They pay the subscriptions, clean out the clubrooms, and organize the raffles. They are characterized by their participation in club competitions, which are important to them. Their involvement is usually as regular as clockwork. For a few it's intermittent, although always ongoing.

Club competitors are good sport/time managers and show evidence of this by doing such things as giving up music lessons to make hockey practice or working earlier or later to generate a long lunch hour for competition training.

The typical sport inhibitors for club competitors are a stated lack of time (how many thousand time have you heard *that* one!), participation in other sports, and minimal financial input. They're not usually interested in the higher-quality training or the more expensive gear. They're middle-of-the-roaders, out for some entertaining Saturday afternoon competition, with a serious eye on winning.

The principal dropout factors for these athletes are other interests that better fulfill their competitive needs, and ceasing to win at the club level.

■ The second threshold: This divides the club competitor from those involved in open competition, up to (but not always including) state championship level.

Open Competitors

Open competitors show evidence of having made some significant choices to focus their lifestyle toward supporting their sport involvement, although other involvements are still heavy. For instance, although their major commitment may be to their studies, or perhaps to their families, they may have accepted a basketball scholarship at college to ensure that their skills improve.

Also typical of this group is the teenager who has selected sport at the expense of other activities (although education and socialization are still relatively high priorities). These young athletes are usually supported emotionally, logistically, and financially by their parents, at least for the time being.

Sport inhibitors for this group typically include low motivational status, financial constraints, and social relationships. Young athletes are always compromised by parental *non*involvement. Dropout factors are educational, career, or family pressures; the technical demands of the sport; insufficient winning; poor coaching; and the perceived pressures of a higher level of competition. Anyone with a low tolerance for risk or stress will be content to stay right here!

■ The third threshold: This one marks the distinction between the essentially good competitor and those who are true championship material.

Championship Athletes

This is where sportstyle starts to get serious. These athletes are moving toward the medal end of the continuum where they're expected to—and will need to—commit a large chunk of their lives and resources to their sport if they are to succeed.

Characteristically, the commitment portrait of championship athletes includes the following:

- Decisions on general life direction in connection with their sport (e.g., has chosen a job that accommodates their sport)
- Evidence of tenacity and single-mindedness of purpose (e.g., they have a track record of resuming competitive campaigns *at the same level* following injury or adversity)
- Evidence of shaping their lifestyles around their sport (e.g., has moved to an area with better training facilities)
- Development of specific goals *and evidence of adjustments to them* (e.g., has taken vacations to enable them to participate in state or national meets)

- Specialization in their sport. Typically these athletes will also have well-developed tapering skills and well-established competition routines.

Sport inhibitors for athletes in this group are any negative lifestyle factors that they knowingly and directly allow to continue to influence their sporting lives *and do nothing to change.* These may include any combination of the following:

- Smoking
- Any kind of substance abuse
- Being overweight
- Excessive socializing when in training
- Neglecting any aspect of competition preparation (e.g., mental skills training)
- Habitual lack of care of sport gear, which may compromise the competition outcome
- Loss of confidence
- Fear of injury

■ Champions shape their lives around their sport.

Typical dropout factors for championship athletes are fear of failure, fear of the task, insufficient coaching, or overtraining. Since financial pressure is substantial at this level, lack of sponsorship and/or logistical support may also contribute to their withdrawal. Burnout is rare.

Those who may have been apparently "coached through" their deficits, while being a monument to skillful training techniques, will ultimately prove a disappointing investment. They may perhaps be likened to a senior executive who is promoted on the basis of previous good performances to a level at which she is neither truly comfortable nor truly competent.

■ The fourth threshold: This is the watershed for those who may be outstanding championship material but will not become elite athletes.

Elite Athletes

An elite is an elite is an elite. Isn't that how it goes? Not so! It may surprise you to know there are three groups of elite performers, and even within these groups there is a big range of skill, motivation, and commitment.

Elite Improvers

Elite improvers are athletes whose sporting lives are unknowingly or indirectly influenced by lifestyle factors that they do not have the skills or resources to control. Their commitment portrait reflects this—despite an apparent potential to improve their performance, it is typically inconsistent. They live by the motto, "Hang in there, boys! You're about to hit the Big Time!" but alas, they are not always destined to do so.

The sport inhibitors for elite improvers are usually personal, such as inappropriate diets, poor sleep habits, unstable or disruptive emotional relationships, and the like.

Elite Mainstreamers

Elite mainstreamers are athletes who, when informed of the possibility of not making it, make immediate and appropriate changes. Compare the commitment portrait of these mainstreamers with that of the improvers, who know about these factors *but take no action* to set them right. Mainstreamers produce *consistently* high quality performances. If this is you, you're among the best we have.

Sport inhibitors for elite mainstreamers include poor athlete/coach relationships and frustration through injury or lack of winning the really big events.

Dropout factors for both elite improvers and elite mainstreamers include lack of status in comparison to superelites (see the next section), burnout, injury, and career mismanagement.

Superelites

Superelites are athletes whose lives are entirely built around their sport. This is the group from which the household names and real greats of sport emerge. *Sport would not be sport without these athletes.*

Superelites typically have long careers and retire while still at the top, getting—and giving—the max. Negative inhibitors are minimal, and competitive withdrawal is usually the result of natural wastage through age, physical breakdown, or changes in personal circumstances or family responsibilities. Many retain a lifetime involvement in the coaching or administration aspects of their sport; others branch out into business, join the media, or enjoy careers on the celebrity circuit based on their sporting success. They are the stars in our sporting sky.

Whether you are an athlete or a coach, you will benefit greatly from clear and *early* identification of your commitment portrait. Commitment is a most seriously influential commodity, which we need by the bucketful if we are to succeed. Measuring it gives us, *for the very first time*, a handle on that bucket. That's got to be progress.

Recognizing Your Commitment Portrait

Not everyone is born a superstar. In fact, most of us are just born mortal. We generally aspire to staying alive, with some of the comforts of our time. A few of us decide to challenge this and set off on ambitious and eventful courses that we commit to with gusto, may live to enjoy, or may later regret or abandon. Brandishing a low tolerance for mediocrity and a high tolerance for risk and disappointment, we play for high stakes. By investing our lives in curious and unconventional pastimes, such as hurling small cannonballs into the middle distance, we create an outside possibility that though we won't be rich, we might be slightly famous. Shot put is not everybody's idea of how best to spend a sunny afternoon, but at least it demonstrates an abiding passion to be different.

We often make seemingly ridiculous adjustments to our lifestyle to continue these pastimes, adjustments others may consider sacrifices. We know, however, that these things don't feel like sacrifices at all because the bottom line is that we *want* to do it. We do it because we like it! Somewhere along the line we gave ourselves credit, others gave us credit, or we got some kind of warm, fuzzy feeling from our pastime, call it sport. So we make another "sacrifice" and do it again.

Anyway, does it matter why we do it as long as we're enjoying it? What better reason do we need to do anything, until we either drop out or drop dead! We enjoy any activity because it satisfies us, fulfils us, challenges us, frightens us, thrills us, soothes us. Whatever it is, it hooks into our personality and leaves us feeling so happy that we are prepared to bypass a lot of other things in life to experience that happiness once more. When we do this over extended periods of time we call it commitment. Excelling in sport takes so much practice that it's simply not possible to be that good without also being committed to the sport.

Along the way we need to be motivated. Now and then our motivation is likely to falter as we experience the normal pressures of life. We know about that. But commitment to our sport may be lifelong, and few things may take as big a place in our life. So next on the agenda is to find out the size and shape of your commitment.

You now have a bright new picture of who you are. You can see at a glance your current level of commitment to your sport and in a minute or two you'll also be able to assess your level of unfulfilled potential—if any. Don't worry if this is different from what you expected. That's normal if you have previously been confusing motivation with commitment. You have now corrected that mistake, so stand by for a few more surprises!

Coming to terms with finding that you are not currently very committed to train or compete in a sport in which you have already invested a good deal of your life and resources can be difficult. But at least you're no longer living an a myth. As a last glance at perfection will remind you, you've long since decided you can live without that item!

Coaches' Corner

Understanding your own, and your athletes', commitment portraits can make your coaching life easier in many ways because . . .

- It's easier to identify performance ceilings. This helps prevent the "square peg in a round hole" syndrome, in which you ask more, or less, than the athlete can give.

- You are better able to match the demands of the athletes' sports with their personal resources and their abilities through more appropriate content and tempo of training. So athletes will stay with you longer and perform better because they are *happier*.

- Selection of elite athletes is clarified. High levels of both commitment and motivation are prerequisites for success, but an abundance of one may easily mask a lack of the other.

- Selecting out subelites from elite candidates becomes possible much earlier.

- Coach/athlete compatibility can be enhanced if each acknowledges the commitment portrait of the other.

- Mistakes in reading your athletes' commitment portrait will be clearly evident in the results that you jointly achieve. If these are disappointing, don't hesitate to comb through the criteria for the different groups of athletes outlined in this chapter, trying as you do so to put aside any assumptions and all of what you know about an athlete other than what you can substantiate through hard *facts*.

It's quite a simple matter to establish a commitment portrait. There are three steps:

1. Gather information on the athlete's sport participation.
2. Compare that participation with those of the different groups.
3. Find the closest match; this is the group to which the athlete belongs.

This will soon tell you whether the athlete has fulfilled his potential and whether he has shown the necessary commitment for the level of competition at which you intend to coach him. Remember, we're only talking commitment here. As tempting as it may be, again, *do not confuse commitment level with motivation status.* And while we're talking traditional assumptions, you might question whether the athlete's goals accurately reflect all the qualities required to reach them. *Do not confuse goals with aspirations.*

Parity Levels

If you're not already in overload, we can draw a number of useful conclusions from all of this information.

1. If the athlete's commitment portrait already matches that required for her present level of competition, *she will go no further*, regardless of technical ability, physique, training, or ambition.

2. If her commitment portrait is compatible with a more committed group than the one she is currently in, *she has the potential for progress*, provided her other skills have the necessary potential for development. When trying to determine whether an athlete has star potential or is simply a precocious physical talent, it is often more useful and ultimately more accurate to look for a *package of abilities*, one of which needs to be commitment. Where precocious motor skills or outstanding physique, fitness, or agility eclipse the commitment potential, it is particularly important to establish the athlete's commitment portrait to avert later performance disappointments.

3. If a performer's commitment portrait is compatible with a less committed group than either that of his current competition level or his stated goals, then *he will drop out of the sport in the short/ medium term* and is therefore a poor coaching risk and an embarrassing selection.

4. You will occasionally meet an athlete in misleading circumstances in relation to his ultimate level of achievement. Perhaps he has not yet been exposed to a sport at which he will later excel. This has been the case in many talent identification programs that have discovered future champions based on bio-metric or psychometric data. His commitment portrait will identify his true commitment potential, regardless of those circumstances and in addition to the standard data. This is important for the successful identification of an elite performer who not only has what it takes but will withstand the training.

Consequences of Knowing an Athlete's Commitment Portrait

Matching an athlete's commitment portrait with the commitment required for the upcoming task can be very useful.

1. In team sports it leads to . . .
   - Development of a more homogeneous group who will train at a more even level and tempo
   - Reduction of injury by selecting out those team members who will be overstretched by the training regimes
   - Higher team morale and improved team spirit built on a cohesive commitment level, with players who are working within their appropriate commitment group
   - Fewer disgruntled athletes who turn sour when the training load gets tough
2. In individual sports it leads to . . .
   - More appropriately defined competitive goals
   - Lowered rates of athlete wastage/withdrawal
   - Higher levels of athlete comfort in heavy training through better selection of individuals who can withstand such loads
   - Fewer competitive disappointments and frustrations for the athlete
   - Fewer coaching disappointments and frustrations (surely just as relevant to performance as those of the athlete)
   - *Substantial* savings of time, effort, and resources by selecting out undercommitted athletes

Looking back on some of your best and worst selections can be an interesting exercise. With the benefit of 20/20 hindsight see how you could have made different decisions had you applied what you know about commitment portraits. Learning from your mistakes here may be the best thing you ever do if it helps you to reassign athletes to levels of involvement at which they are comfortable and at which they can excel. Such moves decrease the pressure on everyone, or at least only apply it to those you know can handle it.

When all is said and done, this chapter may have been hard work, but in practice you'll find it will repay your effort many times over. Oh, and if you need to just run through it again, now's the time.

Summary

There is a big difference in the everyday life of the sportsperson between commitment and motivation. Neither is necessarily appropriate to our current level of competition. Confusing commitment with motivation leads to, and accounts for, a number of predictable and *preventable* mistakes.

Athlete or coach, we all have a commitment portrait that is made up of our

- participation pattern,
- sport inhibitors (positive and negative),
- dropout factors, and
- sportstyle/lifestyle mix.

There are huge advantages for all of us, in both team and individual sports, in understanding our commitment portraits. This helps us compete at a level appropriate to our commitment resources. Looking at these commitment portraits, we find there are five major groups of sportspeople:

- Recreational players
- Club competitors
- Open competitors
- Championship athletes
- Elite athletes

Separating these groups are four commitment thresholds, which constitute very significant divisions between the different participants. By recognizing the group to which we belong, we can assess our true level of commitment, irrespective of our current competition level. This will tell us whether we have

- already reached our competitive potential,
- are trying to compete beyond our true abilities, or
- have real but undisclosed potential to withstand the rigors of a more demanding level of training and competition.

There's no place left to hide if we want to make it to the winner's circle.

18

Taking Charge of Your Personal Growth

For the superstar (er, that's you), stress is a normal and necessary part of being good at what you do. You like it, you go looking for it, you want it, and you need it in your life. Handling it well is part of your job. You are good at this too. Now don't be shy. This is no time to fade into the wallpaper—just come out in your true colors and confess to the world that you are a phenomenon. It is a considerable mistake to see yourself in any other light or to believe for even a moment that you are anything less. To adopt such a persona is to instantly turn much of the contents of your "too hard basket" into trivia. With one toss of your head, you will cease worrying about a whole fistful of incidentals, which will free up brain space, lower blood pressure, and otherwise helpfully contribute to enjoyable stress levels and other feelings of well-being. You not only have a marvelous body but also a magical brain to go with it. All you need to do now is remember to use it. It's refrigerator time again.

■ Think your way around stress.

We *need* stress, unless we want to be dead! Every living creature experiences stress as a normal, healthy part of everyday living. It is useful to feel hot, cold, hungry, uncomfortable, itchy, sleepy, and a thousand other minor stresses in the course of a day. In fact, if we are kept in too bland an environment that does not stress us enough, we go cuckoo. Stress in the right amounts is essential for a healthy life.

We enjoy stress unless we want to stay in that armchair forever. We do not enjoy being limited in what we do—we talk of being *confined* to bed or to a wheelchair, or of being *restricted* to light exercise—and in fact find such limitations a good deal more stressful than normal healthy movement, with whatever stresses we choose to add to that in the form of wheels, skates, runners, or spikes. If we can't find a satisfactory level of stress in what we're doing, we go looking for ways to induce it. Anyone who has had a broken leg will know that when you can't do the things that normally give you the level of interaction with your environment that you are used to, you start trying to invent new ones. One thing is certain—you won't be staring at the wall just because you can't get down to the gym.

Since stress is our own *individual* response, we can *control* it—unless we believe we can't! We normally regulate our stress levels about as automatically as we regulate our breathing or our body temperature. It's only when we overload our system that symptoms of *dis*tress arise and we have to consciously step in and restore order. To do this, we may use any of many tension management techniques that may include relaxation or meditation techniques to take the levels down or imagery and self-talk to take them up.

That's no more difficult than regulating our eating. If we were to over-eat as a way of life, we would end up becoming obese; if we were to become overstressed as a lifestyle choice, we would end up with high blood pressure and heart disease. We can avoid these unpleasant consequences either one bite at a time or one choice at a time. We can choose to control our exposure to stress and to regulate our response to it before it gets to unmanageable proportions. We can then reasonably expect to live better and somewhat longer lives.

So now we are agreed—stress is a normal, healthy part of life. We see that problems only arise when we become *dis*tressed because we go looking for too much of it, find too much of it, generate too much of it, or control too little of it. Because you are a superstar (well, maybe not quite yet, but you're on your way, aren't you?), you actually *like* stress, and you have a bigger appetite for it and a higher tolerance of it than most of us do. With this in mind, you will therefore make bigger, riskier mistakes. You play for generally higher stakes than the average person and enjoy the company of others with a similar habit. Your willingness to risk bigger mistakes will deliver stunning goodies if all goes right and cataclysmic consequences if all goes wrong. Who needs to go to the amusement park when you have your very own roller-coaster built into your head! Furthermore, it's all free—just enjoy the ride up on the slopes or out on the track. Your only serious decision here is whether to hang off a trapeze or a parachute, to climb the mountain or jump off it. When you're done, you can join Thrill Seekers Anonymous for a quieter way to spend your Saturday afternoon!

The only plausible conclusion to arrive at after all this is that your stress is a matter of *choice*.

You *choose* to feel stressed.

You *choose* how much to be stressed.

You *choose* what to be stressed about.

In short, *you stress yourself!*

Only when you are entirely comfortable with that statement will you be ready to take control of your stress and adopt a proactive approach to stress management. Up until that time you will continue to make stress-related mistakes. Forgive yourself for these and regard them as no more than developmental hiccups. You will deal with them in due course when you are ready, and since no one on the planet can hurry this process, don't listen to anyone who says you—or they—can because they'll just add to your stress. A calm recognition of the fact that you always were—and very much still are—in the driver's seat of your life is ultimately what will give you the confidence to steer a smoother course.

Relaxation Versus the Rest

Sometimes you just need to turn down the heat a bit from thrill mark 4 to thrill mark 3. You don't want to relax into a lull, but you do want to shed excess muscle tension to organize your upcoming thrills more efficiently. It's a matter of choice, too, which tool you pull out of your toolbox to do this, whether its progressive relaxation, meditation, physical exercise, or a half a day at the beach. Whatever works for you! When you feel your stress levels are restored to normal (whatever "normal" is for you), then go drive another racing car or climb another mountain. If you're working on a shorter time cycle and need to make these sorts of adjustments when it's not convenient to actually take time out (perhaps between events or just before a major performance), you may have to get good at letting your mind slip into neutral on its way into overdrive, being superfocused before you get too stressed, or maybe just imagining that beach. It is a mistake to ignore these skills, for they will be valuable additions to your toolbox and will help to keep your competition machinery in top running order. Don't let excessive stress spoil your fun.

Flotation Tanks

Sometimes a nice little tool simply won't do the job. We need a big heavy-duty wrench! That's where flotation tanks come into play. You can use them just as they come from the factory, or you can customize your floating by adding your own music or video. Sometimes a float is just what the doctor ordered immediately after training, while at other times you'll want to go with the sport psychologist's idea to float before a massage. Find your own line here; it's just a matter of which regime works the best for you.

Floating can certainly give you a glorious respite from the superstress of competition, but it's not for everybody. The environment is deceptively aggressive, and with the sure touch of a practiced thief it robs you of all your ifs and buts and gets straight down to the business of disinheriting you from the outside world. If you're anything of a control freak, you may find it uncomfortable to be disenfranchised in this way. You might just need to jump off a slightly smaller cliff instead.

Body Scans

If you need a more portable alternative to floating, try doing a body scan. Imagine the sweep of the arm across a radar screen, picking up as it goes on any object within its field; that's exactly what a body scan does. Mentally scan your body for hot spots of tension (knotted muscles, locked joints, clenched fingers, scrunched toes), and you'll be quite amazed at what you find. One shoulder will be tight, one hip will be higher than the other, your tongue will be in a knot—all of these are manifestations of tension. That's not the problem. The problem is that you didn't know about it. Of course, that's not a worry unless you need to use that part of your body. If it's otherwise occupied being very tense, then you're not going to get a sensible answer from it if you start asking tricky questions. Scanning to find these spots will give you the option of releasing them, cooling them, or otherwise rearranging them in such a way as to bring them back into the workplace. If you find it easier to imagine one of those wands used to frisk people at airports, then it is the same idea with different scenery.

Mind Scans

You can do exactly the same with your mind. Following a mistake you can scan your mind to see what you were thinking about, where your focus was, how your energy was organized, what emotion you were experiencing, and so on, and then decide whether you were in the right space for the job. If you caught yourself thinking about what you had for dinner last night or discover you're wired up to run for the nationals, then clearly neither of these would be helpful for learning a new technique in training. It's a case of right time, right place for the job at hand. Doing the mind scan will bring you back to where you need to be and help you shed distractions and refocus. Anyway, don't miss out on the fun.

Wall Charts and Worry Beads

A more pragmatic approach to defending your comfort zone at times of potential *di*stress is to plan your way out of trouble. With only a small amount of luck such planning will ensure that you don't get in too much trouble in the first place. Your choice of wall chart is entirely up to you, as is the color of your worry beads. If you need five wall charts and three different sets of worry beads, that's OK too.

Typical mistakes to avoid are . . .

- Using your planner as a social diary
- Not planning beyond breakfast
- Leaving your worry beads at home
- Failing to ignore any local comment (especially from the opposition)
- Taking any free-floating derision personally

Essential Alternatives

Always have a plan B and a spare set of worry beads. Building in alternative courses of action will impart a maturity to your plans from which you will benefit substantially. Even if you don't ever have to use your plan B, at least you know it's there. Imagine the top 10 tennis pros staggering onto the court under the accumulated weight of a whole *bagful* of plan Bs (What if this string breaks . . . or that one's too slack?) Cover all bases if you want rock-solid peace of mind. Never mind wishing for a caddy; manage without one and buy a bigger bag instead. Meanwhile, do not be talked into, or out of, using whatever works best for you, and on no account *ever* lend your caddy, bag, or worry beads to anybody else.

Moving From the Bad to the Beautiful

There is no way you're going to be out on your own through all this up-stressing or down-stressing or destressing or restressing. Sooner rather than later you're going to have to communicate with folks around you, and here lies a world just waiting for you to misread, mis-say or mis-hear! How many times have you gotten your wires crossed in the most innocent of conversations at times of ease and entertainment? So how huge is the potential to get them into a monumental tangle as the heat is turned up on your sporting effort?

Apart from making you slow, clumsy, and uncharacteristically stupid, one of the things excess stress does is compromise your ability to listen. Maybe you're just too busy, preoccupied with your world at the expense of sorting out incoming information. For whatever reason, we've all made a fistful of these kinds of mistakes.

Imagine it is a bright and sunny day. Competition day. You are discussing with your coach how and why you made a mess of your first event.

"I know you believe you understand what you think I said, but I'm not sure you realize that what you heard is not what I meant," you say, to which your coach's obvious reply is, *"If you think you know you heard me say what you thought I meant, then how come I don't think you realize I believe you didn't understand?"*

It's easy to see—or hear—how these problems can escalate until effective communication is successfully scrambled at both ends. The solution is not where you might suppose (in the communication) but is squatting neatly in the shadow of your stress! It is to this solution that we now turn.

The first thing to do is to set some ground rules. You need to decide just how far outside your comfort zone you really are. This can be a reassuring process because often you find you're only *slightly* beyond the pale; although it may feel terminal, it is really quite a temporary state of affairs. You now have an ever-increasing arsenal with which to address the situation, and although you may still be on an alpine incline instead of your normal learning curve, you do have significant skills to bring to bear.

Should you have any problems knowing where to start in all this, try to take them in your stride. Naturally, you are in a muddle, so naturally you start in the middle of your muddle. There is no "right" place to start other than wherever you find yourself. *Finding* yourself is the important part. Once you've done that, setting yourself on a new course is a stroll down Easy Street.

The next thing to do is to revise your plans to be stressed. Plan to be magnificently and *normally* stressed. Equally, plan to surmount your stress with ease. Feel successful about this (which is a *normal* and positive state, and one to which you are accustomed). Incorporate this self-management into your usual training and competition routines. Once you can *normalize* the situation, your performance will be securely on track again, and you will be firmly back in control of your day.

The last thing to do is to package up all that excess stress and conduct a brief ceremony to bury it either under several tons of concrete or out at sea. It is a mistake to delay these proceedings since you need to engineer a sense of closure on the issue and to enjoy the wake, which should begin immediately. Now you can get on with the rest of your sport.

Managing the Reluctant Hero

It would be nice to think that from here on out you're not going to get stressed any more, but we already know differently. Take a reality check. When was the last time you felt *really seriously challenged*? If you can't remember, then clearly you're cruising and possibly seriously underextended. If an incident springs immediately to mind, then obviously all nerves are alive and well and your stress response is on a hair trigger. Thought so . . . you need a *plan*.

Here is where we introduce the Rule of the Three Ps. This will become your blueprint for self-management. You can adapt it any way you like to suit your individual style. The three Ps are:

- Plan to succeed
- Prepare to excel
- Perform to win

Let's take a closer look.

Plan to Succeed

This is a training exercise and it belongs in your day-to-day work-up to competition. Start by drawing up an inventory of the particular skills you'll need to have up and running to manage yourself successfully. Then make sure these skills will all be operational on your competition day. Needless to say, if they don't have legs by then, they're not going to sprout them on the way to the venue! We'll take these skills one at a time.

Goal Setting

Goal setting is here to stay. Revisit, revise, review, and revamp your goals if you haven't already done so in response to chapter 5. If you haven't read it, that's disappointing, but not as devastating as if you did and have since carried on as usual. But you know all this stuff. Your goals are your responsibility, end of story. No need to fry in your own juice if you haven't done anything about them. Is there?

Time Management

You can over- or underplan and the results come out about the same. It's as if you'd done no planning at all. The same goes for your time management. Squash too much in and you feel like a sardine in an overcrowded can; leave too much out and suddenly you're alone on a desert island. Superstar that you are, you nonetheless have only and precisely the *same* amount of time in each day as lesser mortals. It's up to you to put it to the best use. That means maximizing the positive and useful time and engaging it to your advantage, and minimizing the wasted or poor-return time. It's the *quality time* that counts.

Here's how to begin a rewrite of your time management skills. With your planner in one hand and your worry beads in the other, write down the nuts and bolts of your life. You'll probably include . . .

Training time   Travel time
Time out   Work (?)
Rest   Study time (?)
Family time (?)   Recreation
Sleep

The easiest way to make this list is to go back over your diary for the last week or two and categorize how you spent your time. If you don't have a diary, fix that today. It will soon get to be like wearing a watch; you'll wonder how on earth you managed without it! Once you've

■   Champions match their time to their goals.

sorted out the various activities that make up your life, take a look at how long you spend doing each one. Then decide if you like what you see or whether you'd like to change it. Perhaps you could spend more time training and less time eating. Or maybe if you studied harder you could finish sooner. Look at the pockets of "dead" time in your day, such as waiting for a bus, and see if you can find small activities to fill them, such as drawing up a list or practicing a body scan.

Quite often we experience an odd sort of time warp. For busy people, time seems to hurry by at a fearful rate, with never enough of it to do all there is to be done. For unbusy people, time hangs in the air like a bad smell. This time warp must be in our heads because if you look at the clock (or your new watch), you'll see that exactly the same amount of time has gone by for you as for the rest of us. Do not be disconcerted by this. It is a common occurrence. You can also make all sorts of more unfortunate adjustments to your sense of time. How about that dropped catch, the missed shot, or the short pass—perhaps one you've practiced a thousand times, only to be too early or too late when it mattered most. What about when your hand–eye coordination gets out of sync and you can't seem to be able to do anything about it? Then there's your reaction time: Just when you want to be razor sharp, your body takes a nap. What a litany of ills! And the trick is . . .? Get a grip. What you need are some training strategies to turn all this around.

Strategies

With a little thought we can *all* improve the way we organize our day, and the results are free. Many people say if you want something done, ask a busy person. You'd be better off asking an *organized* person. So see what you can do to better arrange your life.

A simple, more useful tool to help you organize your day is a sheet of paper divided into four quadrants headed *Urgent*, *Important*, *Chores*, and *Still to Do*. First decide which items should be in the Urgent quadrant; this is anything that absolutely *must* be done today. Separate these items from the Important ones, which still need to be done today but can wait until you've done the Urgent ones. Then there are the Chores, which have to be done if your life is to run smoothly, so they also need to be factored in. The Still to Do items, which are last on your list for today, must either move up into the Important quadrant tomorrow or get scrapped as unnecessary.

It is also essential to have a *Too Hard Basket*. That gives you somewhere to put things that are possibly, or definitely, too difficult to do in the foreseeable future. It includes any task about which you need more information or resources before you can complete it and any task that has somehow fallen in your lap but actually belongs to someone else (such as your tax return, which belongs to your accountant). This is a good foil against procrastination and other evils arising from not knowing what to do next.

You will need to empty the Too Hard Basket at least weekly. Anything that does not fit into the four categories or the Too Hard Basket is nonessential to your newly streamlined life. Put it in the trash can. This means crossing it off all future lists and refusing to think anymore about it.

Self-Talk

Check on your chatter. Take another check during and after a crisis. Do not manufacture a crisis for this purpose. You will need a genuine pothole in which to flounder if you are to get a representative sample of what the little voice in your head has to say about it—not only the words but also your self-healing skills. How kind and understanding are you? Do you have valid reasons for your demise, or are they imaginative excuses? How do you help yourself? Do you create options? Do you beat yourself up? Only you will ever know.

Sometimes the little voice in your head could use a little discipline. Unless you set some ground rules, it will chatter away day after day and often night after night, causing you to toss and turn into the small hours.

Sharing your headspace with someone else can inevitably make you feel crowded. The first thing to do is put in some dividing walls. Decide when you are to get airtime and when the Little Voice can have its say. It's really that easy. Don't be discouraged or dissuaded when the Little Voice protests (as it surely will). Just be firm with it. Decide that . . .

- You will listen to the Little Voice only when it is in positive mode.
- You will listen *only* at appointed times.
- You will listen *only* for a given length of time.
- You will identify the issue(s) you need to address.
- You will do *whatever is necessary* to shut the Little Voice up when in negative mode!

As a result of doing these things, you can then make a plan. Remember that a conversation with the Little Voice when it's in negative mode is always one-sided and that the Little Voice doesn't even talk *to* you; it talks *at* you, or even *past* you. There is absolutely no chance to talk to *it* because there's no right of reply here. If you try, the Little Voice just doesn't listen! So what are you to do? Let's eavesdrop on a typical conversation with the Little Voice in negative mode.

> **Little Voice (LV):** I don't think I'm going to be fit enough for the next competition.
>
> **You:** It's 6 weeks away!
>
> **LV:** That's . . . um . . . 6 times 7, er . . . 42. . . *42 days!* There's no way I can be ready in *42 days!*
>
> **You:** Should I pull out now?
>
> **LV:** Cathy Freebody will wipe the track with me.
>
> **You:** But—
>
> **LV:** . . . and Mom's coming! It's a *disASter!*

And so it goes on and on and *on!* Until you *do* something about it, the Little Voice will chatter away every single moment it can elbow its way into your mind, waking or sleeping, invited or otherwise, busily intent on making your life a misery until that disaster really does happen. You have plenty of choices here, including:

1. Get someone else's opinion on your fitness; talk it over with your coach.
2. Reassess your training program; reorganize it to squeeze more out of your body than you currently are.
3. Withdraw from the competition.
4. Reschedule and enter a different competition.
5. Do nothing and keep worrying.
6. Send Mom on vacation.

You can probably add to this list.

It is important to consider these options. Just knowing they are there will go quite a long way to changing the tone of the Little Voice. You'll also want to find out who its conspirators are. Who else does the Little Voice talk to? Is Mom in on it too? What is the tone of voice—kind, sarcastic, angry, patronizing? What is the language like? Is it curt, kind, or abusive? Are you being beaten up? What does the Little Voice actually say?

At the end of a session with the Little Voice, are you enlivened and encouraged or miserable and demoralized? Have you solved a problem or merely chewed over one you've munched on a hundred times before? Have you moved forward or just gone around in a circle to arrive at the point where the chat began? It's all very disconcerting, isn't it? But do try to get a handle on the Little Voice's agenda because only when you've done that will you be able to tell later whether you've nailed it to the wall.

When you've found out who the Little Voice talks to, the next job is to find out who it's quoting. Is it someone you know, with a name and a face, or is it a vague figure who hangs off the sidelines, someone with whom you are forever shadowboxing and who won't own up to his opinions and differences with you? And what does *he* say? Perhaps there are several of them, like a bad choir on a bad day! Call their bluff. If they won't own up to a name, give them one. Call them anything you like, but make them real, kickable, hitable, strikeable, *shrinkable, very destroyable icons.* Then imagine Little Voice lives in a box. The box is plugged into your brain. Now just unplug it! You will immediately feel better. You will immediately *be* better. You will suddenly find yourself very much more in control, which will altogether enhance your sense of fun. Remind yourself that having serious fun is what this is all about.

Energy Management

How well do you muster your energy and use it for what you really need it for? Do you create enough of it, or having done so, do you waste it on unnecessary things such as getting angry? Of course we're not just talking physical energy here. We're talking mental and emotional energy too. The whole man. The whole woman. The full picture. This includes, of course, management of your tension levels to match the job at hand, because maintaining excessive tension levels drains energy from more useful projects. There's nothing more challenging than managing yourself, but there's nothing more rewarding than doing it well.

Mind Maps for the Very Lost

Tip of the week: If you write it down, it's one less thing to think about. This is a simple and effective way to raise your energy levels. To do this, just keep a notebook in the car, keep lists beside your pillow, or swing a walkman off your hip. When you don't know what to do, write it down. When you don't want to forget it, write it down. When you can't think how to fix it, or you've quietly lost the plot, panic if you must, *but write it down.*

It's astonishing how different things look on paper. It's amazing how they read an hour later. Creating your very own flow chart or mapping out your ideas if only to see where the gaps are will quickly and painlessly release hours' worth of emotional energy that you had been using to try to remember all the things you didn't want to forget. You will soon find your way through what appeared before to be a tangle of ideas and information that was catching on your clothing and scratching through your reserves of patience and good humor. Getting a route mapped out that takes you around these hazards will prove to be a lot more comfortable and make for much more energy-efficient traveling.

Concentration

By now your concentration skills are probably in the top 3% of the population. There is little need to do anything more than a running maintenance check on them to see that all is well. This will include a few centering exercises, moving from one type of attentional focus to another, and checking your ability to hold any one focus for a designated length of time. It's unlikely you will make many mistakes here for these are now much-used skills that are very much a part of your daily training. (Am I right?)

Body Awareness

Here's a surprise! All of a sudden we're back into bodies again, as if they haven't caused us enough hassles! The reason for this is that the best person on the planet to tell you what your brain's deepest and darkest secrets are is your body. No other body knows your brain better, for somehow the two seem to be wired up in a way that defies even the best explanations. But like a good marriage—or even a bad one—nobody else has to understand it; they just have to respect it. So have a chat with your bod' and check that it feels as good as you think it should. If its stomach is sore, or its back aches, then ask it what it doesn't like doing or what it's worrying about. Get to know yourself. There's no one better placed than you to do that. And nobody who'll benefit more.

Prepare to Excel

Engrave this one on your soul: *Preparation is the hallmark of professionalism.* Like it or not, that's the name of today's game. You need to map your strategies out with care, and plenty of attitude! We can usefully borrow from the business world again here and use the SWOT analysis. SWOT stands for . . .

Strengths

Weaknesses

Opportunities

Threats

Just ask yourself:

- What are your *strengths* and how will you best use them?
- What are your *weaknesses*, and how will you defend yourself against or overcome them?
- What *opportunities* can you create for success?
- What, or who, are the main *threats* to your success?

You might then like to do the same thing from the point of view of your opposition, asking . . .

- What are their *strengths* and *weaknesses* (and how can you play them to your advantage)?
- What *opportunities* do they offer that could further your success?
- What *threats* do they pose to your success?

When you've answered these questions, you will have the foundations of your game plan. As a member of a team you will, of course, do this as a team exercise. But that's only the beginning. What about those lists of all the small-but-essential things? What about the maps and timetables that need your attention to sort out the logistics of it all? Are you training for *every* element of the competition (the heat/cold, altitude, distance, skill level, ground surface, etc.)? Suddenly the task seems bigger than you expected. Hang in there and get busy. Hone your technical skills, your physical fitness, your mental skills, your emotional control, *and your mistakes management.*

Tactics

Tactics are *how* you propose to make these strategies happen. Just decide now what you have to *do*. Take care not to get lost in the details because in the heat of the competition you won't be able to remember convoluted, overplanned proposals.

■ Motto: Keep it simple.

Perform to Win!

This is the last of the three Ps. All that's left is for you to do is put your plan into action. Follow your strategies, use your tactics, and get out there and *win!* And you're going to do even better than that—privately or publicly *you're going to win the way you want to.*

Stay away from outcome-based goals. Keep your multiple *process-based* goals in your sights, have a simple, effective plan B, and smooth out any ruffles in your routines. You're ready now. Add a little attitude and go grapple with the best.

Coaches' Corner

We've spent a lot of time in the athlete's camp during the last chapter or two, so now it's your turn. Not many people consider the coach when it comes to stress. But you only have to watch a bit of TV footage to see you all out there chewing your fingernails down to the elbow, one loss away from a coronary, and your job and your life on the line. Of *course* you get stressed, because the results matter just as much to you as they do to the athletes. Otherwise you wouldn't be coaching them in the first place! The best thing to do here is to recognize that you are nervous and then do one of two things. Either fix it—or stay away from your athletes. There's no middle ground here. Nothing guarantees the demise of an athlete like the sight of a wobbly coach. So get into your own head and fix your own programming before you go meddling with anybody else's.

Having done that, you can help a wobbly athlete in a number of ways. First, find out to what extent his brain has seized, or whether it is still at least partially functional.

Underdone Competitors

Underdone competitors are the ones who are too flat for their competition. They are so laid back, they'd look good on a beach. This can be the result of . . .

- Having a laid-back temperament
- Being insufficiently challenged by the opposition or the competition
- Making assumptions of winning
- Being insufficiently engaged with the competition
- Having too casual an attitude about preparation
- Being excessively stressed

It's a bit late for deciding which of these is the cause of the trouble, but you'd better do so in a hurry if you hope to salvage the competition because it's not something the athlete is likely to do. You need to rev her up, put some high-octane fuel in her tank, and send her roaring out of the pits, firing on all eight cylinders. If you don't do this, it's an absolute given that her performance will never get off the ground. We sometimes hear of this in the early rounds of a tournament, when a highly seeded player loses "for no reason" to an unknown, unseeded opponent. There was a very good reason, but the mistake here was in not recognizing what was happening before the tournament ever started. It was a coaching mistake. All yours. Better athlete management will ensure that it doesn't happen next time.

Overcooked Competitors

Overcooked competitors are the ones the competition has gotten away from. They need a calm, firm hand on the tiller to help them steady their ship. Since some of them won't even let you on board by this stage, getting anywhere near the bridge can be a bit of a challenge. This is where you need to proceed very much at the athlete's pace and resist the temptations to either take control or overcoach. The first of these is particularly important because one of the athlete's principal concerns right now is that he is experiencing a lack of control. To sweep in and assume command will therefore solve nothing for them. *He* is the one who needs to take control. Your job is to work out how to give it to him.

Overcoaching doesn't help either. Right now, the athlete does not have the brain space to follow instructions or evaluate feedback; neither does he have the wherewithal to try. Anyway, if he hasn't cemented the skills in training, now is no time to do so. Recognize here that this athlete is already extremely busy. He is busy at a whole lot of inappropriate, unproductive activities, but nonetheless busy! To reduce his stress levels, you have to offer him less busy options, simpler ideas, *one* thing at a time to think about.

Overcooked athletes are also lost. They have so much going on in their heads that they often don't know what to think about now, or next. They have lost their way through all the glitz and hype of the competition, like a small kid in the crowd. They need to be told where to go and how to get there one step at a time. This often means reminding them of *their* goals and helping them to refocus on a simple, practical, technical aspect of the performance that they know will help them to achieve those goals. If you're not too immediately close to the performance, you may get the chance to take time out together and walk them through some self-management. Anything that helps them get their breathing or pulse rates lower, helps them center or ground themselves, slows the whole show down, or helps to make them feel less scattered and more in control will be useful. See, *you* really don't have time to get nervous, do you?

Contingency Plans

While athletes will certainly have a plan B, it's really not reasonable to expect them to also carry plans C, D, and E out there onto the field of battle. Back at base camp, high command, or whatever else you care to christen the nerve center of your operations, it's got to be another story. You need to have other plans, arranged in descending order, and you need to know when to use them. In sports in which contact with the coach is prohibited during the competition, clearly this is not a viable strategy, but if you have access to the players, obviously you'll have the opportunity to have input. Knowing when to smoothly adopt a different plan of attack or change the pace of a game, or how to throw your opponent's game off the rails, are not things that are always so easily visible to the players. You get a quite different view of them from the sidelines, and it's the smart coach who takes advantage of that perspective and learns how to use it well.

The Endless Importance of Fun

There's been a lot of serious head-scratching here. Should you feel at risk of developing a little brain-ache, now is the time to remind yourself, and if necessary your athlete too, that once upon a time we did this all for fun. If the fun isn't still around, it's time to lighten up. Only you know what works best here, whether to go find yourself some serious fun by fixing the problems and sorting out the mistakes until the joy of the performance is restored, or to take a break and distract yourself from it all with some frivolous fun. Either way, there's only one watchword . . . *Enjoy.*

Bear in mind also that it takes two to communicate, and although it's a hard call to smarten up your communication skills when you're probably feeling almost as stressed as your athletes, see what you can do. This is a time to celebrate having a little more life experience, not to mention a few gray hairs, and to draw on your maturity and ability to maintain your equilibrium.

Maybe you might have said, *"I realize you believe you've understood what you think I've said, but I hope you don't think that what I meant might not have been quite what you thought you heard"*? Wise words in anyone's language!

Summary

If you aren't a superstar now, then you certainly will be later—so by definition the following statements are true:

- You need stress.
- You enjoy stress.
- You look for stress.
- You can control stress.

It is important to take responsibility for the fact that

- you choose to be stressed,
- you choose how much to be stressed, and
- you choose what to be stressed about.

In short, *you stress yourself.* Relaxation is useful on the beach; regulating your energy is more useful in competition.

- Flotation tanks are not for the fainthearted.
- Body scans are mind-blowing.
- Mind scans are body-building.
- Worry beads are essential.

To develop formidable coping skills . . .

- Decide what you're going to get stressed about and bury the rest.
- Plan to be magnificently, successfully, and *appropriately* stressed.
- Develop your time management until it is an art form. It's quality time that counts.

The best antidote to becoming an overstressed sportsperson is to use the Rule of the Three Ps:

1. Plan to succeed. This includes

   - goal setting,
   - time management,
   - self-talk,
   - self-management,
   - concentration,
   - mistakes management, and
   - body awareness.

2. Prepare to excel. This includes

   - competition strategies,
   - competition tactics, and
   - logistics.

3. Perform to win. This includes

   - winning the way you want to.

19

Exploring Your Confidence

What exactly *is* confidence? Take your time, now . . . relax . . . focus. Wrap your head around this one because *nothing* is more fundamental to your success than getting the right answer to this question. Make a mistake here and you will consign yourself to mediocrity for the rest of time. Scary? Yes. Difficult? No, but if you'd like a little help, read on.

Everyone knows that confidence is vital. Everyone knows that you can't succeed in sport or much else without it. Everyone knows it's something you have, or get, as a result of being successful, but how do you get it in the beginning when you need it the most, and *before* you get buoyed up by success? You establish it, build it, find it, lose it. It's here today and gone tomorrow with not so much as a how or a why, and it can change within the day, grow or lapse within the hour, and save or sabotage your greatest moments. Sometimes there are warning signs that it's on the wane; at other times it evaporates as furtively as the morning mist, or just deserts you with all the speed of a departing rocket. So how do you get a handle on this confidence thing?

Perhaps it's time to revisit our definition of success (see chapter 4). Not only is confidence necessary for success, but also success is the foundation of all your confidence. If you make a mistake here, it will be a biggie. Building anything on shaky foundations is a recipe for disaster in most walks of life, and success is no exception. If you misunderstand success, or worse still, refuse to let go of unrealistic ideas of it, you stand to undermine all your efforts to become confident, and therefore to become successful.

The first thing to do is to define success in your own terms. It doesn't matter now, and it never will matter, how anyone else chooses to measure it, so long as you have your own yardstick that is related to your own capabilities.

Decide what success means *to you.*

Set goals *you* can reach.

Reward *yourself* when you achieve them.

You'll find that your confidence grows daily when you live the life of an achiever. Not only do you reach an ever-growing number of your goals, but *you also begin to expect to reach them.* Those expectations are the seeds of your confidence, and carefully nurtured, they will grow and flourish. As your performances meet your expectations, so you begin to *believe* that you are going to meet them. Then you progress to *knowing* you will meet them. This is confidence. Not wishing, hoping, or dreaming, not even expecting or believing, but *knowing* you will succeed.

Confidence is a pact you make with yourself to believe that your life will happen in a particular way. Confidence is an undertaking to see the world in a particular light—one that shines in a special way on things you want to happen. It is also an intensely private, personal, *intimate* commodity. No one else on the planet can ever know how your confidence behaves. Appearances are often deceptive, and although others might think they can read your behavioral signposts, they may often misinterpret them. Anyway, nobody else will ever know how it *feels.* Sometimes we deliberately disguise or hide uncomfortable feelings from others and sometimes from ourselves. Even if you could explain how your confidence works, the only performance it's ever going to influence is yours. Therefore the only person who ever needs to make sure you have the right amount of the right kind of confidence behind a performance is you. And, the only person in the world who can choose to influence, change, adjust, or reinvent your confidence is you. How's that for putting the responsibility for your confidence in *your* ballpark.

The next thing to understand about confidence is that it's always plural. Confidence is an umbrella term for lots of different confidences, in lots of different things. The following are the principal things in which you're going to need confidence:

Yourself	Your skills
Your sport	Your coach
Your teammates	Your gear
The competition	The officials

Other factors especially relevant to you (e.g., significant others)

Some things only you know about (e.g., old injuries, bad experiences, etc.)

So now we're going to think in terms of *confidences*—plural! This is a very good idea. From now on, if you lose confidence, you can think in terms of only losing one of them. That means you still have all the rest of them. That makes it much easier to rebuild or relocate the part that's damaged, missing, or temporarily mislaid. Also, it means you can feel *permanently* a whole lot more secure because you know that you always have most of your confidence intact most of the time. You never have to fear losing your confidence lock, stock, and barrel again! Your worst-case scenario will only ever be misplacing some of it some of the time.

The more securely your knowledge of these things is grounded in reality, the more rock-solid your resulting confidence will be. Information is the key to your confidence. Once you have accurate, up-to-date information on any one of these factors, you can draw realistic conclusions on where each one is. You will then know what realistic, achievable goals to set. This is positioning yourself to experience success. Of course, you can choose to ignore all this and set yourself up for failure. Some people do. Watch out because these choices can become a habit.

Now you know that the only thing keeping you from being the proud owner of the most marvelous, shining confidence in the world is information. Gathering that information is not difficult or even particularly time consuming. Start now. Get to know yourself and your world better than you have ever done before. You can never have too much information on anything pertinent to your performance. Develop a monstrous appetite for it.

Overconfidence

Overconfidence is not very useful because it inevitably ends in disappointment. It is characterized by skill blindness, in which athletes perceive no gap between their actual skill level and the real skills needed for success in the sport. Such players are very hard to coach since they genuinely believe they already have all the skills they need to get where they want to go. Even a video session often fails to convince them otherwise. It's a case of "love is blind," and in this case they love themselves.

When is confidence not confidence?
When it's bravado.

Overconfidence is also often accompanied by a disregard for risk, which is in fact genuine since the athlete's view of reality is so skewed that he really can't accurately perceive risks. In some sports this can be dangerous. Don't ever go diving, for example, with an overconfident scuba buff.

Underconfidence

Underconfidence tells the world you haven't done your homework. You haven't revised your mind-set, you haven't started your quest for success, you haven't done a reality check, you haven't reset your goals. Why go public with your procrastination? Get busy instead!

Adjust your goals, fine-tune your deadlines, and go out to bat! If your goals are appropriate, *you will achieve them.* It follows that if you're not achieving them, they are not appropriate. They may be good, they may be exciting, they may be the stuff stars are made of, but as your life is clearly demonstrating to you, they are not right for you right now. So change them, and keep changing them until you *are* achieving them. This may mean rerouting them, revising them, lowering them (temporarily), or otherwise adjusting them to better suit whoever you happen to be right now. Goals need to be so current that sometimes those you had at breakfast look out-of-date by lunchtime. These are good goals. They are realistic, achievable, and without being too bendable, flexible enough to be suited to you right now. But you'll need no convincing once you've met your first few targets because you'll actually physically *feel* your confidence growing. Quite out of the blue you'll want to smile. Quite unexpectedly you'll want to run rather than walk. Others will begin to notice too until soon there'll be no holding you back at all.

The Promise of Potential

To be successful, you must be confident in a number of different things, *but it is not necessary to be confident in everything.* So choose what you would like to be confident in and decide right now to enjoy that idea and to stick with it. Choose what you're sure you can be confident in—right now. Choose to stand up and be counted.

Successful sportspeople are strikingly confident in two things:

- The *potential of their sport* to give them satisfaction
- Their own *personal potential* to realize this satisfaction

Potential of the Sport

Successful sportspeople don't just hope that hitting an ace will feel good; *they know it will feel fantastic.* But is the buzz from kicking a good goal the same as that from winning a marathon? That depends on the athlete. Some athletes enlist a dozen strong men to help them feel that sense of satisfaction, while others trudge 26 miles to find it.

This is where confidence starts to get mixed in with motivation. Some experts say that sport gives us confidence, which helps our motivation grow. Yes, but *which* sport, and *what sort* of confidence? Anyway, such thinking is backwards because motivation is all about setting goals and confidence is all about achieving them! If you're half as confused as the established world seems to be on this one, then let's try to make things a lot simpler.

Let's agree that only your particular sport is going to deliver what for you are satisfactory feelings of success. Of the vast number of sports out there, it is up to you to choose one (or however many) that suits you. Do not make the mistake of thinking that just because you're doing it, you must be in the right sport. There's an outside possibility that it wasn't your idea in the first place.

Example

If you are a table tennis player, how often is ski jumping going to soothe your soul? It's horses for courses and risks, games, and gambles for each of us out there. If your sport is not delivering what you want from it, then find another one that does.

To each his own, so the place to start is with a sport you are absolutely 110% *sure* will at the end of every sporting day have delivered whatever you need to feel satisfied. This will be your own very individual mix of physical effort, intellectual challenge, technical complexity, emotional challenge, risk, and social interaction. The bottom line is that it makes you happy.

Personal Potential

The second thing in which successful sportspeople are very confident is their own potential to make it happen. They don't just think it would be nice—they are absolutely drop-dead *certain* that they can or will be able to do it to their own satisfaction. This belief in themselves seems to be as much a part of them as the nose on their face and doesn't necessarily relate at all to any particular level of achievement or to their current level of achievement. Do not mistake this for arrogance. It does not have the foolhardiness that goes with an arrogant performance. What it does have is the *surety*. So join the stars of your universe and choose to be as successful as they are. Know that in your own way you can make your life happen. Learn to be confident in your sport, and in yourself, by looking in the right place for the right goals and then achieving them every day.

Self-Confidence

What are the other pieces of the confidence jigsaw? Well, we hear a lot about self-confidence, which is usually taken to be a heady mix of self-worth and social poise. Our degree of self-confidence undoubtedly contributes greatly to how others see us and is fundamental to the images we portray of ourselves. We all know the young man full of bravado—10 feet tall and bulletproof and bluff all the way to the middle when it comes to actually trying out for the team. What happened to *his* self-confidence? Perhaps he has yet to discover that there's an important difference between being confident in ourselves as people and being confident to perform a particular task.

Don't go looking for self-confidence to give yourself a boost because it is not something you will ever find. It is something that rises up like a flower that blooms on a healthy, vigorous plant. Go looking for that plant in the right place, at the right time, and sure enough that plant will be in flower. It's like that with self-confidence. It's only once you've put everything else together and all the small confidences are happening that your self-confidence will bloom. It's a natural result. But having started at the end of the confidence story, let's take a look at the beginning. This is where we learn about a few other aspects of this thing called living, which impacts so dramatically on our sporting lives.

Self-Efficacy

Self-efficacy . . . what's that! Well, it's just another kind of confidence. Self-efficacy is confidence in your ability to achieve. It's how sure, or otherwise, you are that you can actually *do* something. A high sense of self-efficacy means that you are sure of your skills, whether they be racing down the fast lane of the local swimming pool or playing host to the media after your best-ever win. The higher that sense is, the more you feel in control of your own destiny. This imparts an air of authority to you that is difficult to define but instantly recognizable by those around you. It will open doors faster than the best set of keys in town. Enjoying a sense of self-efficacy is like nothing else. It's not just about being captain of your ship—it's about being 110% sure you have the skills to sail her. If you still have doubts, ask the man on the Harley how he'd feel astride a horse.

Self-Belief

Self-belief is the hallmark of all successful people no matter what their particular claim to fame may be. From the very start they have an unswerving belief in themselves. This is also not to be confused with arrogance. It's just an unshakable that's-the-way-the-world-is state of *knowing*. Somehow there's just no other point of view to have. When you believe something as utterly as this one, there's no plan B. Whatever the rest of the world thinks, whoever says it can't happen, and whatever obstacles lie in your path, it just doesn't occur to you to change course. That's being your own best fan. That's self-belief.

Confidence in Your Skills

If you're to make a success of your sporting life, you need to be confident in many other things. One of the most important is your skill base. There's nothing quite like the confidence that comes from knowing you've done the practice and the laps and the circuits, and that you're the best you can be *at that moment*. Such a feeling doesn't care where you'll be next week or next year, but it does reassure you that right now you've done all your homework and jumped through all the hoops you could reasonably have been expected to go through to get where you are. Security is the next best thing to eternity! Security in your skill base—knowing that your skills won't let you down when you call on them—is the next best thing to creating your own little heaven.

Social Confidence

Social confidence has to do with how confidently you address social situations and interactions with others. If your skills here are a bit wobbly, then all you need to know is that these too can be learned, practiced, and perfected. Social confidence is very much a part of your successful sporting life because *people* are a part of your sporting life. It's quite simple. Becoming a good team player and a good competitor is all part of the show. So let's get the curtain up on a bit of the action!

Competition Confidence

A rather different type of social confidence that generally comes a little later in the story is competition confidence. We usually refer to those who have developed this quality as "seasoned" competitors. It certainly takes a bit of exposure and several successful forays for most of us before we get used to the sense of occasion that surrounds the competition scene, but this is another foundation stone of our successful career. Performing under the gaze of a thousand eyes will tax even the most weathered veteran if the occasion is big enough. Don't forget that we all started out feeling nervous and overawed once upon a time. Skill in planning successful competition campaigns is vital to developing competition confidence, and carefully orchestrated programs against appropriate competitors gradually facilitate your progress into the upper echelons of your sport. Mistakes here will make big dents in your confidence. Only careful, sequential training and progressively more challenging competition outings will help you avoid such pitfalls.

Confidence in Your Gear

A somewhat overlooked aspect of confidence is confidence in your gear. Many sports have highly specialized gear that has been developed to optimize and enhance performance skills. The only problem is that your performance then becomes dependent on the sophistication of your gear. Consequently, you have to learn to trust it. That trust may be put in the strength of a trapeze or the technology of a racing tire.

Anyone who has watched a high-performance sportsperson prepare for a match, game, run, or performance of any kind will witness the respect accorded to the gear. The fastidious checking of straps, goggles, helmets, gloves, and every conceivable kind of clothing is amazing to watch. In many sports the reliance on it is total. In some, it is critical to survival.

Perhaps living in such a relatively safe environment, we have become used to controlling risks to our survival. Sport challenges that comfort zone and invites us to move out of it. As we pick up that challenge, we also pick up our gear. The result is that it's a short step to knowing we rely on it, and to do that we need to have it function effectively and flawlessly enough times for us to become rock-solid confident in its performance.

Confidence in Your Teammates

There's nothing quite like being part of a team. Whether that means being named to the next football squad, the anchor man on a bobsled, the pacemaker in a 1500 meter run, or the partner to a horse. Mind you, there's the downside too, when you let your partner(s) down and lose the game or match with resounding embarrassment. Nevertheless, every competition is a bright new day. Every *successful* competition is another notch of confidence in your teammates—one or all. Smart people include their coach in the team. It halves the hassles and doubles the resources. We're all team players when it comes down to the line. But we don't all have team skills. Developing them needs to be in your mission statement.

Confidence in Officials

In the heavy contact sports and some of the higher-risk sports a peculiar need arises for confidence in the officials. This is because they not only protect you from abuse of the rules, but also insulate you from accidents by setting good, safe—if difficult—courses with appropriate safety measures, medical backup, and rescue procedures. Good officiating and sound administration and management of events will often encourage good-quality competition and help to minimize injuries. We all hope to live to play another day, but that depends on being confident that those responsible for staging our appearances really do know *their* job too.

Confidence in Your Coach

This is a big one, and it is not a given. It is something every coach has to earn from athletes. It rests on the coach's credibility every step of the way, and that in turn is a product of skills in a whole battery of different departments. We all know that there's no such thing as an overnight success—in anything. So by definition, success means a long, hard haul. When you're anywhere else but at the end of it, you need to be confident that *somebody* knows where all your effort is going. That somebody is your coach. You may question, argue, challenge, and dispute a thousand issues along the way, but despite all that, you need to feel an unshakable faith in the vision, technical skill, and organizational abilities of your coach. Lack of confidence here will lead to serious cracks in the superstructure of your career. Better to face up to them early and avoid the disappointments later on.

Confidence in the Athlete

So the coach has to have confidence in the athlete? Well, yes, otherwise it's time we all packed up and went home! A coach needs to feel that, ultimately, the athlete will deliver. Without that, who's going to vouch for *his* (or her) motivation?

Caring for Your Confidences

So exactly how much confidence do you have? Probably lots. Possibly too much. Occasionally not enough. But be careful here.

■ Confidence is not an infinite resource.

Rather, each confidence is a hungry beast with an ongoing appetite for positive affirmations, proof of performance, validation of skill, and displays of memory, fitness, flexibility, adaptability, and creativity. Confidence needs feeding at short and regular intervals. It is like a large and hungry cat that does not do well waiting for its next meal. Caring for such a beast requires, first of all, a total lack of fear of it. You must be unabashed as you accost this lion in its den. You must address it with respect but without reserve. You must minister to its needs but not pander to its whims. Above all, you must recognize that confidences are *living entities*. They may grow and thrive, but like the rest of us, they are subject to injury, trauma—and death. They will respond to care and attention, suffer from grievous injury, or die from accident, abuse, or neglect. Your confidences are the springboard for everything else you do in life. Without them your life would be sadly bereaved. So keep enough written affirmations on the fridge, stuck to the bathroom mirror, or pinned on the back of your closet door to keep you positive and cheerful. Put a shine on your confidences every day in every way.

One of the most necessary life skills is being able to recognize when repairs to your confidences are in order. One may be fine, while another is in tatters. Don't be afraid to address the problem and jump to your own rescue with a lifeline of affirmations and plans B, C, and D, if necessary. Enlist the help of friends when nothing less than a team effort will repair the damage. Can you translate this into action and incorporate it into your everyday training?

Imagery

One of the most powerful tools for repairing any one of your confidences is imagery. We're not about to reinvent that here, but if you make sure your imagery skills are up to scratch, they'll deliver a cast-iron guarantee to improve the quality of some—if not all—of your confidences. Can't say much better than that, eh? Everyone knows that our minds can't distinguish between fact and fiction, so now is the time to indulge in mountains of the best fiction you can manufacture. Relive, redream, redraft, revisit, reinvent, remember, restore, and recreate yourself and your performance in the full glare of the spotlight of success, and be sure to enjoy every moment of it! You'll find imagery is a product with no need of a guarantee. If you use it regularly, before you know it, your confidences will grow. What more could a successful person want than a successful strategy for staying successful?

There's not much you can't take on in this world if armed with a fistful of confidences. The trick to having them all in working order is to take advantage of daily opportunities to keep up the running maintenance on them. Naturally enough, this takes practice just like any other skill, but if that's all that is coming between you and your successful life, get very busy, very soon!

Active Listening

So how do you know which confidences are in good shape and which ones you need to build, rebuild, or repair? It's quite easy—you begin with active listening. Well, we've all heard of *that*. It's been in the picture since Adam was a boy. But the thing is, because we're always being told to learn to listen to somebody else, *we don't realize that the most important person to learn to listen to is ourselves.*

■ Self-talk is *the* key to a confident life. And there it is, right inside your head.

Learn to listen to yourself very carefully indeed! When your Little Voice is positive, constructive, or trying to be helpful, don't drown it out, argue with it, or justify or rationalize or become selectively and very suddenly deaf. Take your own messages to heart by becoming your own best friend, your own best coach, your own best *everything! And don't let the listening stop you from getting in on the action, because only when you ACT will your confidence grow.*

■ *Action* is the catalyst of confidence.

We dream, wish, hope, and wonder about so many things. By comparison we actually *do* very few of them. Confidence comes with the doing. Confidence will not grow in the long shadow of your armchair—or of your opponent. If it is to flourish, confidence needs to see the sunlight and a slice of the action.

So start by giving your Little Voice your undivided and most passionate attention. Nobody knows you better than that Little Voice. Nobody knows how you feel except that Little Voice. Nobody else on the planet is privy to your thoughts except that Little Voice. Develop a dialogue with your Little Voice and snip negative comments or unhelpful hints out of the conversation with at least as much vigor as you'd use to abandon a sinking ship. If you need some help with this, write out a list of positive affirmations, and when you feel your Little Voice challenging your confidence, just repeat an affirmation until you can really say it with conviction and feel good. Think yourself into any of your most challenging situations and repeat those affirmations until you feel thoroughly in control of your Little Voice. Continue to school your Little Voice until it is always positive and always kind, and is your resident 24-hour cheering squad. It's the best coaching you'll ever have, or ever do, so get to it and coach *yourself.* Your confidence will flourish like never before, and the world will seem an altogether friendlier place.

Letting Your Confidence Grow

You've now learned to recognize how you feel and know what to do when your confidence is being challenged. As we have established, knowing is the single most useful tool for building your confidence. So all that's left to do now is to let your confidence grow. Whether it's only

■ When you know you will achieve your goals, you have the confidence to do it.

slightly dented (and responds almost immediately to this treatment), seriously battered (in which case you may need some more practice to screw it back together again), or shattered into its component pieces (which it isn't or you wouldn't be reading this book), plan A is as follows:

- Flag your feelings.
- Listen to your Little Voice.
- Reply with your affirmations.

Plan B is to get quicker off the mark next time. Remember, you don't have to get it *right*—you just have to experiment and have fun trying. If you find you're hanging back on the trying, then just reread this chapter until your curiosity to see if it all works gets the better of you!

Coaches' Corner

Getting the confidence part together takes time. Give your athletes lots of it. Give them the chance to come to terms with just how hard they have to work to become a very successful person—or even a moderately successful person. No sooner do they reach that lofty status than they too become a role model for somebody else to measure their dreams by.

If there's one thing that's harder than getting to the top, it's staying there. By the time you've made it, you've become sufficiently good at "it" that "it" all starts to look easy. Very deceptively easy. This belies the effort and skills involved. Being a role model for your athlete is a nice measure of your achievement, but it's also ongoing, ultrahard work. You leave a mighty awesome gap behind you. If you too once contemplated that gap, stretch out a helping hand to others who also want to make it to the other side.

Summary

Confidence is short-speak for a fistful of confidences in a whole bunch of different things. Confidence has *nothing* to do with nerve, courage, guts, or any other challenge to your man- or womanhood. Confidence has *everything* to do with what you define as success and your expectations of achieving it.

Confidence is a result. First you need information. Then you set your goals. Finally, you *know* you will achieve your goals, and so have the confidence to do so. Bingo!

Confidence is a living entity. It needs to be fed and cared for if it is to prosper. Confidence is *your* responsibility, to have and to hold, for richer or for poorer . . .

Confidence is a finite resource. You do not inherit a bottomless pot of it, nor will it automatically survive your neglect or abuse. If you want it to have a long and illustrious career, you must nourish the confidence you already have and create new confidence to meet new goals as you set them. If you don't do this, you may find that your confidence grows jaded and thin, or you may risk running out of it altogether.

Confidence must be *task specific* and *situation specific.* Above all, it must be *current.* This means you need to put a shine on it by reviewing your recent achievements. If your confidence is not in fit and running order sufficient to facilitate rather than handicap your performance, it is not your confidence that needs reviewing. It's your goals. These need adjusting to be within what you *know* you can achieve.

Getting your confidence into shape then becomes merely a matter of once more engineering and then experiencing your success by achieving your goals.

Sports Thought for the Future

This book has done what you as coach or athlete do as a way of life: in search of the winning edge, it has pushed back the boundaries of sport today, challenged established views and values, refused to be beaten when the going gets tough, and bounced back in time to turn another idea on its ear. It's your turn now. It's up to you to put it all into practice.

To all athletes and all coaches: Be out there and be first because winning *is* everything. Make no mistake about *that*! It is possible, however, that one thing is more important than winning, and that is *how* you win. Just as you aim for excellence in your technical skills, aim for excellence in your mistakes management and you will find that you win more often and more easily. Maximizing your winning by minimizing your mistakes has to be a top strategy for a high-power future! It's all up to you now. Take this to the gym and into the pool and onto the court. *Nobody* has ever developed their "sports thought" in this way before, so rewriting the record books is up for grabs. But be quick, before the rest of the world wakes up to mistakes management as the smart way to success. And don't forget to add some *attitude.*

What's the difference between errors and excellence?
Mistakes worth making.

Index

Note: The italicized *t* following page numbers refers to tables.

About the Author

Sue Halden-Brown is a sport psychology instructor, coach, and examiner and educator with the Australian coach accreditation system. As a coach, Halden-Brown has lent her expertise to help both national and international equestrians and pentathletes to Olympic competition. She is the coauthor of the central text for the Australian equestrian coach education system and the director of the Five-Star Equestrian Training Centre, a training and education facility for equestrian athletes and coaches.

Halden-Brown holds a bachelor of applied sciences in sport studies (coaching) from the University of Canberra and was the recipient of the Australian Coaching Council's Coaching Excellence award in 1994. She resides in Bungendore, New South Wales, Australia.